The
Imaginary
Reminiscences
of
SIR MAX BEERBOHM

The Imaginary Reminiscences of SIR MAX BEERBOHM

Ira Grushow

Ohio University Press
Athens, Ohio   London

Grushow, Ira, 1933-
   The imaginary reminiscences of Sir Max Beerbohm.

   Bibliography: p.
   Includes index.
   1. Beerbohm, Max, Sir, 1872-1956—Criticism and
interpretation. 2. Caricature—England. 3. Art and literature. I.
Title.
PR6003.E4Z683   1984   824'.912   83-19504
ISBN 0-8214-0723-6
ISBN 0-8214-0766-X pbk.

© Copyright 1984 by Ira Grushow
Printed in the United States of America
All rights reserved

To the memory of my father and mother

Contents

Illustrations ix
Acknowledgments xi
Introduction xiii
    Chapter I.   The Quest for Form 1
          II.   Toward the Imaginary Reminiscence in
                Prose 23
          III.   Toward the Imaginary Reminiscence
                in Caricature 59
          IV.   "The Mirror of the Past" 93
           V.   *Seven Men* 125
          VI.   *Rossetti and His Circle* 165
         VII.   The Fading of Memory 208
Notes 255
Bibliography 271
Index 279

Illustrations

NOTE: All illustrations are by Max Beerbohm unless otherwise indicated.

1. Mr. Balfour — a Frieze. c. 1912 69
2. Revisiting the Glimpses. 1911 73
3. Henrik Ibsen and William Archer. 1904 76
4. A quiet morning in the Tate Gallery. 1907 83
5. An illustration for "Hail and Farewell." 1911 85
6. "The Mirror of the Past," MS p. 37 110
7. Princeps Triplumiferus. 1916 118
8. *La Bella Mano* by D. G. Rossetti. 1875 119
9. Lord Morley of Blackburn. 1911 121
10. Oil painting attributed to Walter Greaves 123
11. Half-title page of presentation copy of *Seven Men* 135
12. Felix Argallo and Walter Ledgett 161
13. British Stock and Alien Inspiration — 1849. 1917 172
14. Benjamin Jowett and D. G. Rossetti. 1916 177
15. Design for Oxford Union, from a copy by H. Treffrey Dunn . 178
16. D. G. Rossetti in childhood. c. 1916 180
17. *Gabriele Rossetti* by D. G. Rossetti. 1853 181
18. William Bell Scott wondering. 1916 185
19. William Morris and Edward Burne-Jones. 1916 187
20. A momentary Vision that once befell young Millais. 1917 . 190
21. *Ferdinand Lured by Ariel* by John Everett Millais. 1849 ... 191
22. Mr. Morley introduces Mr. Mill. 1917 194
23. English Fiction — Ancient and Modern. 1923 238
24. Lord Balfour: The Old and the Young Self 248
25. Mr. Cunninghame Graham: The Old and the Young Self. 1924 250

Acknowledgments

I am profoundly grateful to Eva Reichmann for her generosity in allowing me to quote extensively from Max Beerbohm's published and unpublished writings and to reproduce his drawings.

Scarcely less deep is my indebtedness to the curators and librarians of the following institutions, who have made the physical objects available for my perusal and have permitted me as well to duplicate many of them: Ashmolean Museum, Oxford; Henry W. and Albert A. Berg Collection, New York Public Library, Astor, Lenox and Tilden Foundations; British Library; William A. Clark Memorial Library, University of California, Los Angeles; Delaware Art Museum; Houghton Library, Harvard University; Library of Congress; Merton College, Oxford; Tate Gallery, London; Robert H. Taylor Collection, Princeton University Library; Victoria and Albert Museum, London; and Yale University Library. Special thanks are due to Oxford University Press for permitting the reproduction of D. G. Rossetti's drawing of his father.

To Franklin and Marshall College, its faculty and administration, I owe an incalculable debt of gratitude for the financial and psychological encouragement granted me over the years in preparing my hobbyhorse for the steeplechase.

At all points along the way I have been aided by persons whose assistance I delight to acknowledge: Mary Brubaker, John Burgass, Lord Cottesloe, Charles E. Greene, the late Stephen Greene, Lucretia Hammond, Sir Rupert Hart-Davis, Roger Highfield, Bruce Holran, Mrs. David Karmel, Alvin B. Kernan, A. Walton Litz, David Redston, Claudia K. Ritter, Lord Sherfield, Robert H. Taylor, and Joseph C. Voelker.

Finally, I wish to record my thanks to my family. To my daughter, Sophia, who never ceased to find Max's drawings

Acknowledgments

amusing even after I explained them, to my son, Alexander, who is eager to proceed with the compilation of the index on the computer, and above all to my wife, Jane, who punctures pomposity with gentleness and whose critical ear has caused me to recast many a paragraph, I owe special gratitude for having borne my obsession with patience.

Introduction

It is now over one hundred years since the birth and over twenty-five years since the death of Sir Max Beerbohm. Though hardly in the mainstream in the history of English literature and at best a meandering rivulet in the history of English art, he has nevertheless continued to engage the attention not merely of scholars but of practicing artists themselves as well. Edmund Wilson, W. H. Auden, and John Updike, vigorous stylists in their own right — likely candidates for inclusion in a latter-day *Christmas Garland* — have all written penetratingly about him,[1] and at the height of his career he exacted from the caricaturists such greater and lesser tributes as a whole book of appreciation from Bohun Lynch and smaller acknowledgments of admiration from David Low and Osbert Lancaster.[2]

While still alive Sir Max came to be "collected," a condition that he found not altogether to his liking[3] and which subjected him to the scrutiny of bibliographers, whose labors, particularly in tracking down fugitive drawings, have been immense.[4] After his death additional collections of Beerbohm's work began appearing, including items both out of print and never before in print.[5] And the concomitant of the publication and republication of minor works is that of correspondence.[6] There has even appeared a book that extracts from Beerbohm's published writings, drawings, letters, and conversation his attitudes toward Americans and America.[7]

All of these books contribute materials to our knowledge of Beerbohm's life and work, and a feature of many of them is their illustration by hitherto-unreproduced sketches done by Max. One senses, however, that they have been lovingly compiled and edited more for the delectation of those already addicted to Beerbohm than for the definition of his accomplishment to the

Introduction

benighted or partially enlightened. What is absent from them generally is a critical perspective — as though to classify, to describe, and to edit were the ultimate ends of scholarship. To be sure, an editor or bibliographer must scrupulously abstain from evaluative criticism himself; yet he should subtly convey some sense of the uses to which his work may be put. Despite all the writing about Sir Max Beerbohm in the last twenty-five years, he is still a figure who is essentially appreciated and admired — loved even — but not taken very seriously.

This uncritical and rapturous attitude is particularly apparent in the two full-length works that try to portray the living man. S. N. Behrman, the American playwright and essayist, had in many ways the more difficult task. In 1952, in his sixtieth year, he finally met Max Beerbohm, then in his eightieth, and from his conversations with him emerged a series of *New Yorker* articles later published in book form.[8] As a general introduction for the uninitiated, Behrman's book is unsurpassed, and it is generously illuminated with excellent reproductions of sketches and drawings. Like Boswell, Behrman allows his subject to reveal himself wherever possible in his own words (and pictures) and takes extraordinary pains to project himself as little as possible. Like Boswell, too, Behrman is suffused with hero-worship, if not idolatry. But an intimate portrait is not possible through a series of interviews, however carefully edited. In the final analysis Beerbohm told Behrman no more than he wanted to, and the encounters between the two men are essentially devoid of drama. Although he invokes Beerbohm's own reminiscence of the elderly Swinburne, "No. 2. The Pines," Behrman has written essentially a book of information rather than one of impression or interpretation. The general reader is perhaps given more information than he wants; the aficionado regrets perhaps that the opportunity was lost for finding out even more than is available from other sources. *Portrait of Max* remains a popular book about a figure who could never be truly popular.

Lord David Cecil's limitations were largely self-imposed, the result of choice. As Beerbohm's "official" biographer, he was extraordinarily conscious of the kind of work that was expected of him; and although the work is certainly affectionate, it is not

Introduction

characterized by the intimacy and poignancy of his other literary biographies. Because he finds Beerbohm's life, in terms of external happenings, essentially uneventful, Lord David conceives his task as primarily that of an editor, an archivist, "making use as far as possible of Max's own words and of those who knew him well, to compose, as it were, a succession of detailed portraits of him and his mind during the successive phases of his life." Curiously, he feels that the emphasis on quotation relieves him of the obligation of documentation and that passages of literary criticism introduced into a biography, even of an externally uneventful life, "dissipate its atmosphere and interrupt its narrative flow."[9] What emerges is a not unreadable, but perhaps too reverential, portrait, a biography of the last century rather than of this one.

This state of being much considered, of having many admirers and many books written about one, yet of not being pinned down and classified, would have pleased Max Beerbohm greatly. He would have been delighted that his mask had not been pierced. All his life he posed as a dandy and a trifler, depreciating his own work, despising all forms of publicity, identifying himself even in London with no literary group. Yet the grand subject matter, the ambiance of his best work, is the society of writers and artists, their quest for imaginative worlds to inhabit, their conflicts with the commonplace world, and their thirst for fame. Moreover, in all his work the persona is always a manifestation of himself — not a projection, but the literal self. Obviously this is so in his essays, but in his fiction as well he is always present in his own guise. In *Seven Men* he appears in all the stories, not merely as a linking device but as the ironic creator of all the characters, including himself. And in his only novel, *Zuleika Dobson*, Beerbohm invests self-conscious narration, proposed originally by Fielding in the eighteenth century as a burlesque of epic convention, with a preciosity that is not only screamingly funny but subversive of the very foundations of realistic fiction as well. "Just how far," he challenges his readers, "are you prepared to accept my characters as real?" A similar challenge is posed by the caricatures, which also reflect his persona. To draw a representation of a particular man in a deliberately dis-

Introduction

torted way is to disdain an objective for a subjective view, to prefer the private to the public judgment. Beerbohm's caricatures do not offer us likenesses; rather, they emit attitudes.

How is it, then, that this conflict between the outward demeanor of the man and the richness and intensity of his work has never been resolved? For one thing, Beerbohm rarely offered any help, preferring to talk about others and their work rather than about himself and his own. For another, most of the studies of Beerbohm have been executed by people who knew him personally, by friends and admirers whose attitude for the most part has been uncritical and unanalytical — not necessarily out of reverence, but as much out of ignorance, because Sir Max was a very formal and reserved man. Genial, humorous, benevolent — but not, it would appear, intimate. "To be interesting," he once wrote, "a man must be complex and elusive."[10] These are adjectives eminently descriptive of him, and in the words of his biographer, "Max remains for posterity a puzzle."[11] In Beerbohm's case the traditional advantage of the memoir writer over the later biographer who cannot use himself as a primary source of information is almost negligible.

An embarrassing but very real suspicion is raised in the absence of a solution to the puzzle: Is Max worth puzzling over? To friends and acquaintances, certainly; but when they die off and the last anecdote or *bon mot* has been preserved in the amber of print and duly cross-referenced, when a Beerbohm caricature of George Moore will have to be annotated as extensively as one of William Watson, will it still seem quite the same useful enterprise? Will our interest in Beerbohm be merely historical (as he suggests, perhaps ironically, in "Enoch Soames"), or is there a substantial core of art in his accomplishments? The very nature of those accomplishments baffles criticism. As a writer *and* a caricaturist, alternating between two media, Beerbohm is easy to follow in his career, though his development is difficult to chart. As a writer, he practices in many forms, in none of them quite like anyone else; as a caricaturist, he shows relatively little growth in technique. His work, moreover, seems to be made up not of whole pieces but of fragments composed at various times and periodically collected into books of essays or albums of drawings. There is no immediately apparent handle by which they can be lifted up and examined.

Introduction

One critic has, however, fashioned such a handle. John Felstiner's brilliant exposition *The Lies of Art: Max Beerbohm's Parody and Caricature* posits a dialectic of creation, criticism, and parody upon which it is possible to array not only Beerbohm's public art as writer and caricaturist but also his private art manifested in his hoaxes, impromptu sketches, and other amusements. Felstiner relates the word to the line, the historical figure to the fictional one, the parody to the caricature, and is able to demonstrate a progression through Beerbohm's career, a maturing conception of self and art. The study that follows owes an incalculable debt to Felstiner, largely for his courage in undertaking to break Max's butterfly on the wheel of criticism and in venturing to transgress the laws of generic criticism in order to do so.

My own approach to Beerbohm is perhaps more conservative and less daring than that of Felstiner, who is concerned ultimately with the *source* of Beerbohm's art, the impulses to expression and how they were tempered. Mine is more with the form, the generically unique vehicle of Beerbohm's art, whose invention and refinement in writing and drawing I designate the "imaginary reminiscence," a vehicle that serves not merely to contain his art but also to comment on the nature of art itself. My assumptions are that Beerbohm's work, while generally of high quality throughout, is not all of a piece and that it can be evaluated if the right measure can be found. My belief is that the right measure is to be sought in contemplation of the imaginary reminiscence, whose most successful manifestations are in *Seven Men* (1919) and *Rossetti and His Circle* (1922). These, I would confidently maintain, are Beerbohm's most accomplished and enduring works, and their careful study will serve not merely to illuminate the whole of Beerbohm's canon but to reflect as well the crisis of art in the twentieth century.

CHAPTER I

The Quest for Form

In their treating of Max Beerbohm's work, critics have inevitably tended to consider his achievements as a writer and as a caricaturist separately. That his work is cast in different forms is obvious; but that this distinction, which bids us search in different parts of a library (even under so enlightened a system of classification as that of the Library of Congress) for the productions of an integral artistic consciousness, should pervade so thoroughly even the most sensitive criticism is less readily understood. John Felstiner himself, who more than any other critic has explored the unity of that consciousness, still feels impelled to discriminate between the effects produced by the two media. Excepting *Rossetti and His Circle,* he observes:

> Generally Beerbohm's caricatures tend to ridicule, while his judgments in writing are less direct — the rough distinction is between satire and irony.... For one thing, Beerbohm's virtual presence in stories and essays, as character or self-conscious stylist, inhibits outright satire. And a comment Beerbohm himself often made clarifies the distinction further: he insisted that drawing figures was delightful and natural for him, compared to the labor of writing prose.[1]

But Beerbohm is often the subject of his own caricatures (he is the principal figure in nearly one hundred of the slightly over two thousand listed in Hart-Davis's *Catalogue*) and appears frequently in conjunction with others, so the distinction is not altogether clear-cut; moreover, the captions to Beerbohm's caricatures are often so mannered and stylized as to constitute the narration of a "self-conscious stylist." More significant, however, is that Felstiner's observation implies that irony is a more complicated affair than satire and one generated through labor rather than through delight. Although he sees the two as complementary, there is no question but that he rates the achievement of the writer as more significant than that of the caricaturist. For Edmund Wilson, in contrast, if we accept the presence of imagination in art as desirable, the evaluation is the reverse. He writes of Beerbohm that "his work as a caricaturist is in general on a higher imaginative level than his stories, his essays and his parodies."[2] For Felstiner, led into his elaborate thesis through study of Beerbohm's presentments of Henry James, the parodic and critical would naturally be of more consuming interest; for Wilson, the astute critic of the fiction of several national literatures, Beerbohm's attempts to create characters and dramatic situations in prose must have seemed feeble indeed. The point is not that for different reasons each evaluates differently, but that the evaluation proceeds naturally on the basis of the medium rather than upon the achieved intent of individual works. Not only was he himself a practitioner of two arts, Beerbohm was also fascinated by others who were so, and he wrote of their plight in an early essay:

> When a man can express himself through two media, people tend to take him lightly in his use of the medium to which he devotes the lesser time and energy, even though he use that medium not less admirably than the other, and even though they themselves care about it more than they care about the other. Perhaps this very preference in them creates a prejudice against the man who does not share it, and so makes them sceptical of his power. Anyhow, if Disraeli had been unable to express himself through the medium of political life, Disraeli's novels would long ago have had the due which the expert is just beginning to give them. Had Rossetti not been primarily a poet, the expert in painting would have acquired long ago his present penetration into the peculiar value of Rossetti's painting.[3]

The issue is not just quibbling over whether one prefers the drawings to the prose or the prose to the drawings or which involved the greater care or pains. For unlike Disraeli (it is interesting, by the way, that Beerbohm elevates politics to an art — or, at any rate, to a medium of expression) and not quite like Rossetti, Beerbohm practiced both arts simultaneously; he pursued a single career rather than two. Nor is it particularly helpful to seek out separate lines of development, using one medium to illuminate the other. J. G. Riewald, in his introduction to a selection of caricatures from several of Beerbohm's books of different periods, writes: "Though [Beerbohm] disapproved of the illustration of literary texts, he often supplied his own drawings with exquisitely apt and elaborate captions and legends. His later caricature volumes especially contain numerous examples of this rare combination of visual and verbal artistry, to such an extent even that it is sometimes difficult to say whether the legend illustrates the drawing or the other way round."[4] But why should it be necessary to say? In a comic strip or a cartoon by Jules Feiffer the pictorial is unquestionably subservient to the verbal; these are truly illustrated texts. But in Beerbohm's caricatures the legends in most instances do not really explain or illuminate so much as give titles to the drawings, however lengthily. They are verbal equivalents and complements to the drawings, probably conceived in the same instant of time.

A simple example should suffice. The frontispiece to *A Survey* (1921) is a color reproduction of a drawing of Joseph Conrad done a year earlier.[5] The novelist is shown on a deserted beach, legs apart, hands thrust into the pockets of a tightly-buttoned officer's jacket, contemplating a snake winding its way through the eye socket of a human skull. The caricature is titled "Somewhere in the Pacific," and the legend on the drawing itself reads as follows: "MR. JOSEPH CONRAD: *'Quelle charmante plage! On se fait l'illusion qu'ici on pourrait être toujours presque gai!'*" This is translated on the legend sheet as, "'What a delightful coast! One catches an illusion that one might forever be almost gay here.'" Visually the humor arises from the incongruity of the carefully groomed and monocled Conrad dispassionately gazing upon a sight from which most men would shrink with horror. The legend, which by its circumlocution compounds the contemplative posture in the picture, further intensifies that incongruity by revealing the subject's attitude of exhilaration at

3

the scene. Taken together, picture and legend constitute a criticism of Conrad's art. In 1920 Conrad had not achieved the stature of moralist and technical innovator, bright god in the pantheon of modernism, to which he has since been elevated. Beerbohm's caricature, though not irreverently, fashions him as a somewhat tedious tale-teller, whose subject matter is remote and distasteful to cultured men and women and whose style is equally foreign, attenuated by endless qualification: ". . .illusion . . . might . . . almost. . . ." Such a reading may seem harsh but can be tested by an examination of the last plate in the volume, "Mr. Conrad Again" (HD 360; BLC 86), also executed in 1920. The scene is best described by another caricaturist:

> Here are various sea-captains, all woe-begone, each in his individual way. Max seems to have introduced every known attitude that subtly suggests dejection. There is a depressed nigger, . . . and an old lady in a cap with a small tight bun of faded hair. Her profile not merely shows her misery, but proves it to be an irritating misery. The slightly frog-like mouth and eye, the pallor, make you feel that sadness is her occupation in life; and you want to shake her. The lamp is smoking, on the table a skull lies on a green woolly mat beneath a glass dome, and two untidy and sluttish young women lean sulkily against chairs. Mr. Conrad, very spick and span, widely grinning, is coming in at the door.[6]

The legend is in part a quotation from Wordsworth's "Peter Bell," significantly from the stanza cited by Shelley in his satire "Peter Bell the Third" and omitted by Wordsworth in later editions: "'A party in a parlour, all silent and all damned' — and, as usual, Mr. Joseph Conrad intruding." Neither Bohun Lynch, who has described the picture so extensively, nor Professor Riewald, who has annotated it, has ventured an explanation of its meaning. Riewald implies that the damned souls are in some way both auditors and subjects of Conrad's fiction, but the idea is rather vague: "In spite of his dark vision of life, Conrad had a tremendous power to charm. He was a spellbinding storyteller, not only in his novels and short stories, but also when he was in company. As a writer and as a storyteller he often allowed his personal experiences to coalesce imaginatively with episodes about which he had read."[7] It seems more likely that rather

The Quest for Form

than entertain or cheer up this doleful congregation, Conrad "intrudes" for the purpose of learning the source of their misery. As in "Somewhere in the Pacific," there is a contrast between Conrad's reflective self-assurance and the rest of the picture. Neither is the allusion to Wordsworth altogether casual, for Wordsworth too sought out the company of the abject — illiterates, beggars, idiots — as the inspiration for his art. Beerbohm is amused by the idea and reduces it to absurdity.[8]

The relationship of picture to text in these Conrad caricatures is thus quite intimate, and this is generally so in the best of Beerbohm's drawings — not because words make up for the deficiencies of his draftsmanship, but because the criticisms he generates have both visual and verbal components. One of Felstiner's principal assertions is that parody is caricature of a person's utterance and caricature is a parody of a person's appearance. It should not surprise us therefore to find that with but one exception (that of A. C. Benson) the writers parodied in *A Christmas Garland* are among the most frequently caricatured in Beerbohm's albums. Occasionally a caricature will actually have its origin in a visualization of a quotation (as discussed in chapter 3) or in a bit of prose that works better as a drawing. "The Mirror of the Past," Beerbohm's abandoned novel of reminiscence, is a mine of such nuggets. And often the obscurity of a caricature may be dispelled when its source is found in some figurative language in an essay or a drama review.

At the outset of his career the case was rather different and there was little connection between Beerbohm's writing and his drawing. As elaborate and ornate were the essays in *Works* (1896) and *More* (1899), so chaste and uncluttered were the portraits in *Caricatures of Twenty-Five Gentlemen* (1896). Even the subject matter was sharply differentiated. Caricatures were of the living — eccentric portraits of the prominent; essays, where they dealt with real people at all, concerned the dead. As a very young man Beerbohm simply accepted the stipulated provinces of the two genres. A caricature resembled the drawings of Ape and Spy in *Vanity Fair*; an essay, though it had no rules, had as its chief aim the exposure of the writer's personality — and Beerbohm set out to establish a flamboyant and dandified one. But with the entry into the twentieth century a gradual change began in Beerbohm's work. Ten years passed before the publication of his next book of essays, and although *Yet Again* (1909) does not seem strikingly different from *More* in general content, the style is more subdued, more workmanlike and less flashing. The slower pace and soberer tone may have been a result of the demands of journalism: from 1898 to 1910 he wrote weekly drama criticisms for the *Saturday Review*. The same period saw a startling alteration in his caricatures. He published two books of these and laid by a third, which was brought out in the wake of the success of the 1911 exhibition at the Leicester Galleries.[9] In *The Poets' Corner* (1904) Beerbohm departed from his earlier work by introducing figures from the past and by replacing static portraiture with more or less dramatic situations. In *A Book of Caricatures* (1907), even though the subjects were all contemporaries, they are often seen in groups and against backgrounds. *The Second Childhood of John Bull* (1911) is a group of political cartoons, allegorical in style, relating to the Boer War.

With his departure from England in 1910 and the subsequent completion of *Zuleika Dobson*, he began to purge his prose and his drawing of their journalistic quality. It was not merely that he worked no longer to meet deadlines or the specifications of his employers, but a genuine imaginative element, hitherto present only in traces, now began to suffuse all his work. He started to create fictions. To be sure, they are the fictions of an essayist and a satirist: their purpose is the objectification of a personal view and personal comment rather than of some larger vision of the way things are. *Zuleika Dobson* is an obvious instance. But the parodies in *A Christmas Garland* (1912) may also be considered fictions invented for the purpose of criticism in ways that the essays of the earlier volumes were not. And the drawings of *Fifty Caricatures* (1913) advance even further than before Beerbohm's tendency to place his subjects in interesting situations, often in confrontation with others, rather than draw them in isolation.

There is another curious development in Beerbohm's work that seems to date from his retirement to Italy: the blurring of traditional generic distinctions. Clearly classifiable are the achievements before 1910; however idiosyncratic, the essays are undeniably essays and the caricatures are caricatures. But what is a librarian to do with *Seven Men* (1919), which has the *look* of essays about it, which seems to insist that it is nonfictional, yet is clearly invented? And if the librarian happens to be mathematical, the presence of only five divisions in that work, even allowing for the doubling in "Maltby and Braxton," is even more unsettling.[10] In terms of the central situation of the narrator — a young aspiring writer invests his memories, his earlier thoughts and apprehensions on encountering established ones, with life in his pages — is there all that much difference between "Enoch Soames," the first piece in *Seven Men*, and "No. 2. The Pines," Max's recollections of Swinburne in *And Even Now* (1920)? They were actually composed at about the same time. Would Tenniel or Thackeray have recognized as caricature — as distinct from illustration, designed to accompany a significant text, or cartoon, composed out of conventional symbols and time-worn biblical or mythological allusions — the meeting of an author (Arnold Bennett) with a character in his fiction (HD 132; BLC 96) or another (George Moore) with a prototype of a character (HD 1050; BLC 90)? Both of these drawings appeared in *Fifty Caricatures*.

Clearly Beerbohm had leaped the bounds of genre. It is now obvious that he had both developed new and unique vehicles and radically adapted others to contain his thought and feeling. But it was not equally apparent to his contemporaries. Parodies were expected to be good-natured and shallow likenesses, rather like the impressions of public figures produced by stage comedians. One reviewer of *A Christmas Garland* wrote that "we are hardly disposed at this time of day to take too kindly fun poked at George Meredith, Mr. Thomas Hardy and Mr. Henry James. It may be that I am old-fashioned, but I prefer not to laugh at sacred subjects."[11] Another found that Beerbohm "imitates least well the authors whose methods and manner are the most strongly marked" and, having applied his rigid mimetic standard, determined that the parodies of Henry James and Rudyard Kipling, generally considered among the best, are among the least distinguished of the group.[12] For a third there was "nothing irresistibly comic about imagining Mr. Kipling reading [the] story of Santa Claus arrested by P. C. Judlip, because he might easily have written the greater part of it."[13] The reception of *A Christmas Garland* was on the whole favorable, but few of the reviewers suspected the full richness of the work. *Seven Men* was even more baffling to one reviewer, who observed that "the fairy who made Mr. Beerbohm an artist made him a queerly incomplete one. In equal doses she endowed him with fancifulness and sense of form, and then left the two to fight it out between them. . . . In other words she made him incapable of writing a good short story."[14] And while critics were generally applauding the brilliance and penetration of the drawings that make up *Rossetti and His Circle,* one of his greatest admirers as a graphic artist was having qualms about the direction in which Beerbohm seemed to be heading: "Here for the first time in bulk, though single instances were to be observed in *Fifty Caricatures,* Max has shown a tendency . . . to make portraits rather than caricatures. True, the portraits have in them all manner of subtleties, quiet appreciations, recondite disparagements, as indeed have serious portraits by accomplished artists. But that, speaking with humility combined with confidence, is not Max's art."[15]

Beerbohm was engaged in nothing less than the rearrangement of the boundaries between essay and story in prose and between serious and comic portraiture in art. Before *Zuleika Dobson,* when he represented human beings at all, he dealt principally with historical figures in prose and contemporary figures in caricature in situations that were essentially real, however exaggeratedly or ironically presented; after *Zuleika Dobson* the subjects became reversed: he began to treat contemporary figures in prose and historical figures in caricature in *imagined* situations. Without the living face before him, Beerbohm's sketch of Yeats would work better in words, even if it were not altogether appropriate to publish them at the time; and his observations on the mannerisms of Lord Balfour before he was prime minister could be incorporated into the tale-within-a-tale of the fictional Maltby in *Seven Men.* But since the impulse to caricature had been a strong one with Max since boyhood, it was not to be overcome merely through the absence of live models. Sources for his drawings could be found in the photographs and portraits of men who were not contemporaries.

The Quest for Form

Such a mechanical explanation fits the facts and is in a large measure true. But the retirement and exile were voluntary and suggest that Max, whether he attained it or not, had some artistic goal in mind and was not simply the victim of a change in his environment. What he found in Rapallo principally was time to reflect on his past experiences, though it is also true that he became essentially unreceptive to new ones. Auden explains this lack of receptivity as a consequence of Beerbohm's having matured early, formulating his tastes and exercising his talents without having had to undergo a long painful process of discovery. But early development, argues Auden, exacts a price. "The price which Max paid was that after about the year 1910 he became incapable of responding imaginatively to anything happening about him, whether in society or in the arts."[16] Had Yeats, who was seven years older than Beerbohm, similarly become impervious to new experiences in life or in art in 1910, we should not have had the extraordinary and innovative poems of the middle and late years; he would, indeed, be no more than the member of the Rhymers Club, the showman, the dabbler in mysticism that Max recalled and continued to represent him as.

But although we may genuinely regret the absence of Beerbohm caricatures of James Joyce and D. H. Lawrence and for them perhaps would willingly trade some of the many of Shaw and Kipling and although we might wish that Beerbohm's admiration of the Bloomsbury writers had extended beyond an appreciation of Lytton Strachey, we cannot actually assert that the quality of Beerbohm's art, apart from the subjects he deals with, was in any way diminished by his abstraction from contemporary literary and social life. As a very young man with a professional career to establish, a life outside the capital was unthinkable, for it was in London, and in London only, that he could meet and be encouraged by such friends as Frank Harris, Robert Ross, and Edmund Gosse. However, London was a place merely of apprenticeship; it was, moreover, full of expenses and full of distractions. But so removed from the daily practices of contemporary writers and artists were his mature essays and caricatures, so relatively free from suggestions and influences, that, however stimulating the company of such men and women might be, it would contribute little to Beerbohm's intellectual and technical development.

The truth is that Beerbohm cared very little for ideas in themselves and was dubious of their presence in art. As a septuagenarian, looking back over his life, he spoke as follows to an unseen radio audience in the middle of World War II: "I have always thought that a young man who desires to know all that in all ages in all lands has been thought by the best minds, and wishes to make a synthesis of all those thoughts for the future benefit of mankind, is laying up for himself a very miserable old age."[17] His own preference is asserted in one of his few essays of straight criticism (apart from drama reviews), written when a young man of twenty-five: "I am a dilettante, a *petit maître*. I love best in literature delicate and elaborate ingenuities of form and style."[18] Between these two assertions lay a lifetime of reading, but reading of books chosen for their beauty and companionability rather than for their profundity or breadth of vision. Even his favorite writers were preferred for accomplishments that may seem peculiar to modern readers. Thus he finds Meredith's historical romance *Harry Richmond* far superior to "the tedious, crack-jaw, arid intellectual snobbery of *Diana [of the Crossways]*."[19] The "gaps" in Beerbohm's appreciation seem immense, but as he revealed them largely in conversation rather than in words and drawings he published himself, they seem less damning.[20] They are a consequence, I think, not of a closed mind, but of one that sees art pre-eminently as personal expression, however outrageous, presented in recognizable and acceptable form. Even if not wholly understood by them, the artist must be approachable by his admirers. Beerbohm could envision sitting down to dinner with Trollope; he could not imagine doing so with Dostoevsky. And his account of his several dinners with Swinburne reveals not the flaming radical, the rhapsodist of atheism, but the aged and fragile man of letters, the retired scholar in whom the lyric impulse has been drained by time but not completely extinguished.

Beerbohm is very much a child of the nineteenth century for whom art is the dress of the artist — not a personal or a social necessity, but a performance, whose graceful and sensitive execution he records in his writing and drawing. And so George Moore comes off in Max's portraits rather like his fellow countryman Oliver Goldsmith in Boswell's *Life of Johnson,* as a talented oaf; the talent is asserted, but the oafishness is demonstrated. Beerbohm's writings and drawings deal less with the *substance* of art than with its manner; he is less concerned with books and paintings than he is with writers and artists, less with social and economic policies than with the style of their advocates. Like Dr. Johnson, he sees literary life as an arena in which heroic battles are fought — battles for fame and success against a multitude of contenders for honor, battles demanding sacrifice and self-discipline. But although he shared with Dr. Johnson a preference for the biographical part of literature, it was for aesthetic and not for moral reasons. His heroes — Rossetti, Whistler, Lytton Strachey — are heroes by virtue of their panache; his villains — Noaks of *Zuleika Dobson,* for example, or Rudyard Kipling — are villains by virtue of a tawdry and unspeakable vulgarity.

Indeed, how one perceives one's standing in society is virtually the only trait of personal character with which Beerbohm seems concerned. That it is an element of character, that one can be vulgar by choice and not merely inheritance, is evidenced in his treatment of Edward VII, of whom he drew more caricatures than he did of any other person (except himself). But it is the artists, poets, and statesmen, whose accomplishments can transcend class, who interest him most. These are the lives and accomplishments on which he comments. Zuleika Dobson's artistry is no more than a few conjuring tricks she has stolen from a youth passionately in love with her, and these she converts into a source of power; Enoch Soames tries desperately to escape his Preston background by becoming a poet, but he achieves no more than an ironic posthumous recognition; Hilary Maltby, the society novelist, is destroyed as an artist by his own snobbery; Rossetti constructs for himself an alternative world of art, one that not even Ruskin, and certainly not the pedestrian artist William Bell Scott, can enter.[21] In each instance artistic achievement is perceived of, not in terms of objective worth, but as a means of establishing one's identity within society or outside it. The same is true of politicians. Winston Churchill (most of the caricatures date from 1920 and earlier), his head sunk between his shoulders, is constantly portrayed as one who will never achieve the eminence of his father; Stanley Baldwin is shown as too commonplace and unimaginative a man to fill a nation's highest political office. Neither of them has the bearing of a statesman.

It is thus apparent that Beerbohm is concerned less with the actual accomplishments of men and women than with their attitudes and postures, the stratagems they devise to accommodate their need for attention and gratification. The pursuit of art is one such means, the pursuit of power another. All of Beerbohm's best work, whether parody, caricature, essay, story, or review, passes judgment on the beauty and effectiveness of these tactics. That is why failures fascinate him as much as, if not more than, successes. Enoch Soames is a pathetic figure and so is "Savonarola" Brown, whose unimaginative play is a complement to an unimaginative life. But no less pitiable, perhaps, is the Earl of Rosebery, who is arrayed in caricatures that read like a graphic "Vanity of Human Wishes," who had, it was said, but three ambitions in life — to win the Derby, to marry a Rothschild, and to become prime minister — and who realized all three of them but without the satisfaction of fulfillment. Loyalty is conceived of as fidelity to one's own best ideals rather than to persons, and Beerbohm could justify the relentlessness of his satire against Kipling by saying, "He was a genius, a very great genius, and I felt that he was debasing his genius by what he wrote. And I couldn't refrain from saying so."[22] That is why he was perpetually outraged at artists turned businessmen and businessmen turned artists. The popular and commercial success of Marie Corelli and Hall Caine appalled him, for it vitiated taste and diverted rewards from the meritorious.[23] That is also why he had no sympathy with any collective enterprise of men. If he dreaded the decline of culture that would attend government by the far left, he saw through the pretensions of class disinterestedness of the far right, as his last volumes of caricatures would testify.

And because this criterion of judgment, a legacy of the heyday of aestheticism, is not at all a common one yet is enunciated in language and depicted in line that amuses rather than shocks,

The Quest for Form

because its concern is not fundamentally ethical, characters seen from the inside — who grow and develop in response to their traits and their experiences — have no real place in the imaginative world of Beerbohm's creation. If all is performance and the role of the critic is to interpret and evaluate that performance, then traditional history and biography go astray by their too close attention to facts. Beerbohm's tongue is not altogether in his cheek in "King George the Fourth," an ironic rehabilitation of the "first gentleman" after the devastation wrought by Thackeray in *The Four Georges*. He defended his essay, it is significant to note, as a performance in its own right: "To treat history as a means of showing one's own cleverness may be rather rough on history, but it has been done by the best historians, from Herodotus to Froude and myself. Some of my 'George' was false, and much was flippant; but why should a writer sit down to be systematically serious, or else conscientiously comic. Style should be oscillant."[24] Ultimately, then, it is the performance by Max of the act of criticism of the performances of others to which we are responding when we look at a Beerbohm caricature or read a Beerbohm essay. There is no illumination of Rossetti in *Rossetti and His Circle*, or of Swinburne in "No. 2. The Pines"; there is no more inquiry into the reasonableness of the paradoxes of George Bernard Shaw than there is into those of Oscar Wilde. But there is a good deal of concern with the style, in the broadest possible sense of the term, of these men. And in the case of Enoch Soames, the performance of the hero is dim while that of his chronicler and remembrancer, Max himself, is bright.

Given this propensity to perform while criticizing, to judge in an inoffensively self-centered manner, Beerbohm's problem was to find the proper vehicle for creative expression. The task of reviewing plays was clearly not fulfilling. It was not merely that he had no choice of subject but that he was also tied inexorably to a weekly column, a word limit, and a deadline. One could graduate from journalism to literature — he had the example of his immediate predecessor, George Bernard Shaw, to inform him, and there were more conservative examples as well of men of letters who wrote with style and precision whose writing often seemed worthier than the literature they wrote about. But Beerbohm had not the intense moral vision of a Dr. Johnson, nor did he have the scholarship even of an Edmund Gosse. He was, moreover, more interested in men than in books.

So unique were his objectives that the established literary genres were difficult to work in. He continued to write personal essays until late in his career and enjoyed a twilight reputation as a broadcaster, summoning up remembrances of pre-World War I London to radio audiences of the thirties and forties. As the literary form most readily adaptable to his purposes in its projection of an unmediated private viewpoint and in its attentiveness to manner almost as much as to matter, the essay was for Beerbohm a highly favored genre. But flexible though it was, it could not perform all that Beerbohm required of it. The subjects of personal essays were traditionally light and fairly inconsequential. To substitute criticism for mere amusement, to introduce real and imaginary persons, and to explore one's own relations to them in all their complexity would baffle the expectations of the average essay-reader. Such concerns would seem to lie more within the province of poetry. A disembodied voice he might have managed, but Beerbohm's devotion to the syntax and rhythms of prose, and his conception of poetry as essentially lyrical and metrical discourse, kept him away from verse except for relaxation and fun.[25] In Edwardian days verse was comic and poetry was serious. The Horatian urbanity of Sir John Betjeman had not yet come into fashion, nor would World War I hasten its acceptance, but had he been inclined to write poetry professionally, Beerbohm's would probably have resembled Betjeman's.

One would expect that his concern with the social world would have attracted him to drama or to fiction. He tried his hand at both.[26] Nuances and subtleties could certainly be conveyed from the stage, but Beerbohm could never diffract himself into other personalities, could never write himself out of a role or trust wholly to dialogue. The respectability of the self-conscious narrator, even of the meddlesome sort, had been reestablished by Thackeray and Trollope, however much it was despised by the realists. In the novel, therefore, Beerbohm could have given free rein to his essayistic fancy, as indeed he does in *Zuleika Dobson*. Beerbohm's knowledge of life, however, extended little

The Quest for Form

beyond the drawing rooms of the prominent. Lack of scope might have been compensated for with psychological penetration — his admiration of Henry James shows an appreciation of that kind of accomplishment — but again, he conceived his role as an observer rather than as an analyzer of character. His respect for the traditional Aristotelian elements of fiction — plot, character, fable — would have made him skeptical of the experiments of Joyce and Woolf, and as one whose pre-eminent interest was in performance, the wholly private meanderings of mind, the subconscious, and most certainly the unconscious, were areas he did not choose to explore.

If Beerbohm was a displaced person in the province of prose, his status as a visual artist was even more problematic. He never really learned to draw, nor was faithful physical representation what he was after. Serious portraiture, after the manner of his friend Will Rothenstein, was no part of his objective. Beerbohm began his career as a caricaturist inspired by the portrait tradition of Carlo Pellegrini (1839–1889), the Ape of *Vanity Fair*; his successor Leslie Ward (1851–1922), Spy, was considerably more bland and less penetrating in his observation. Portrait caricature in the last decades of the nineteenth century had become very genteel and polite, not at all a vehicle for criticism. Of caricatures of human figures in action, or cartoons, two principal types existed. The first consisted of illustrations of jokes,

> third-rate quips of conversation, which form the staple of most artists on . . . comic papers. "She: 'Who discovered the circulation of the blood?' — He: 'A Johnny called Harvey!' — She: 'Then who discovered Harvey's sauce?'" I have invented this as a fair sample of the jests in the more modern comic papers, or in the sad enclosure which serious papers set aside for purposes of mirth. Whether such jests require, or are in any way strengthened by a picture of a *decolletée* girl sitting in the shadow of a standard lamp, with a bald man bending over the back of her chair, is a question on which I have already made up my mind.[27]

Contemptuous of such practice as Beerbohm was, he did not disdain in some of his work to have his characters engage in dialogue not inevitably suggested by the drawing. Yet even in such instances the dialogue is of Beerbohm's distinct invention, not a

15

standard impersonal joke. The second kind of cartoon was political, where there was indeed greater intimacy between drawing and legend, legend often participating in drawing in the form of labels. The editorial cartoonist created his scene by placing the heads of contemporary politicians onto the bodies of standard mythological and allegorical figures. In one of the few finished passages of "The Mirror of the Past," Beerbohm hilariously characterizes one of his (imaginary) boyhood political heroes as presented by Tenniel in the pages of *Punch*:

> He appeared for the most part in the guise of an Homeric warrior, with great muscular development of calf and biceps. I remember him intervening to knock up the crossed swords of two lesser and evil-visaged warriors, one of whom had a breastplate labelled *Revolutionary*, the other a shield labelled *Reactionary*. I remember him as Perseus rescuing Brittania-Andromeda from a squamous monster whose tentacles were labelled *Anarchy* and *Prejudice* and *Sedition* and *Vested Interests* and any number of awful other things. On one occasion he himself was shown writhing in chains on a rock, and a vulture was hovering near him. He had been adversely criticised by some newspaper or Member of Parliament, thus reminding Mr. Punch of Prometheus.[28]

Clearly Beerbohm's work as a caricaturist fits in neither of these categories. From the *Punch* cartoonists, however, he did learn the value of placing his subject in the midst of a visually arresting action. The great innovation of *The Poets' Corner* was the appearance of men of letters in the kind of vigorous poses that had hitherto been reserved for figures in political life.

Dispossessed in regard to form both in literature and in art, Beerbohm groped for years to discover the vehicle that would perfectly convey his ironic artistic vision. Without dismissing any of the models along the way or ignoring any that come after, we may assert that the richest of Beerbohm's achievements are manifested in his imaginary reminiscences, works characterized by his invention and detailed portrayal of incidents or situations, quintessential scenes in the lives of men (and rarely women) he never knew for the purpose of implied commentary. Subsequent chapters will explore this thesis further, outline the development of the imaginary reminiscence, and discriminate more finely be-

The Quest for Form

tween its characteristics in prose and in caricature. At this point it is necessary to emphasize what these verbal and graphic "memories" have in common and to distinguish them from conventional fiction and comic portraiture. Satire, in conventional literary classification, has no distinctive form; it disguises itself as something else — quite literally in parody, somewhat less obviously in burlesque. *Gulliver's Travels* purports to be an account of the voyages of an actual ship's doctor; *Penguin Island* pretends to be history. By their interposition of an invented persona, satiric fictions much more subtly and thoroughly *manage* the reader's response. There is no participation in or re-creation of the artist's experience, no invitation to compare notes. Rather the satirist imposes his view upon his readers. What alone justifies this tyranny are the obliqueness and the delicacy, the cleverness and the beauty of the execution. For Beerbohm the satiric mask is of one who remembers. If he can remember Swinburne, why not Rossetti as well? If he can parody living writers in *A Christmas Garland,* why not imaginary ones in *Seven Men*?

The successful quest for form had additional advantages for Beerbohm as well. Not only did the imaginary reminiscence provide him with a mask and a perspective, it also enabled him to generate works that had greater substantial unity. Before the perfection of the imaginary reminiscence, all of Beerbohm's volumes were miscellanies. *The Poets' Corner,* it may be argued, is somewhat more specialized than *Caricatures of Twenty-Five Gentlemen* in the subjects under scrutiny, but it is a specious unity for all that: the writers caricatured have nothing more in common than that they were drawn by the same hand, for even the approach to them is inconsistent. The volumes of essays emphasize by their titles that they are but cumulative gatherings of unclassifiable and otherwise fugitive pieces: *Works* (1896), *More* (1899), *Yet Again* (1909), *And Even Now* (1920), *A Variety of Things* (1928), *Mainly on the Air* (1946). Apart from being designed for Christmas giving, *A Christmas Garland* (1912) grew out of a few parodies that had been written for December numbers of the *Saturday Review* six years before their publication in book form. And Christmas in some way, often quite ingeniously, is at the core of each parody. But such unity is quite artificial and mechanical compared to that of *Seven Men,* where the presence of Max as a character in each of the sketches gives the work as a whole a significance greater than the sum of the individual parts, not all of which are equally good. Although the three sketches of literary figures are clearly superior to the two nonliterary ones, the weaker are buttressed by the stronger not merely through association or physical juxtaposition.[29] And *Rossetti and His Circle* is not merely an album, as all the other books of caricatures are, but a narrative in pictures, a profound and subtle comic book. The imaginary reminiscence became for Beerbohm an organizing principle whereby the stray insight, the casual *aperçu,* could be pressed into the service of a larger design. Oscar Wilde, faced with a similar artistic problem a quarter of a century earlier, had sprinkled his epigrams through a series of "well-made" social comedies commercially successful but unimaginative until he found the proper vehicle for them in farce, *The Importance of Being Earnest,* a play that affords a more penetrating analysis of Victorian society than all of Wilde's other plays put together. For Beerbohm, the last of the aesthetes, the answer lay in a seemingly romantic looking back to the nineties — and beyond.

But it would be a mistake to look upon Beerbohm's development as an artist in the wholly narrow perspective of his own achievement. It is true that his themes and subjects are somewhat less than universal and that the peculiar combination of his talents makes his career unique, incapable of supplying a pattern of growth to others. Yet those themes and subjects and that career do not constitute an anecdotal backwater; rather, they run a course parallel to the mainstream of twentieth-century literature. As one contemporary critic observes:

> One now reads Beerbohm with recognitions beyond the powers of those of us who were literary neophytes in the Twenties. The elegant trifler contributed more than one had supposed to literary history. Beerbohm played an essential if deliberately minor role in the famous "revolution of taste" that took place between, roughly, 1910 and 1922. True, he was never a "modernist" in his own tastes, preferring the poetry of Swinburne and the novels of Trollope, Meredith, and James to *Ulysses* and *The Waste Land.* Nevertheless, he discovered before Pound and Eliot did (and in-

dependently of Laforgue) the futility and pathos of the dandy and his lady. As a verbal caricature of the London literary life, *Seven Men* parallels at several points Pound's treatment of the same subject in *Hugh Selwyn Mauberly*.[30]

In the final analysis, however, it is not likely that Beerbohm's themes will assure him a place in literary history. *Zuleika Dobson*, though Beerbohm's most famous work (largely, I suspect, because in its form — "an Oxford love story" — it perplexes readers, outwardly at least, less than his others) may yet not be his most enduring one. The dandy and his lady are not, after all, the central social problem of our time. Neither, for that matter, is London literary life — although at the hands of a writer like Gissing it can be made to seem so. Beerbohm's contribution to literary history lies less in his subject matter, though he is increasingly coming to be regarded as a chronicler and illuminator, than in the implications of his techniques. In his fusion and transfusion of genres and in his perfection of the imaginary reminiscence, he made a number of discoveries about the nature of representation of life in art and made them, moreover, quite independently of the "modernists," to whom, indeed, as Dupee suggests, he had an affinity.

The first of these discoveries, which is subversive of the distinction between the real and the imaginary, is that where any form of representation is concerned, there is no significant difference between historical and fictional personages. In the mind of a twentieth-century reader, Napoleon I of Elba and St. Helena is no more "real" than Edgar Linton of Thrushcross Grange, and possibly a good deal less. For although we puzzle over the behavior and experience of both, we have all the information we need or can ever get about Edgar Linton whereas we are subject to a different selection of facts about Napoleon from each biographer or historian. But in both instances the reader is presented with interpretations, and these interpretations proceed from a conception of life that sees human conduct as explicable, if not predictable. Both Napoleon and Edgar Linton must first become characters before they can mean anything to us. They may be complex and elusive characters, yet they are represented as capable of being understood. This principle is so well appreciated in art that historians do not see any *material* distinction between a Madonna and the *Mona Lisa*. But in literature the question posed to Autolycus as he plied his fantastic ballads — "Is it true?" — has lingered down through the centuries.

All worthy representations of human beings involve interpretation, and all interpretation proceeds from the reduction of persons to characters. Rossetti worked from live models yet produced a kind of human beauty not actually seen before. And Beerbohm produced a kind of Rossetti, his own reflection on the myth of Rossetti, that had also not existed before. So much does the vitality in the public consciousness of Hilary Maltby in *Seven Men* depend upon the antithesis of Stephen Braxton that both fade from the scene when they are separated; one makes no sense without the other. We make characters (and occasionally caricatures) of living persons as well as dead ones, and in they go — Will Rothenstein and the Portuguese Minister, Theodore Watts-Dunton and Walter Sickert — to mingle freely with the "fictional" characters. Are Beerbohm's verbal and graphic sketches of Whistler and Swinburne, both of whom he had met, but not often and hardly intimately, made more perceptive by his having met them or by his having studied them and characterized them? Beerbohm constantly teases his audience into an acceptance of this truth, which many novelists who insisted on the story rather than the telling of it had failed to understand.

Nor can character exist without an author. The second of Beerbohm's discoveries is that the disinterested observer is an impossibility. If the popular notion of the eighteenth-century deist's view of God was untenable — that of a Creator who ceased taking an active interest in His Creation once it was established and set in motion — then that of the eighteenth-century novelist who posed as an editor or a historian was equally untenable. The interpretation not only presupposes an interpreter but it also presupposes one whose interpretation constitutes participation in the thing being interpreted. And so Max includes himself in the picture: he has not merely composed it, he has delayed the shutter release so that he can slip into the photograph as well. In some instances his appearance seems almost as gratuitous as Alfred Hitchcock's in one of his films. When the Duke

The Quest for Form

of Dorset remarks that her speech "has what is called the literary flavour," Zuleika Dobson responds, "Ah, that is an unfortunate trick which I caught from a writer, a Mr. Beerbohm, who once sat next to me at dinner somewhere."[31] Yet even here Beerbohm seems to be insisting that the "source" of his creation is to be found, not in life, but in certain kinds of literature and certain kinds of social occasions. Max imagines and makes a character of Zuleika, but she does the same for him. This is not quite the same as in *The Pirates of Penzance* when Major-General Stanley proudly sings that he can "whistle all the airs from that infernal nonsense *Pinafore*." Beerbohm was enthusiastic about writers like Lytton Strachey and Frederic Manning who interpreted the past idiosyncratically.[32] And he had no sympathy with writers like "Savonarola" Brown, who denied responsibility for their creation. "I don't create," says Brown. "*They* do. Savonarola especially, of course. I just look on and record." The play and the scenario that fill out the sketch in *Seven Men* are not merely parodic of pseudo-Elizabethan drama (or even of Shakespeare himself, as has been suggested), they are illustrative of art that is lifeless and ludicrous because it is not informed by a *view*. Shakespeare's Rome is a historical anachronism but is internally consistent; Brown's Florence is a hodgepodge because it has no imaginative substance.

No amount of historical research could have saved Brown's play. Fidelity to detail and the objective stance may produce the standard two-volume biography but have no part in artistic representation. So much is clear from the foregoing. Art is self-conscious; it imitates but does not duplicate life. "Life," Beerbohm wrote, "save only through conventions, is inimitable. The more closely it be aped, the more futile and unreal its copy."[33] Yet neither could the play be saved by imitation of successful models. Brown's rather scrupulous observation of the conventions of Elizabethan poetic drama and his faultless metrics ("I have searched it vainly," says Max in his own voice by way of preface to the unfinished play, "for one line that does not scan"), together with the rush of echoes from all sides, constitute the very source of the pastiche. And thus we are brought to the third of Beerbohm's discoveries: that artistic truth is a matter of vividness, not clarity of detail, but clarity of vision. If a fiction can be intensely imagined, it becomes true. Jowett's remark to Rossetti,[34] though qualified by the words "likely to have been made," has become an authentic anecdote. Even if he didn't say it, it is the *kind* of thing he would have said had he had the opportunity. Enoch Soames is "dim," but to Will Rothenstein, the serious portraitist, he doesn't even exist. Only Max has the power to make him real. Soames's last words to Max, the only one who seems to have taken him seriously, are flung back through the doorway as the Devil is taking him off to Hell: "*Try* to make them know that I did exist!" And try Beerbohm did. He wrote the sketch, after all. And he drew a caricature of Soames (HD 1842) for the first American edition of *Seven Men,* backdating it to make it look like an early unfinished drawing, for Max preferred in the end to use caricatures rather than to illustrate scenes. Soames also intrudes into Beerbohm's group caricature "Some Persons of 'the Nineties' . . ." (HD 1650; BLC 51), where he is being harangued by William Butler Yeats. And the existence of Soames's diary has even been recorded in a standard reference work.[35] Who can doubt that Soames himself will appear, as it has been written, in the reading-room of the British Museum on 3 June 1997?

The work of Sir Max Beerbohm is in no danger of being forgotten. The delight of his contemporaries has given way to the chuckle of the literary historian, the art historian, the theatrical historian, and the political historian as Beerbohm's portraits in words or lines provide them with footnotes or illustrations. Beerbohm is likely to remain as well the recreation of the student of literature, for whom *The Poets' Corner* and *A Christmas Garland* are volumes in his library as necessary as the *Rejected Addresses* of Horace and James Smith or the *Nonsense Verse* of Edward Lear. Students with interests more specialized in the Pre-Raphaelite and Aesthetic Movements cannot ignore the testimony of Beerbohm. But as an artist, as one whose method and performance are as worthy of study as the subjects he dealt with, Beerbohm has only recently received serious attention. The imaginary reminiscence lies at the core of his satiric vision; it informs his maturest work not merely as a device for delivering himself of criticism but as a reflection itself on the nature of representation in art after realism. It is his own private form of modernism.

CHAPTER II

Toward the Imaginary Reminiscence in Prose

In the spring of 1895, when Beerbohm returned from a brief tour of America with the stage company of his half-brother, Herbert Beerbohm Tree, he found that public curiosity about the scandal surrounding Oscar Wilde's action of libel against the Marquis of Queensberry had been succeeded by the more lurid interest in the criminal charge against Wilde himself. Reginald Turner, Max's Oxford companion and lifelong friend, had been with Wilde at the time of his arrest (as he was to be with him at his death) but had prudently gone abroad before the trial. It was to him that the twenty-three-year-old Max confided his impressions of the affair:

> Ever since I arrived I have been all day at the Old Bailey and dining out in the evening — and coming home very tired. Please forgive me. Oscar has been quite superb. His speech about the Love that dares not tell his name was simply wonderful, and carried the whole court right away, quite a tremendous burst of applause. Here was this man, who had been for a month in prison and loaded with insults and crushed and buffeted, perfectly self-possessed, dominating the Old Bailey with his fine presence and musical voice. He has never had so great a triumph, I am sure, as when the gallery burst into applause — I am sure it affected the gallery.[1]

Although the account is certainly sympathetic, although it is apparent that he abhors the barbarity of the proceedings, it is neither as a loyal friend nor as an enlightened liberal that Beerbohm interprets the event. It is as a critic viewing a performance. Courtroom drama is described almost literally in the language of theater as Beerbohm observes the upstaging of one of the other defendants and his counsel and deplores having to pass through the crowd of witnesses for the prosecution after each day's scene. The letter goes on to describe a social evening with Wilde's friends and sympathizers as a rather incoherent play into which he has somehow stumbled:

> The scene that evening at the Leversons' was quite absurd. An awful New Woman in a divided skirt . . . writing a pamphlet at Mrs Leverson's writing-table with the aid of several whiskey-and-sodas: her brother, a gaunt man with prominent cheek-bones . . . kept reiterating that "these things must be approached through first principles and through first principles alone:" two other New Women who subsequently explained to Mr Leverson that they were there to keep a strict watch upon New Woman number one, who is not responsible for her actions: Mrs Leverson making flippant remarks about messenger-boys in a faint undertone to Bosie, who was ashen-pale and thought the pamphlet (which was the most awful drivel) admirable: and Mr Leverson explaining to me that he allowed his house to be used for these purposes not because he approved of "anything unnatural" but by reason of his admiration for Oscar's plays and personality. I myself exquisitely dressed and sympathizing with no one. (P. 104)

The imperfection of each performance is exposed with almost chilling dispassionateness. It is not enough that Wilde's defenders are all well-disposed toward him. The New Woman's pamphlet is still drivel — composed under the influence of alcohol in the middle of a party by one not responsible for her actions. Lord Alfred Douglas (who was to leave for France the next day) is fervent yet frightened. The Leversons themselves, who took Wilde into their home when he was out on bail, are also flawed: Ada is not above making sly insinuations to Douglas about his homosexuality, and Ernest hastens to affirm the restricted basis of his tolerance. But Beerbohm has sense enough to realize that he too is performing along with the others. The letter closes with Max's plea that Reggie return to England, lamenting the "rather bad luck" that had caused Turner to be present "at that unpleasant crisis," though he recognizes that "you must have been more or less talked about as you were in the garden of Gethsemane at the supreme moment" (p. 104). It may well be that Beerbohm's own low vitality rendered him incapable of comprehending the obsessions of others; yet he saw clearly enough that, whatever else it might come to signify to others, Wilde's ordeal had its origin in flamboyance and theatricality.

I have quoted this letter at some length because, although it was written when Beerbohm was very young, it is thoroughly characteristic of his way of looking at life. It was in their public performance, their actions and gestures, that he judged men and women, not in the tangled and unknowable motives behind that performance. But he did not pretend that these judgments were absolute. They were personal, and they appealed to no moral or philosophical principles for their authority, being grounded in no more than good sense, good taste, and good language.

To a pure essayist, a recorder of his own thoughts and moods or a commentator on social habits and institutions, such an attitude is doubtless essential. But the two literary genres that inquire intimately into the lives of individual human beings, fiction and biography, have traditionally been based on more than the impression of the moment. As the heir of epic, the novel enshrines the fundamental values of a culture or a critical response to those values; recently, it is true, the vision of novelists has become less reflective of public consensus; yet the novel is still seen as a vehicle of truth, not of self-indulgence. We speak of the "personal essay" without thought of what the adjective means, but to speak of a "personal novel" would arouse feelings of contempt. For the novel, given all its peculiarities and the assumption that it deals with the experience of human life, must always instruct, however much it may delight. Even more obvious is the instruction afforded by biography, which we read not merely for information but for moral guidance. Thus, however charming or original, however penetrating and full of insight even such perspectives may be, to view the behavior of men and women as performances and to apply not moral but aesthetic criteria to their conduct suggest attitudes surely not generally found acceptable.

Sir Max Beerbohm

Beerbohm clung to this legacy of the Aesthetic Movement long after the temple had crumbled with the downfall of Wilde and even after the ruins had been obliterated by World War I. Unlike Wilde, however, Beerbohm chose not to exemplify Pater's dictum "to burn always with a hard, gemlike flame" but to analyze the flames of those who did. Increasingly he came to examine the postures and gestures of public men and to invent men to exemplify commonly assumed postures and gestures. For the ruling passion of eighteenth-century psychology, Beerbohm substituted role-playing — only in the literal, theatrical sense. Natural behavior was a myth; men fashioned themselves into the characters they presented to the world. It was therefore neither cynical nor blasphemous of Beerbohm to see Wilde's betrayal and humiliation as an imitation of Christ — not in the sense of St. Thomas à Kempis, but as a portrayal, a characterization. Moreover, he was discerning enough to recognize that Wilde had thrown himself into the part. To appear in public at all is to step out onto a stage. A caricature almost by definition views life theatrically, providing with line the exaggerations of make-up, lighting, and costume. Beerbohm's task was to find a literary way of accomplishing the same thing.

An industrial and egalitarian society distrusts heroism and offers little opportunity for its exercise. The comforts and distresses of civilization alike dull the senses, discourage passionate commitment, and foster unquestioning conformity. Although himself sober and fastidious, Beerbohm was fascinated by those who he believed had dedicated themselves to their roles, not for wealth or fame or power (though these might accrue to them), but as an escape from the tedious, monotonous, and unimaginative — those, in short, who had made an art of life. His appreciation was that of the spectator, but he was not an uncritical one, and this latter fact accounts readily enough both for his personal recollections of the eminent and for their quality of recollecting for us the spectator as fully as the spectacle. Equally accounted for are his unhistorical judgments of figures of the past, judgments that illuminate Beerbohm far more than his subjects. In both instances the reader is tricked into believing that he or she really is reading for information, for in-

Toward the Imaginary Reminiscence in Prose

struction, that the play of imagination over all is mere coloring, that style and manner are subservient to solid fact.

The essayist and satirist, then, is suffered to make his observations about performances as long as they are in some measure verifiable. George IV, "Romeo" Coates, Aubrey Beardsley, and Algernon Swinburne have all been duly interred in the *Dictionary of National Biography*. Whatever Max may write about them irreverently or irrelevantly thus constitutes additional information about real personages. The critic of performances is thus granted a kind of inferior status as a biographer. But no such concession is granted to the critic of imagined performances, for he adds nothing to our stock of information. Of what value is a critique of a play that cannot be seen or a review of a book that cannot be read? Recollections of real men may be fragmental, anecdotal, and apparently inconsequential, but recollections of imaginary men must be coherent and organized — imaginary men must not only perform, they must perform in a drama.

If the essayist or satirist once submits to the tyranny and becomes a novelist, it is all over with him. He is subject to the laws of fiction, to which he can never wholly conform; and he comes to be regarded at best as an eccentric like Thomas Love Peacock or Samuel Butler. Beerbohm, however, saw no real distinction between his real and imaginary reminiscences. That both were deficient in "story," though not in narrative, did not disturb him; and he sought very consciously to obliterate the line between the two. Thus the intrusion of real persons into fictional events and the attribution of fictional anecdotes to real persons are justifiable on grounds that have nothing to do with verisimilitude. We do not, in reading Beerbohm, see things with our own eyes as he describes them; we see them through his eyes as he saw them.

But there is a danger in describing the performance of a living man, and that danger is that no two performances can ever be the same; moreover, performers can undergo changes that completely re-create their roles. A recollection of a performance that has been superseded by another discredits the reliability of the recollection. Perhaps an apprehension of this kind led Beerbohm not to publish the five essays ("No. 2. The Pines" is the sixth) about contemporaries that he mentions in a letter to Edmund Gosse.² One of these essays was "First Meetings with W. B. Yeats," broadcast over the BBC in 1954 and first published in book form in the enlarged, posthumous edition of *Mainly on the Air*. Beerbohm was aware that Yeats was, even in the nineties, an impressive figure; yet he was equally aware that Yeats's spell was one to which he was singularly impervious. To publish impressions that not only would have been received as unorthodox at the time that they were made but which also grew increasingly remote as Yeats shed his earlier masks would have been of service neither to Beerbohm nor to Yeats. But the powerful image of the poet engrossed in diabolism and ready to expound its fantastic lore to any who would listen to him was too precious and too palpable to be effaced. Yeats may have outgrown the role of *fin-de-siècle* decadent; yet it was too good a role to be wholly forgotten. Beerbohm cast Enoch Soames in it instead — or, rather, allowed Soames to try out for the part. Soames too is engrossed in diabolism.

It may be objected that I have urged a rather involved explanation for a rather commonplace occurrence. All writers of fiction, after all, derive their characters and incidents from people and situations in real life. And all put them to artistic uses that may be at considerable variance from the originals. My point is, however, that Beerbohm was not particularly interested in the fiction. He cared less about what happened to Soames (or to Yeats) than he did about recording how they struck him on first and subsequent meetings. Under the guise of biographer and remembrancer he imposed upon us his purely personal impressions and brought off that most difficult feat, the theatrical reminiscence, which he once described as

> the most awful weapon in the armoury of old age.... It is curiously exasperating to hear about a great actor whom we have not seen. So far from honouring, we abominate, his memory. Actors are like pet-birds. When a pet-bird dies, there may be, for those who knew it in the day of its song and its ruffling plumage, some poor comfort in the sight of its stuffed body. For others, there is only a sense of depression.³

A Beerbohm reminiscence is no more depressing than an Eliza-

Toward the Imaginary Reminiscence in Prose

bethan love sonnet. Both are "appreciations," both artifacts of the writers' engagement with living human beings. In both instances what is valued is the artistic representation rather than fidelity to an original. That Beerbohm increasingly indulged in imaginary reminiscence means no more than that years of observation and experience had made it possible for him to distill quintessential characters. It does not mean that he was ready to explore them from the inside or to allow them to interact with any but himself. Max is still the critical observer and ironic participant. Imaginative his reminiscence had always been. If the imaginary reminiscence constitutes the summit of Beerbohm's artistry, then it is because it enabled him to do what he had always done even more imaginatively than before.

It would be tedious indeed to plod methodically through Beerbohm's canon in search of nuggets of reminiscential ore before mining the rich veins of the mature work. Reminiscence is not, after all, a young man's game, and Beerbohm's earliest work seems almost preoccupied with manner to the exclusion of everything else. Yet if the Victorian Beerbohm had not much personally to recollect, in his pose as historian he subordinates the scholar to the raconteur and commentator. He delights to explode the myth of history and perversely to examine the Regency through the spectacles of a late nineteenth-century aesthete. In "King George the Fourth" (1894) the twenty-two-year-old Max attempts to rehabilitate the name of the much maligned monarch from the censures of Victorian respectability, and he balances passages beginning with "it is said" with those beginning with "I like to think." What made the essay so outrageous to his contemporaries was perhaps less the extravagance of its style than the substitution of an aesthetic for a moral judgment of behavior. Beerbohm asserts, for example, that it is not out of any democratic principle that the common man should be entrusted with the reins of government but because "it is horrible to think that, under our existing *régime,* all the men of noblest blood and highest intellect should waste their time in the sordid atmosphere of the House of Commons, listening for hours to nonentities talking nonsense, or searching enormous volumes to prove that somebody said something some years ago that does not quite fully tally with something he said the other day, or standing tremulous before the whips in the lobbies and the scorpions in the constituencies."[4] The witty play on "whips" and "scorpions" serves to remind us that Max is performing for us as well as reviewing the performance of King George. In another "historical" essay in *Works* composed two years later, "Poor Romeo!" Beerbohm purports to find an explanation for the bizarre exhibitionistic behavior of Robert Coates, an early nineteenth-century dandy and amateur actor, in the cruel exactions of the haughty belle with whom he was infatuated. The explanation necessitates Max's purchase from a Bath bookseller of the fragments of a letter hitherto unknown to historians and the fashioning of a *femme fatale* something between Zuleika Dobson and Lucrezia Borgia (from Ladbroke Brown's play, *Savonarola,* of course). The real interest, however, is not in motive, but in the grotesque performance of Coates himself:

> All were eager to applaud the new Romeo. Presently, when the varlets of Verona had brawled, there stepped into the square — what! — a mountebank, a monstrosity! Hurrah died upon every lip. The house was thunderstruck. Whose legs were in those scarlet pantaloons? Whose face grinned over that bolster-cravat, and under that Charles II. wig and opera-hat? From whose shoulders hung that spangled sky-blue cloak? Was this bedizened scarecrow the Amateur of Fashion, for sight of whom they paid their shillings? . . . Those lines that were not drowned in laughter Mr. Coates spoke in the most foolish and extravagant manner. He cut little capers at odd moments. He laid his hand on his heart and bowed, now to this, now to that part of the house, always with a grin. In the balcony-scene he produced a snuff-box, and, after taking a pinch, offered it to the bewildered Juliet. Coming down to the footlights, he laid it on the cushion of the stage-box and begged the inmates to refresh themselves, and 'to pass the golden trifle on.'[5]

Here is theatrical reminiscence with a vengeance; if we doubt that Max actually saw the performance he describes, it is only because it took place over sixty years before he was born. The detail of the central incident, together with the casual citation of sources and the obviously spurious letter that Beerbohm happens upon, inclines one to the belief that the whole thing is an invention. So akin in conception and execution is the character

Toward the Imaginary Reminiscence in Prose

of Coates to Beerbohm's other performers, Soames, Maltby, and Brown, that Behrman was deceived about his actuality until Beerbohm himself put him right and the *DNB* confirmed the assertion.[6] In these two early essays, then, we see adumbrations of Beerbohm's later reminiscential manner chiefly in his concern for persons as performers. The past differs from the present only as a revival differs from a new play.

History is played with in a number of other interesting ways in the early essays. In "1880," which was to be the grain of sand around which "The Mirror of the Past" began forming, the essential joke is that the writer treats this memorable year, which is only fourteen years past, as though it literally were a part of ancient history and as though the Aesthetic Movement were as significant a development in civilization as the rise of Christianity. Slender and impressionistic as the essay is, Beerbohm has sprinkled it with numerous documentary and explanatory notes to establish his credentials as a historian. The same persona of the dandy turned historian is maintained in *The Happy Hypocrite*(1896), a fairy tale that is shamelessly imitative of Wilde's manner and which must surely be unique among fairy tales for being set in Regency times and annotated with spurious historical references. The tale, moreover, justifies the doctrine of masks, for the hypocritical rake Lord George Hell, who dons a virtuous mask in order to win the love of Jenny Mere, ultimately becomes what he has represented himself to be. The most extravagant of Beerbohm's spoofs on "objectivity" must surely be his essay "The Case of Prometheus" (1898), in which a traveler's eyewitness account of having seen that Titan chained to a mountain-top, his liver daily plucked at by an eagle, leads Beerbohm, after due consultation of venerable authorities, to propose an expedition to liberate this victim of ancient injustice. There is a Lucianic wildness to this piece, particularly in its juxtaposition of images of mythology and contemporary civilization:

> I shall hail the captive with words of good cheer — χαῖρε, 'Ιαπετιονίδη! —and with my gun I shall shoot the eagle as it hovers over him at sunset, and with a file I shall free him of the rusty fetters that bind him to the rock. Dodging any thunderbolts that

may be hurled at me, I shall pick up the shot eagle, and shall lead Prometheus gently down the mountain-side. When we reach the inn in the valley, I shall provide him with the tweed suit which I have ordered for him and am taking with me, the fur coat, the dressing-case whose fittings are marked Π. We shall be in London, if all go well, in time for the latter part of the season. I am sure Prometheus will be much lionised.[7]

The madness, however, is not uncritical. There is something more than a schoolboy's travesty in this mixture of ancient and modern heroism and its rewards. Prometheus may find the London season more of a punishment than Mt. Caucasus. Nor is the quixotism of the persona to be overlooked: his desire is not so much to right the injustice as to achieve social success.

Apart from these playful excursions into the nature and limitations of historical narrative, Beerbohm also explores in his early works the capacity of the writer to invent realities of his own, the power of the word to create a visual truth — or to alter one. In "A Good Prince" (1895) Beerbohm skilfully composes a pen portrait of an ideal heir to the throne, simple, blameless, ornamental, a credit to the institution of monarchy and a model of behavior to his future subjects — quite unlike, one must observe, the then Prince of Wales. Encomium upon encomium is piled up until the relevation, which has been prepared for by subtle hints, is complete. The paragon is still an infant: "He stands alone among European princes — but, as yet, only with the aid of a chair."[8] The writer has not merely imposed upon our credulity; he has exposed our folly in expecting to find irreproachable behavior in men born to privilege, insulated against adversity, and placed constantly on view. There is a heightened irony in our recognition that the young prince so eulogized grew up later to be King Edward VIII and Duke of Windsor. In "Prangley Valley" (1897) Beerbohm constructs a beautiful landscape unspoiled by developers and railway builders, which "from Kew Gardens one may reach ... in less than half an hour's walking,"[9] and then immediately laments the praise, for he sees it as the summons for the valley's destruction. But his distress is as imaginary as the valley itself, whose beauty cannot fade. This is Beerbohm at his most Keatsian, finding enduring beauty in art and taunting

Toward the Imaginary Reminiscence in Prose

the literalist and realist with word-pictures that have seemingly more vitality than actuality itself. Beerbohm is very fond of manipulating the reader's response and particularly of baffling his expectation. "Going Back to School" (1897), inspired by the sight of a schoolboy at Victoria Station returning from his holidays, looks as though it is about to develop into a nostalgic reverie, a dream of lost innocence and of carefreeness. But it is nothing of the sort. Infinitely more pleasant are the life and times of an adult than those of schoolboys:

> Were I to meet, now, any of those masters who are monsters to you, my boy, he would treat me even more urbanely, it may be, than I should treat him. When he sets you a hundred lines, you write them without pleasure, and he tears them up. When I, with considerable enjoyment and at my own leisure, write a hundred lines or so, they are printed for all the world to admire, and I am paid for them enough to keep you in pocket-money for many terms.[10]

Beerbohm refuses to yield to the celebration of childhood made fashionable in literature by Gray and Wordsworth. Whatever the condition of children ideally, he knows that in the present state of society an unregimented and comfortable existence is available to no children and to only some adults, of whom he is fortunate to be one. In "A Memory of a Midnight Express" (1902), one of his most introspective essays, Beerbohm marvels at his capacity to experience alternately feelings of terror and sorrow without any real justification for either. The unstated cause, of course, is imagination. But the traveler has communicated his feelings to us — we feel them as palpably as he — just as A. V. Laider does in *Seven Men*. It is precisely this power of imagination, rather than technical proficiency, that makes the artist's rendering truer to life than life itself. Waxworks are depressing to him because they create no illusions, they constitute a "morgue of upstanding corpses,"[11] though a waxen effigy will do well enough to serve the purely ceremonial functions that royalty has been preserved in England to perform.[12]

Art does not copy life directly, then, but creates an illusion of it. But so, to complete the Wildean paradox, does life create an illusion of art. This reversal comes about because a purely "nat-

Sir Max Beerbohm

ural" existence is unavailable to us in a civilized society, where we are constantly attending, to use a contemporary expression, to the image we project of ourselves. Beerbohm explores this notion in one of his most "philosophical" essays, "Pretending" (1898):

> Every human creature weaves for himself and wears an elaborate vesture of illusion. All of us pretend. And we pretend in order that we may impress others, not ourselves, and our pleasure is proportionate to our success in making others believe us to be something finer than we are. We grudge no time that is wasted, no convenience that is sacrificed to that end. Gregarious animals, we are gluttons for effect, and the pains we take to produce effect are the chief tragedy of our existence. . . . We do but want to be envied, and for envy we will pay any price. To enjoy, simply, the things that are ours, is a philosophy beyond us. We value them not, save as material for false display, for deception. . . . For what is ours by natural right we care nothing. In our code possession is nine points of ennui, and we delight only in things alien to us. Our young men ape the wisdom and weariness of eld, whilst eld would fain dance, with stiff limbs, to the joyous and silly tunes of adolescence. What we have not, we simulate; and of what we have, we are heartily ashamed. We pull long faces to hide our mirth and grin when we are most wretched.[13]

There is, of course, pretense and posturing here too, as Beerbohm strenuously tries to suppress frivolousness and to assume the mantle of Dr. Johnson. Yet the idea is a central one in Beerbohm's life and work and provides the justification for his minute inquiry into the pains men take to produce effect. Habitual though our pretense may be, few of us can carry off our acts really well, and Beerbohm is attracted to the inspired amateurs, such as the dandies.[14] Because it is a performance usually attended to with great awkwardness, Beerbohm projects in one essay a service whereby professionals see people off on long journeys.[15] Paradoxically, it is those who act professionally, who in a disciplined way employ their lives as a medium of expression, rather than the rest of us who are amateurs, whose art is the most fragile and evanescent. They are therefore worthy, argues Beerbohm, of the lavish accolades accorded them during their lifetime, for they are certain of none afterwards.[16]

Toward the Imaginary Reminiscence in Prose

The notion that an artificial civilization should elicit artificial behavior is used as a plea for the restoration of standards of politeness and deportment in "The Decline of the Graces" (1905).[17] In this essay, however, there is no hint of irony in his assumption of a posture rather like that of a schoolmistress. But he is rarely so earnest. For the most part, in his early essays, the idea of pretense is played with more lightheartedly, and there is not so much an examination of individual performances as there is of human institutions as theatrical presentations. He interprets this conceit rather perversely in *More*, which contains two essays that overturn our expectations of theater. In "An Infamous Brigade" (1896) he sees the firefighter as a kind of Puritan suppressing the pleasurable spectacle of conflagration whereas "At Covent Garden" (1897) interprets the opera itself as but a backdrop for the more exciting social scene played in the auditorium and the lobbies of the theater. The essays of his subsequent volume, *Yet Again,* are generally less fanciful and more thoughtful in their use of this theme. "Dulcedo Judiciorum" (1908) looks upon civil court cases as a form of drama, and "General Elections" (1909) sees these contests and the interest that they provoke in the general populace as something akin to sporting events. All spectacle is theater to Beerbohm, which belief leads him to wonder in "A Parallel" (1905) why the aggression of two people toward each other, since it can neither instruct nor delight onlookers, should attract paying crowds. The idea of awarding prizes to people for fighting each other in public seems to him as pointless as awarding prizes to people for making love to each other in public. Beerbohm was spared the knowledge that in the second half of the twentieth century the limits of theater would be extended to realize what he had thought a *reductio ad absurdum.*

All are performers, then, and those who train themselves and make a study of their performance are the professionals. But there is something to be said for the unstudied and unpremeditated:

> Art, in a writer, is not everything. Indeed, it implies a certain limitation. If a list of consciously artistic writers were drawn up, one would find that most of them were lacking in great force of in-

tellect or of emotion; that their intellects were restricted, their emotions not very strong. Writers of enormous vitality never are artistic: they cannot pause, they must always be moving swiftly forward. Mr. Meredith, the only living novelist in England who rivals Ouida in sheer vitality, packs tight all his pages with wit, philosophy, poetry, and psychological analysis. His obscurity, like that of Carlyle and Browning, is due less to extreme subtlety than to the plethoric abundance of his ideas. He cannot stop to express himself. If he could, he might be more popular. The rhapsodies of Mr. Swinburne, again, are so overwhelmingly exuberant in their expression that no ordinary reader can cope with them; the ordinary reader is stunned by them before he is impressed. When he lays down the book and regains consciousness, he has forgotten entirely what it was all about. On the other hand reticence, economy, selection, and all the artistic means may be carried too far. Too much art is, of course, as great an obstacle as too little art; and Pater, in his excessive care for words, is as obscure to most people as are Carlyle and Browning, in their carelessness. It is of him who takes the mean of these two extremes, to that author who expresses himself simply, without unnecessary expansion or congestion, that appreciation is most readily and spontaneously granted.[18]

A most Horatian formulation and one that it is difficult to believe follows by but one year the studied extravagances of *Works*. Beerbohm's definition of art may seem a bit too near what Pope would conceive of as "correctness," but he argues elsewhere as well that there are virtues in spontaneity. Amateurism is seen as the source of strength in "Whistler's Writing" (1904) whereas self-consciousness and creeping artistry have brought about "The Blight on the Music Halls" (1897). And the professionalism that turns writing into a trade rather than the occupation of a gentleman is most savagely attacked in "Arise, Sir — !" (1897). The role of artist may be played in a number of ways, and Beerbohm was to explore all of them in his later works.

One other characteristic of Beerbohm's mature style that has considerable bearing on the imaginary reminiscence has its adumbration in the early writings. Under the collective title "Words for Pictures" Beerbohm gathered together in *Yet Again* a number of the fugitive descriptions and impressions of paintings he had published between 1898 and 1901. These often display an engaging whimsy in Beerbohm's probing of the conventions of narrative painting as he later questions those of narrative writing. In Bellini's *Peter the Dominican* one searches vainly in the painting for the words *"Credo in Dominum"* that the martyr wrote in the dust before dying, but the only writing in the picture is on a little scroll hanging from a branch: *"JOANNES BELLINUS FECIT."* Out of this absence and this presence Beerbohm derives his assertion that the artist's work is superior to the subject of his art: "After all, there have been so many martyrs — and so many martyrs named Peter — but so few great painters. The little screed on the fence is no mere vain anachronism. It is a sly, rather malicious symbol. PERIIT PETRUS: BELLINUS FECIT, as who should say."[19] Beerbohm records his response to Corot's *Macbeth and the Witches* as though he had undergone an actual encounter with the figures depicted, and he finds that the power of the scene derives from its originality of imagination, not from its being an illustration. "It is because Corot had no reverence for Shakespeare's text — because he was able to create in his own way, with scarcely a thought of Shakespeare, an independent masterpiece — that this picture is worthy of its theme."[20] Finally, in his piece on George Morland's *The Visit*, Beerbohm imagines scenes both anterior and posterior to the one in the painting, thus rendering his "reading" a highly personal one. In all these instances he has responded to the works as living performances, not as static objects, and has teased reader and viewer alike by his quick shifts from the real to the imagined.

On first consideration it would appear that an extended work of fiction could not fail to exhibit strongly those characteristics of the imaginary reminiscence so prominent in Beerbohm's later work. Yet the truth is that, brilliant though *Zuleika Dobson* is, and memorable — it will undoubtedly remain his most popular work, if popular can be applied to a writer so fastidious as Beerbohm — it is not the most representative of his compositions. In it we see neither the fruition of earlier growths nor the seeds of later ones. *Zuleika Dobson* could be attributed to no one other than Max Beerbohm; yet our understanding of this fantasy novel is not particularly enhanced by a study of his first volumes of essays, nor does it in turn illuminate the later ones. Like *The Rape of the Lock* (to which in its rococo elegance of execution and mockery of literary conventions it bears comparison), it is readily separable from the rest of the canon and perhaps best analyzed apart from it.

What chiefly distinguishes *Zuleika Dobson* from Beerbohm's other work is not that it is given over so utterly to fantastic happenings but that there is absolutely no way in which we can identify with any of the characters; both heroes and villains are preposterous; we care not for their fates, however much we may enjoy the telling of the tale. We do not quarrel with the implausibility of the fable. Zuleika, a theatrical conjuror and *femme fatale,* descends upon staid Oxford, making a conquest of all the undergraduates but chiefly the Duke of Dorset, a dandiacal youth of extraordinary accomplishments. Because Zuleika can love no one who loves her, and because the duke cannot live without her, he determines to drown himself in the river, in which resolve he is followed by all the other undergraduates. Zuleika, unperturbed, departs for Cambridge. It helps, of course, to recognize that Beerbohm's characters may be literalizations of the stock characters of melodrama[21] and that the situations are likewise literalizations of clichés.[22] The myth of romantic love clashes with the myth of romantic Oxford. We delight in Beerbohm's irony and his play of wit. But we cannot join in the laughter because we do not know what has set him off. Like Romeo and his friends amazed at the vitality of Mercutio's fancy and invention in Queen Mab, we cannot quite participate. *Zuleika Dobson* is imaginative but it is not reminiscential. It has the quality, not of a thing remembered or a thing discovered, but of a thing invented or concocted. Max is undilutedly the creator and in no way a participant. That engagement of the critic *in* the performance, which so suffuses his later work, is almost wholly absent here.

Almost. Every reader of the novel is struck by an apparent change in tone that takes place in chapter 11 (the book is composed, by the way, of twenty-four chapters, an epic number), where Beerbohm steps into the book in his own person as the servant of Clio, the Muse of History, and records an Olympian disquisition on the relative merits of history and fiction. Mechanically the interlude may be explained as occurring at the point where Beerbohm took up the novel again in 1910, having originally conceived and begun work on it twelve years earlier. Studies of the manuscripts of the novel support conjectures about Beerbohm's altered conception of the work.[23] Behrman sees in the London manuscript "the struggle between Max's dual careers . . . several times, Max seems to have forgotten that he was writing a novel, and whole pages are devoted to drawings, some of them sketches for caricatures that later became famous."[24] The manuscript written in Italy is full of corrections but no distractions. According to John Felstiner, the intervening years as a drama critic and essayist, his ventures into literary parody, contemporary developments in the novel, particularly those of Henry James, "the remoteness of Victorian Oxford, and Beerbohm's three engagements to actresses . . . made a straight novel impossible for him."[25] But chapter 11 is no mere justification, however humorously executed, of a working novelist's innovations in form. The persona identifies less with that of Fielding in *Tom Jones* than with the more elusive ones of Swift in *The Battle of the Books* and *The Tale of a Tub*. In other words, although the intrusion holds up the story, it is essential to the narration.

In this interlude Beerbohm explains the legitimacy of his pretensions as a historian by telling of how Clio, bored by the politics and military strategy that constituted most of what passed for history and longing for the more romantic interpretation of events by writers such as Herodotus, began scanting the works she was said to inspire and started reading novels instead. When Zeus fell in love with her, he at first wooed her by appearing to her in the guise of various (dull) nineteenth-century historical tomes, until Hermes told him of Clio's predilection. She was no less sickened when he then pursued her in the form of novels. Her deep acquaintance with both forms, however, led her to conceive of the advantage of combining the historian's commitment to fact with the novelist's privilege of understanding character and motive, and she pleaded with Zeus that a trial might be made of it. "He admitted the disabilities under which historians laboured. But the novelists — were they not equally handicapped? They had to treat of persons who never existed, events which never were. Only by the privilege of being in the thick of those events and in the very bowels of those persons, could they hope to hold the reader's attention." But Zeus's principal objection appeared to be economic. "If similar privileges were granted to the historian, the demand for novels would cease forthwith, and many thousands of hard-working, deserving men and women would be thrown out of employment."[26] Nevertheless, Zeus allows himself to be persuaded to make an exception in a single instance. Clio chooses Beerbohm as her historian, and Zeus confers upon him "invisibility, inevitability, and psychic penetration, with a flawless memory thrown in." But Beerbohm refuses the full exercise of his commission; he is too much the gentleman to spy upon the Duke of Dorset in his humiliation; he discreetly draws the curtain over the scene, using the hour instead to hover over Oxford and reflect upon it. We are returned to the story in chapter 12 but now the narrator is very much more the eyewitness than before.

The interlude functions certainly as a bridge from the early chapters to the later ones, as a means of reconciling the original idea of the novel with its final form. But it is reflective too of Beerbohm's grave reservations about the ability of fiction and history to create the illusion of life. The make-believe of novels becomes as tedious to Clio as the dry details of what actually happened — neither seems vital. And if a character fails to persuade from his exterior, no amount of penetration into his motives will make him seem any more real. The historian, on the other hand, does not pretend to be all knowing, but all that he does know must be put down and all that he fancies must be kept out. In the novel generally and in the interlude particularly Beerbohm seems to be arguing that the only subjects that a writer really has are his own impressions. The novelist rejects them in exchange for omniscience; the historian rejects them in exchange for objectivity and impartiality. In *Zuleika Dobson* Beerbohm toys with the conventions of fiction and history. The historian with the privileges of the novelist is but a conceit of Beerbohm's attributed to a mythological Muse. But that conceit was to be realized fully in the imaginary reminiscence.

Zuleika Dobson, then, is a comic exposure of the insufficiency of the conventions of the novel, including its portrayal of charac-

Toward the Imaginary Reminiscence in Prose

ter, to account for life. Zuleika is as mythical as Prometheus, as out of place in Oxford as he in London. Beerbohm was to deliver the same kind of criticism in another way in *A Christmas Garland* (1912). Like the novel, *A Christmas Garland* was essentially some unfinished business that he had brought with him from England to Italy. Of the seventeen parodies of living writers, seven had already been published in the *Saturday Review* in 1906 and an eighth ten years earlier than that.[27] It is possible that another, the parody of A. C. Benson, may also belong to the earlier batch; for although purporting to be fiction, it is imitative of Benson's rambling, and not very illuminating, reflective essays *From a College Window,* which had been published in 1906. Half of Beerbohm's book, including some of the best parodies, those of James, Kipling, and Wells, had already been written while he was a journalist in London. This is a point well worth remembering: Beerbohm's first two books published after he had settled in Rapallo are but completions of works conceived and considerably advanced while he was writing essays and drama reviews. Italy provided him with leisure, not inspiration.

To mimic someone, and to do it successfully, is one of the most devastating kinds of criticism. Even if the mimicry is appreciative, there is an implied reduction of the victim to the status of automaton. His attitudes and behavior, what he does and says, are not only explicable and imitable, they are predictable — and if predictable, then controllable. The mimic constructs a simulacrum of the original, as the voodoo witch doctor constructs a doll. What afflicts the simulacrum also afflicts the original. Parody, the imitation of a writer's manner, is a particularly excruciating kind of mimicry; a gait or a twitch, the timbre of voice or the movement of hands, all are fundamentally involuntary personal characteristics, but a writer's style is his essence: it constitutes not only how he talks about life but how he sees it. Successful parody, like all satire, is more than clever entertainment: it is the invitation of a writer to a sophisticated reader to submit the work of another writer to the test of ridicule. And Beerbohm's parody is undeniably successful. The generally enthusiastic reception of *A Christmas Garland* by his contemporaries has not appreciably lessened over the years, though some of the writers under scrutiny, like Maurice Hewlett or G. S. Street, are hardly known today. That Beerbohm chose not merely prominent but enduring writers to parody is only a partial answer to the continuing appeal of *A Christmas Garland*. Mere likeness or suggestion of the original, which is usually all that the casual parodist can bring off, gives way to studied composition. In the words of a contemporary reviewer, "He has not so much copied his models as extended them. He has projected the mind of each writer into a theme of his own invention, and, but for the subtle touches of exaggeration, and an occasional reduction of the method of absurdity, he has written as they would have written."[28] In this projection of the mind of each writer he creates a performance that passes as a specimen of the original — something he would have written if the test were set to him. With Christmas as the general theme, each goes about his work in his own way: Frank Harris links the subject up with Shakespeare, Chesterton propounds logic-chopping paradoxes, Shaw writes a preface to a play, and Gosse engages in a chatty, urbane recollection of how he brought together Robert Browning and Henrik Ibsen. What results are reminiscences of literature that are wholly imaginary. If they were not all written about the same subject, if there were not these touches of absurdity, these parodies might be taken for authentic compositions.

The method is particularly effective in respect to the novelists, in whose work the parody not merely imitates the outward style but becomes critical of the writer's vision of life as well. In the parody of Henry James, "The Mote in the Middle Distance," Beerbohm presents us with two children, Keith and Eva Tantalus, wondering on Christmas morning what are the contents of the stockings at the foot of their beds and debating in an exaggeratedly elliptical way whether or not they should investigate. Felstiner, who devotes a whole section of his book to Beerbohm's responses to James as man and writer, in caricature as well as in prose and verse, observes:

> Beerbohm's title and the rest of his parody develop the way of registering perceptions which James developed in his later novels. All the turns of style Beerbohm invents for Keith and Eva can

> be found in *The Wings of the Dove* and *The Golden Bowl*. They sometimes seem to be done better by Beerbohm, sometimes less well done: the broken sentences, roundabout simplicities, syntactical quibbles, colloquialisms made genteel by inverted commas, italics for delicate intonation, stunning double negatives, accumulated homely adjectives, abruptly placed, vague adverbs, banal metaphors worried and reworried, the narrator's unsettling glances into the future and his intimacy with "our friend" Keith, the exasperating, magnified scruples, and, at last, the vibrant moral renunciation by Keith and Eva — "One doesn't violate the shrine — pick the pearl from the shell!"[29]

The imitation is superb, the mastery of the master's tricks is complete. But we honor forgery no more than we honor plagiary. In seeming to duplicate James's achievement, Beerbohm is questioning its worth — specifically by extending the introspection and the tortuous psychology of James's adults to children. If the verbal and moral complexity, rendered with such loving fidelity to the original, seems absurd, ill placed, in the instance that Beerbohm invents, is it any less so in James's novel itself? To pose the question is not necessarily to provide the answer. But the parody of James is a test of the validity of the author's style as an instrument for conveying the illusion of life.

No such ambiguity attaches itself to the parodies of Kipling and Wells. In "P.C., X, 36," Santa Claus is apprehended by Constable Judlip as a burglar because he is seen carrying a sack late at night and is obviously German. The situation is funny enough but is preceded by several pages of Kiplingesque dialogue between Judlip (whose aspirates are all represented by apostrophes) and the narrator, his somewhat more educated admirer. The arrest is thus seen not merely as a case of mistaken identity but as a natural consequence of the brutal, authoritarian, and jingoistic attitudes of the lower-class Judlip and his more privileged champion (presumably a projection of Kipling himself). It is obvious that Beerbohm cares neither for Kipling's style nor for his illusion of life. The imitation of Wells is a little more complicated, for here we have a parody within a parody. The outrageousness of the takeoff on Wells's visionary blueprints for the future, entitled "Sitting Up for the Dawn," is compounded by demonstrating the inspirational effect of that work on the young idealist Perkins, who is in danger of being seduced by High Society. The effect is a little like that in "'Savonarola' Brown," where Max is shown to take quite seriously his role as Brown's literary executor. At a Christmas party given by an unnamed duke and duchess, Perkins is near despair at the recollection of his inability in the past to gain support for his progressive schemes from his fellow guests and other members of the class to which they belong. "He reflected, while he was dressing for dinner on Christmas night, how odd it was that he had ever thought of Using them. He might as well have hoped to Use the Dresden shepherds and shepherdesses that grinned out in the last stages of refinement at him from the glazed cabinets in the drawing-rooms."[30] With the gift from the Duchess of a pair of diamond and sapphire cuff links, Perkins realizes that he is in danger of being Used by Them. Retreating to his bedroom, he dips at random into the influential book, which not only frees him of temptation but rekindles his zeal for utopian reform. Until we are presented with the extract that so moves him, the narrative is not really all that ludicrous, except perhaps for the mention of Perkins's pet scheme — a Provisional Government of England by the Female Foundlings. We are more struck by the fact of the aristocracy's resistance to change of any kind. Perkins's situation invokes our sympathy rather than our derision. That is, it does so until we read the chapter on General Cessation Day, which describes what Christmas will have evolved into in the fully regimented, classless society of the future: it will be a holiday in which citizens who have reached the prescribed age (thirty-two in the new reckoning, which involves a ten-day week, a fifty-day month, and a thousand-day year) will "make way" by availing themselves of the Municipal Lethal Chamber, accompanied on their final journey by friends and relations. The whole idea is set down with a chilling rationality reminiscent of Swift's description of the Houyhnmns:

> You figure the wide streets filled all day long with solemn processions — solemn and yet not in the least unhappy. . . . You figure the old man walking with a firm step in the midst of his progeny, looking around him with a clear eye at this dear world which is about to lose him. He will not be thinking of himself. He will not

be wishing the way to the lethal chamber was longer. He will be filled with joy at the thought that he is about to die for the good of the race — to "make way" for the beautiful young breed of men and women who, in simple, artistic, antiseptic garments, are disporting themselves so gladly on this day of days. (Pp. 45–46)

Whether or not Beerbohm doubts that mankind can ever develop into the selfless and unemotional beings so described, he certainly wants no part of their society. The ridicule falls in double measure: first, upon the naive, chimerical, and authoritarian ideas for the reorganization of mankind, which, even if feasible, are inhuman; second, upon the feeble and inartistic use of fiction as a device for propagating these ideas. Beerbohm rejects what Kipling and Wells stand for by turning against them their very instruments of expression — their styles.

The best parodies in *A Christmas Garland* may begin in the aping of linguistic mannerism, but they generally extend to an implied criticism of the writer's basic outlook. In the parody of Conrad, "The Feast," there is the recognition that the writer's style is unique not merely because English is not his mother tongue but because Conrad's unremittingly moral perspective and heavy, humorless irony have imposed themselves on the very process of generating sentences. In the following passage we see the fusion of the two in the grammatically acceptable but odd locutions (such as the unemphatic postpositioning of adjectives) and in the momentarily arresting but unnatural similes and figurative language in Conrad's search for the *mot injuste*:

> The roofs of the congested trees, writhing in some kind of agony private and eternal, made tenebrous and shifty silhouettes against the sky, like shapes cut out of black paper by a maniac who pushes them with his thumb this way and that, irritably, on a concave surface of blue steel. Resin oozed unseen from the upper branches to the trunks swathed in creepers that clutched and interlocked with tendrils venomous, frantic, and faint. Down below, by force of habit, the lush herbage went through the farce of growth — that farce old and screaming, whose trite end is decomposition.[31]

Moreover, Beerbohm seems to suggest in the tale itself that the hero is hardly interesting enough as a character to merit the elaborate production that is contrived for the working out of his fate. The same may be said of "Scruts," the parody that attempts to capture in miniature the epic pretensions of Arnold Bennett. It is full of invented local color and invented local history, and presumes to take seriously Bennett's belief that the traditional novel was a fit vehicle for the chronicling of sagas of the working class, that the introspection of Anna Karenina and that of Emily Wrackgarth were qualitatively the same, the only difference being that one had to be rendered in Staffordshire dialect. And in "Endeavour" Beerbohm zeroes in on the self-indulgent, impractical, hand-wringing liberalism of Galsworthy's aristocratic intellectuals, whose endless discussion of the world's injustices brings about no alleviation and has no greater consequence than resignation.

This detailed and practical scrutiny of style as an index of a vision of life is carried out in a general way in two other pieces composed around the same time as *A Christmas Garland*, though not published in book form until 1920. The first of these, "'How Shall I Word It?'" (1910), expands a group of model letters upon emergent occasions found in a manual that Beerbohm had picked up at a railway bookstall. Beerbohm's examples provide patterns of expression for some of the less noble human sentiments and include a blackmail note, a gentleman's refusal to pay his tailor's bill, letters of thanks for an unwanted inscribed copy of a book and a hideous wedding present, and a letter of congratulation to a member of Parliament unseated in a general election. The samples are hilarious in themselves, not least because the occasions hardly seem proper ones for seeking out models of composition. And that observation causes the reader to wonder whether there are *any* occasions on which it is appropriate to do so. To accept another's words as an expression equivalent to one's own is not merely an act of laziness or indifference but one of self-abnegation as well. In "Kolniyatsch" (1913) Beerbohm purports to offer an appreciation of a minor Eastern European writer, one of a "seemingly inexhaustible supply of anguished souls from the Continent — infantile, wide-eyed Slavs, Titan Teutons, greatly blighted Scandinavians, all of them different, but all of them raving in one common darkness and with one common gesture plucking out their vitals for exportation."[32] Whether, as has been suggested, Kolniyatsch is a composite of Dostoevsky and Gorki[33] is of no particular importance. Beerbohm thought that the extravagant emotionalism of the Russians was alien to the British temper and that the lavish praise bestowed on them also had in it more than a touch of the trendy and chic. "Kolniyatsch" is therefore written in a kind of glib critical journalese, a barrage of words that gives the illusion but not the substance of a thing comprehended:

> As one of the critics avers, "It is hardly too much to say that a time may be not far distant, and may indeed be nearer than many of us suppose, when Luntic Kolniyatsch will, rightly or wrongly, be reckoned by some of us as not the least of those writers who are especially symptomatic of the early twentieth century and are possible 'for all time' or for a more or less not inconsiderable period of time." That is finely said. But I myself go somewhat further. I say that Kolniyatsch's message has drowned all previous messages and will drown any that may be uttered in the remotest future. You ask me what, precisely, that message was? Well, it is too elemental, too near to the very heart of naked Nature, for exact definition. Can you describe the message of an angry python more satisfactorily than as *S-s-s-s?* Or that of an infuriated bull better than as *Moo?* That of Kolniyatsch lies somewhere between the two.[34]

Unless we recognize that the criticism falls more heavily upon his witless adorers than upon Kolniyatsch himself, the essay will strike us as merely an exposure of another of Beerbohm's literary blind spots. Actually, however, it marks a considerable advance on his road to mature satire. In 1900 he had written an essay that attacked the ponderous clichés of journalism in an expostulating way.[35] In it he presented the reader with virtually a catalogue of worn-out phrases, sterile allusions, and what passes for fine writing among the imaginatively impoverished. Here, in "Kolniyatsch," the group under attack is not quite the same one, but the assault is more effective because it is more oblique and more inventive. Both writer and critic are imagined. And the reader is invited to respond not to an abstraction — the abuses of journalists — but to a performance.

Sir Max Beerbohm

Zuleika Dobson and *A Christmas Garland*, which only by an excessive teasing of language can be considered reminiscences, were both, as we have seen, conceived during Beerbohm's years as a journalist in London and merely brought to completion in Italy. But he took with him as well the material for another project that, though he did not advance it very far, was to signal an important shift in Beerbohm's point of view both as an essayist and as a caricaturist, a shift from the viewpoint of observer to that of remembrancer. S. N. Behrman, noting that much of the material for Max's radio broadcasts had actually been written before World War I, mistakenly believed that the source of Beerbohm's recollections of his contemporaries was "The Mirror of the Past."[36] It is possible that the octogenarian Max believed it as well. But his literary remains auctioned in 1960 revealed two distinct sets of manuscript notes, one of real and one of imaginary reminiscences.[37] "The Mirror of the Past" (SC 329) will be discussed in chapter 4; many of the real ones are contained in a manuscript notebook (SC 332) now in the Berg Collection of the New York Public Library. Alphabetically indexed, the book contains the names of about a hundred celebrities whom Beerbohm encountered socially or professionally during the last decade of the nineteenth century and the first decade of the twentieth, from William Archer and Winston Churchill to Mark Twain and William Butler Yeats.[38] About a fifth of these entries are blank but for the names themselves, among which are Gosse, Galsworthy, and Shaw; wealthy hosts at whose homes Beerbohm was a guest, Lady Desborough and Sir William Eden; and even his half-brother, Herbert Beerbohm Tree. Another third, including Hilaire Belloc and Auguste Rodin, have entries of fewer than five lines. Most of the entries range from only a few lines to about half a page, whereas those of three, George Meredith, Algernon Swinburne, and Oscar Wilde, are a page or more in length.

The statistics may be a little misleading, however. The essay on George Moore, which runs to eighteen printed pages,[39] has its apparent source in no more than a third of a page of manuscript notes; no character studies were ever written (or at any rate preserved) of Meredith and Wilde; and the entry under Yeats is a single word, "Written," implying that the notebook

Toward the Imaginary Reminiscence in Prose

was not the exclusive record of Beerbohm's recollections of prominent literary and social figures. With the possible exception of the entry on Swinburne, these laconic and terse notes, the hasty setting down of physical characteristics, bits of conversation, and hints of anecdotes offer little insight into Beerbohm's methods of composition. They do, however, suggest much about his literary intentions. They reveal, for one thing, that there was a verbal counterpart to the sketches he kept drawing of people he met, and, for another, that quite early in his career he had come to regard these observations not merely as a part of his own growth or development but as the raw material of future compositions as well. Instead of proceeding through diaries or fictional sketches, the men and women Beerbohm encountered made their way into his literary consciousness as distinct entities and in their own persons. That the purpose of the notebook was more grandiose than that simply of an *aide mémoire* is clear from two separate pieces of evidence in Beerbohm's own hand. The first is in the notebook itself, on whose last pages, amid the inevitable sketches of faces, there are several lists of the names of those entered on the earlier pages, arranged unalphabetically but apparently by profession. On the last verso leaf five categories seem established. The first, and by far the largest, is that of literary figures; the third and next largest, that of statesmen and diplomats; the fourth and fifth groups, each smaller than the last, those of artists and theatrical folk. The second column has but a single name, that of Barney Barnato, the South African mining tycoon. In the lower right-hand corner of the page are two more lists, presumably of essays actually completed or seriously worked out. The second of these reads as follows:

No. 2 The Pines
Conder
H. B. Irving
Soveral
Lang
Nat Goodwin and — [Hall Caine]
Moore
Yeats.

"No. 2. The Pines," the reminiscence of meetings with Swinburne and Watts-Dunton, was the only one published within a reasonable time after its composition.[40] Beerbohm kept the others aside, and only many years later did the essays on Irving, Goodwin and Caine, Moore, and Yeats, composed in Italy before World War I, find an audience. Max broadcast them on the BBC between 1949 and 1955; they were published posthumously in the enlarged edition of *Mainly on the Air.* "An Incident," the recollection of a personal anecdote about Beerbohm and Henry James, written up as late as 1954 and broadcast two years later, also derives from the autograph notebook.[41] What clinches the conjecture that Beerbohm planned to present his recollections not as autobiography, in the manner, say, of his friend Will Rothenstein, but as highly wrought artistic composition comes from a note penciled on the first page of the extract from the Swinburne essay he sent to Edmund Gosse in December 1914: "An extract — very long!! — from a sort of essay which I have called 'No. 2. The Pines.' (I have already written several essays — or sort-of-essays — of a similar kind, a 'remembering' kind. Them and this one and some others I shall probably publish some day; but not yet.)"[42]

Leaving aside for the present "No. 2. The Pines," the published essays of the "remembering kind" constitute a very slight portion of Beerbohm's canon, and the fact that they appeared between boards only after his death suggests also that Beerbohm himself may not have thought all that much of them. If we look into them at all, it is for information, for anecdotes, or for passages that will corroborate some theory we may have had about Beerbohm's attitude to this or that. If, however, we are prepared to see them as prototypes of a new kind of writing, something between autobiography and biography, with which new form his other friend Gosse had experimented in *Father and Son* only a few years before, then they take on a new significance. A comparison of any of these "remembering" essays with the much earlier "Aubrey Beardsley" (1898)[43] would not be quite fair to either, for the Beardsley piece is an obituary tribute to a coeval (Beerbohm and Beardsley were born within a few days of each other) cut off in young manhood. Its tone is serious; its cadences, stately. Personal memories are not absent, but

Toward the Imaginary Reminiscence in Prose

they are invoked as illustrations of Beardsley's limited physical vitality or extraordinary industry, his kindliness or his scholarship. Beerbohm does not linger over scenes, nor does he introduce himself in any capacity other than as witness. *De mortuis nil nisi bonum.* But the "remembering" essays, dealing as they do with yet living contemporaries and hence free of the obligation to be wholly laudatory, display as well the extraordinary engagement of the writer in the scenes he describes. We experience his terror at dining with H. B. Irving, a formidable presence at Oxford, yet an undergraduate only two years Max's senior.[44] And we experience too the subtler emotions, the psychological exquisiteness almost worthy of the master, when Beerbohm contrives to avoid the company of Henry James himself in order to read James's latest story, preferring the literary to the living presence.[45] Whatever else they may do, these essays preserve emotions recollected in tranquility.

Immediacy is what is principally conjured up by these essays — what Max (not "it") felt like to be in the presence of the people he was describing. But he is fully aware that his own imaginative powers invest these scenes with their intensity: "Life seemed wonderful (though really, of course, it was I who was wonderful in being able to secure romance on such cheap terms). Had I been a conspirator in a strange land, finding my way towards some appointed spot for some fell purpose, I could not have been prouder of myself."[46] To achieve that immediacy and to convey that intensity, Beerbohm eschews the kind of organization and development of ideas expected of the biographer, charting rather the flow of his own impressions. Nat Goodwin, the American stage comedian, and Hall Caine, the popular English novelist, seem unlikely mates for a single essay of recollection. It is not merely that Max encountered them in the same house, though years apart. That, of course, is the physical, but not the psychological, connection. Goodwin, with his drawl and his artless assumption of what he conceives of as the style of the English country gentleman, actually becomes in Beerbohm's fancy the squire of the manor, and Hall Caine, the alien intruder, all the more fearful a presence because Beerbohm is deeply conscious of the injury he has done him through his caricatures. Beerbohm builds up his sense of dread of meeting Caine with all the vividness that he bestowed on the nervous apprehension of Maltby at the spectral appearances of Braxton. Caine proves surprisingly sympathetic, however, and Beerbohm's anxiety is allayed. Actually meeting Caine and conversing with him brings to Max a greater understanding of the man and how his career developed. It is significant that Beerbohm thinks no more highly of Hall Caine's accomplishments in literature than he had before. But the experience has desymbolized him as Popular Novelist for Max and made them both seem more human. The essay turns out to be a poem — in reading it, we undergo an extraordinary intellectual and emotional journey — only with people instead of primroses as catalysts.

Reminiscences are not generally poems. They are either a wave of memory that overwhelms the senile, leaving debris strewn all over the beach, or a carefully documented compilation of filecards assembled for the purpose of self-justification. By conceiving of his reminiscences as art, as beautiful objects that convey an illusion of life, Beerbohm liberates himself from traditional restraints and achieves a rare kind of candor, enabling him to make observations about his friends that would be devastating out of their context. His portrait of George Moore, for example, is constructed around the idea that Moore was dear "to all people who had the wit to enjoy in the midst of an artificial civilisation the spectacle of one absolutely natural man."[47] Beerbohm does not despise naturalness (though he is far from it himself); yet he recognizes at what tremendous disadvantage it must appear in the presence of cleverness and sophistication and how ineffectually it endeavors to conceal itself in their company. In the following passages we can see how Moore's virtues of energy and openness turn against him, making him look like a buffoon:

> No one but Ruskin has written more vividly than he, more lovingly and seeingly, about the art of painting; and no one has ever written more inspiringly than he, with a more infectious enthusiasm, about those writers whom he understood and loved, or more amusingly against those whom he neither understood nor liked. Of learning he had no equipment at all; for him everything was a discovery; and it was natural that Oscar Wilde should com-

Toward the Imaginary Reminiscence in Prose

> plain, as he did once complain to me, "George Moore is always conducting his education in public." (P. 86)

The tribute to Moore's natural gifts is sincere, but it is a defect to be unable to learn from others and a bore to reveal it. Hence Wilde's complaint, however cruelly phrased, is not only deserved, but "natural." With painters — Walter Sickert, Wilson Steer, and Henry Tonks in particular — Moore was most at home.

> To them he could talk, with the certainty that they would sympathise, about painting, and about literature without being interrupted. They, on their side, revered him as the one mere critic with whom they could talk as with one of themselves. His face, too — that face transferred to canvas by so many painters since Manet — always entranced them with those problems of "planes" and "values" in which it abounded. He was always a sort of special *treat* to them. They went to him as children to a pantomine. Even more than his felicities of thought did they love those sudden infelicities which he alone could have uttered — those *gaffes* hailed with roars of delight that grew in volume while Moore stared around in simple wonderment (P. 89)

From the society of *literati* Moore flees to the companionship of painters, less exacting in their intellectual demands and seemingly more polite, for they listen without interruption to his literary talk. But of course he is not really one of them — however sympathetic, he is not a painter, but a "mere critic." Yet he does interest them professionally — as a subject. Beerbohm implies the inferiority of their craft in portraiture relative to his own by referring to the terms of their mystery, which are words common enough, in inverted commas. And finally Moore, having escaped the witty taunts of a Wilde or a Gosse, is now consigned to play the clown, the butt of their childish glee. What wonder then that Moore assiduously cultivated his Parisianism, that he boasted of his amours to even the most casual of acquaintances, that he almost unconsciously appropriated the *bons mots* of others as his own? These were the pitiable defenses of a natural man in an artificial civilization. For Beerbohm, as for the others, George Moore was in public a figure of fun. And because he was so, Beerbohm is better able to appreciate the dedication and courage of Moore in persevering, in willing himself to be a writer:

> No young man — nay, no young woman — ever wrote worse than young Moore wrote. It must have seemed to everyone that here was a writer who, however interesting he in himself might be, never would learn to express himself tolerably. Half a crown, we know, may be the foundation of a vast fortune. But what can be done without a penny? Some of the good writers have begun with a scant gift for writing. But which of them with no gift at all? Moore is the only instance I ever heard of. Somehow, in the course of long years, he learned to express himself beautifully. I call that great. (P. 98)

The simple word *great*, appearing without qualifiers after the elaborately wrought depreciation, shines forth like an absolution from sin. Moore is redeemed from all his acts of folly or pettiness; his critics, including Max himself, stand abashed at his achievement.

The image of Max that emerges from the "remembering essays" is of a man seriously engaged in exploring his generally first impressions and setting them down in an artistic way. He does not psychologize, nor has he any axe to grind. He is frank without being apologetic or defensive. The authority of his judgments rests, not upon his own eminence or any fancied superiority to those about whom he writes, but upon the authenticity of careful observation, cultivated sensitivity, and thoughtful reflection. These alone validate the almost Proustian association of sensations he achieves in "Nat Goodwin — and Another," the imaginary dialogue he fashions in "George Moore," and the persistent doubt that, however theatrical the procession, the Emperor is wearing any clothes in "First Meetings with W. B. Yeats." Such exploration of one's first impressions, while artistically justifiable, may still give personal offense. Beerbohm was undoubtedly wise in delaying publication until his subjects could be looked at as characters rather than as persons, and he was fortunate in finding the perfect medium, radio, to convey his subjectivity. But all the same, it must have been frustrating to write for, as it were, a time capsule.

Toward the Imaginary Reminiscence in Prose

No such frustration attended the composition of "No. 2. The Pines." Although the essay grew more or less out of the commission of Edmund Gosse, as Beerbohm explains in a prefatory note,[48] that was hardly the sole impetus, and it is obvious from the evidence cited earlier that in overall design it is one of the "remembering" kind. Since both Swinburne and Watts-Dunton were dead before Beerbohm even began writing the piece, one inhibition to publication was removed; another disappeared when Gosse's *Life of Swinburne,* which incorporated the extract made from the original essay, was published in 1917. Accordingly, "No. 2. The Pines" was included in Beerbohm's next collection of essays, the only representation of the experiment in genre whose source was the autograph notebook. Like the others, this essay records the impressions of a young man, a beginner in literature, in his encounters with giants — the plural is used advisedly, for Watts-Dunton looms almost as large as Swinburne.[49] The scenes he recalls are not merely memorable for him but instructive as well. They inform him, caution him perhaps, of what becomes of men who devote themselves to literature. While maintaining a highly qualified awe-struck and self-effacing posture, Max evokes a picture of the two old men curiously dependent on each other that is at once heroic and comic, noble and pitiable. And, as with the other "remembering essays," what is remembered has more of the truth of art than of strict fact.

The essay turns on a series of simple but highly marked contrasts. Geographically, it begins in Putney High Street with Max, full of trepidation, about to pay his first call on the aged and retired poet and his scarcely younger companion and nurse. It ends with Max reintroducing himself to them in Elysium, where their spirits are freed of the restrictions of flesh and environment. The central part of the essay deals with their attempts, not always successful, to transcend those limitations in this world. In his novel *Aylwin,* if one can discount the Celtic supernaturalism, Watts-Dunton had opposed two attitudes: one of "acceptance," the rational and practical approach to life; and one of "wonder," the spiritual and poetic approach, which seeks to transform the commonplace. The household of The Pines reflects the conflict between the two. Firmly planted in genteel suburbia, indistinguishable in its exterior from its staid Victorian neighbors, the house is to all intents another unit of conformity and respectability. "But," Max writes, "as that front-door closed behind me I had the instant sense of having slipped away from the harsh light of the ordinary and contemporary into the dimness of an odd, august past" (p. 62). The wondrous and unearthly beauty of Rossetti's women gazing languidly from their portraits on the walls clashes with the homely utility of the Tupperesque furnishings. Even the physical appearance of the two men belies their inner vitality: Watts-Dunton, shaggy and gnomelike, always engaged in some mysterious literary activity, and Swinburne himself, small and malformed, but capable of movements of extraordinary speed and agility. Beerbohm marvels at the contrasts and the transformations. Prevented from participating in dinner conversation by his deafness and by the solicitousness of Watts-Dunton, who would not allow him to speak until he had eaten well, Swinburne "smiled only to himself, and to his plateful of meat, and to the small bottle of Bass's pale ale that stood before him — ultimate allowance of one who had erst clashed cymbals in Naxos" (p. 66). Yet these ordinary aliments having been consumed, the equally ordinary occurrence of a morning walk, during which he saw a baby in a perambulator, inspires him:

> He spoke to us of his walk; spoke not in the strain of a man who had been taking his exercise on Putney Heath, but rather in that of a Peri who had at long last been suffered to pass through Paradise. And rather than that he spoke would I say that he cooingly and flutingly *sang* of his experience. The wonder of this morning's wind and sun and clouds were expressed in a flow of words so right and sentences so perfectly balanced that they would have seemed pedantic had they not been clearly as spontaneous as the wordless notes of a bird in song. The frail, sweet voice rose and fell, lingered, quickened, in all manner of trills and roulades. (P. 68)

That childlike enthusiasm is perpetuated in Swinburne's love of books — in books from too remote a past for Beerbohm fully to appreciate. Max's mention of the contemporary Rostand's *Cyrano de Bergerac* sets Swinburne off into a rapturous praise of

Toward the Imaginary Reminiscence in Prose

L'Histoire Comique des États et des Empires de la Lune. On another occasion, embarrassed by his inability to respond knowledgeably when Swinburne displays his library to him, Max in desperation wildly mistakes one old play for another, thereby failing in his intent to please Swinburne. What he realizes much later, of course, is that Swinburne's enthusiasm requires no external reinforcement. One is tempted to wonder what would have happened had Swinburne chosen to show Beerbohm some of the choice volumes of erotica his library is said to have contained. That of course would have been irreconcilable with the portrait of Swinburne in old age that Max means to draw — or rather, not of Swinburne, but of himself, of a votary who, having come to pay homage at a shrine, is struck by what he finds there of the purely human qualities of frailty, tenacity, and loyalty.

The adoration, even passed through the filter of their humanity, is yet allayed with gentle reservations. The strangeness of the two companions at The Pines will never wear off for Max, however removed in time:

> I see that dining room. . .; the long white stretch of table-cloth, with Swinburne and Watts-Dunton and another at the extreme end of it; Watts-Dunton between us, very low down over his plate, very cosy and hirsute, and rather like the dormouse at that long tea-table which Alice found in Wonderland. I see myself sitting there wide-eyed, as Alice sat. And, had the hare been a great poet, and the hatter a great gentleman, and neither of them mad but each only very odd and vivacious, I might see Swinburne as a glorified blend of those two. (Pp. 73–74)

Wonderland has no street address; we suspect that Max has indulged his fancy. But no; there are Swinburne's helplessly fluttering hands, an uncontrollable nervous disorder from earliest childhood, the price the gods exacted for giving him genius. And there is Beerbohm's profession of his personal inability to inhabit a world so exclusively literary as Swinburne's, an imperfection in himself that he artfully contrives to be the occasion of a prose parody of Swinburne, replete with balanced phrases, alliteration, and consonance. All these instances proclaim a simultaneous sympathy and distance. The inmates of The Pines are worthy of respect and love, but they *are* rather peculiar.

Sir Max Beerbohm

The significance of the "remembering" essays for Beerbohm's artistic development is far greater than their bulk would suggest. For one thing these essays revealed to him that even a relatively young man could frequent the Temple of Memory rather than that of Prophecy. And for another, he found in them a more effective and less cumbersome way than in *Zuleika Dobson* for fact and fancy to mingle, for the narrator to involve himself in the narration without the sacrifice of his own identity. Reminiscence need not be the exclusive privilege of the old but was the birthright of the reflective; reminiscence need not pretend to objectivity — it was but the self contemplating its experiences in a nonabstract way; reminiscence need not be haphazard, it could be ordered and shaped; and finally, reminiscence could be as imaginative as the fictions that were refined and distilled ultimately out of the same experiences. As the last of the "remembering" essays, "No. 2. The Pines" is particularly illustrative of these truths. More specifically, in his treatment of Swinburne as one who transfigured or transcended the commonplace, Beerbohm found — at last — a theme that could be adapted to the verbal and lineal styles he had been perfecting. Two lines of growth emerge from this essay: the first led to those other mockingly admired artists directly remembered in *Seven Men;* the second extended even further back in time, bringing Max to remember obliquely through the memory of others, and even more ambiguously, the characters of *Rossetti and His Circle*. These developments constitute nothing less than the transformation of the imaginative to the imaginary reminiscence.

CHAPTER III

Toward the Imaginary Reminiscence in Caricature

Any attempt to discuss Beerbohm's caricatures is immediately bedeviled by their multitude and their limited accessibility. Sir Rupert Hart-Davis lists over two thousand drawings in his catalogue, acknowledging the deliberate omission of some juvenilia, the less finished sketches that appear in manuscripts and letters, costume designs, straight portraits, and other items that depart from pure caricature.[1] Dispersed literally all over the world, even when available for inspection at public libraries or museums such as the Tate Gallery or the Ashmolean Museum, the originals of Beerbohm's caricatures are rarely on permanent exhibition. Essentially, when one speaks of Beerbohm's caricatures, one is speaking of reproductions that even in the albums first presenting them to a general public were reduced in size and distorted in color from their originals. With the exception of *A Survey* (1921), no edition of Beerbohm's albums ever exceeded five thousand copies.[2] Of his first book, *Caricatures of Twenty-Five Gentlemen* (1896), only five hundred copies were issued. Eleven years later the figure for the handsomely produced folio *Book of Caricatures* barely doubled that figure. Consequently almost all of Max's albums of caricatures have attained the status of rare books. Moreover, apart from what might have been realized from the sale of the original drawings, only the two-shilling wartime reprint (considered as a book rather than as an album) of *The Poets' Corner*,[3] augmented by four plates from *Rossetti and His Circle,* appears to have had even a brush with commercial success. Fifty thousand copies of this popular edition were printed; and although the plates are only one-fourth the size of the originals, the fidelity of reproduction to the ink and wash of the original drawings compares favorably with the lithographs of the 1904 printing. But apart from this reprint, only one of Beerbohm's other books of caricatures appears to have undergone republication.[4]

In view of all this limited publication it is the more surprising that Beerbohm's work as a caricaturist is as well known as it is. To a large degree this familiarity is due to fairly frequent reproduction of single drawings as illustrations. Sale catalogues continually bring new drawings to light; newspapers and magazines enliven their pages with appropriately selected old ones. Where a caricature by Max exists, it may illuminate far more searchingly than a photograph the subject of a volume of memoirs, biography, or history. Mention has already been made of the practice of illustrating books about Beerbohm with hitherto unreproduced caricatures. And since his death books of his drawings have been published which are quite independent of Sir Max's original selections. The Ashmolean Museum has reproduced in an attractive booklet[5] twenty-nine (or nearly half) of the drawings in their collections, the contents of which booklet range from 1894 to 1925 and include both the previously published and the unpublished. To date only the first volume of a more ambitious undertaking has appeared: "Some months before his death Sir Max Beerbohm gave his blessing to a project for the recovery and presentation in book form of some of the best and least available of his caricatures. He also approved the plan of a series of such volumes, each devoted to a decade of his work, and made known his preferences for the contents of this first volume."[6] Like the Ashmolean booklet, this collection gathers together both familiar and unfamiliar drawings, but its chronological arrangement and selectivity make it a more useful instrument for the study of Beerbohm's artistic development. Finally, J. G. Riewald in a newly published selection assembles over one hundred caricatures of literary subjects (by far the most significant class of Beerbohm's work), chiefly from the major albums, and annotates them extensively.[7] This republication of Max's drawings should make them available for delight and study to a far greater public than the original albums could ever reach. That such regrouping and rearrangement violate Max's original preferences in the matter and obscure the line of his growth may be argued, but not too strenuously. For with the exception of *The Poets' Corner* (of which Riewald includes all but one plate) and *Rossetti and His Circle,* each Beerbohm album comprises no more than his selection of his best work since the last album. They have no more integrity than that. As long as reproductions of the caricatures can be obtained in some form, analysis of individual drawings and theories about general characteristics can proceed. In the discussion that follows, I have tried to restrict my illustrations to drawings most frequently reproduced, though I have not hesitated to refer to others when they are particularly significant to the argument.

It is well at the outset of this discussion to indicate its limits. Although there is doubtless a place in some future history of caricature for a technical consideration of Beerbohm's work, it is primarily as a satirist that he is here under scrutiny. For the purposes of this study, the specific medium of his drawing and how he employs it — ink or pencil, wash or hatching — are purely descriptive characteristics. Doubtless with accumulated practice came increased skill. There is no question that *Rossetti and His Circle* is technically superior to *The Poets' Corner.* But the maturity and complexity of its conception are only marginally dependent on that increased skill. Greater effort, greater care, greater ambition, and greater confidence were lavished on the later work, but all would have been wasted had they been uninformed by ideas more profound and subtle than those apparent in *The Poets' Corner.* For it is certainly not as a technician that Beerbohm is admired as a caricaturist. It is generally conceded that he is not a very good draughtsman. "We are sure," writes one critic of caricature, "about the drawing of a Daumier, a Caran d'Ache, a Charles Keene — we are not so sure of Max Beerbohm; but it does not matter, for we know that few great caricaturists are so certain of saying, with a few strokes, precisely what they want to say."[8] The concern here, then, will be with what his drawings appear to be saying, and it is not as pleasing forms but as icons that they will be read.

Sir Max Beerbohm

Beerbohm himself resisted the notion that his drawings could be interpreted, that by the simple act of deliberate distortion in physical representation some criticism — as opposed to mere comment — is conveyed to the spectator. "Caricature," he wrote in an early essay that aspires to lecture, "implies no moral judgment on its subject."[9] The caricaturist is merely one who has habituated himself to drawing portraits hyperbolically. "Caricature consists merely in exaggeration" (p. 127). The caricaturist "exaggerates instinctively, unconsciously" (p. 124). Obviously, then, caricature is of persons, not of ideas. And though a caricature ought to have about it an air of spontaneity, it must nevertheless be a product of careful observation and study. To an interviewer he once indicated the intent behind his work:

> I always endeavor to convey the man's life, to give an idea of his history, to show his characteristic attitude. I give a sort of *précis* of people, boiled down, like an arithmatical problem, to the least common denominator. . . . A caricature, to convey any real idea of the subject whatever, ought to be a synthesis of acute observation of the man as he is. . . . And it is the casual attitude, the unstudied expression, that best conveys the whole man. It is these things that I seek to reproduce in my caricatures.[10]

These observations, however, constitute more the manifesto of a man at the beginning of his career than the distillation of principles from a lifetime of practice. It is significant that Max made no such grandiloquent pronouncements about his craft once he was reasonably established as a caricaturist. Although he doubtless sincerely believed that the caricaturist's gaze preceded the moralist's squint, there is yet a criticism implied in the very choice of subjects for caricature and in the mode of exaggeration. The Portuguese minister, Marquis Luis de Soveral, with his orbicular head and bushy cyma-curved eyebrows and moustache, may, in his extraordinary self-satisfied ugliness, have well appealed to just such a disinterested gaze. At any rate Beerbohm never tired of drawing him.[11] But it is hard not to read censure into the presentments of Wells and Kipling. In the case of Wells, there are at least two instances in which physical distortion of the subject is subordinated to backgrounds that

Toward the Imaginary Reminiscence in Caricature

burlesque his visionary idealism, and the results are fairly close to editorial cartoons (HD 1755–1756; BLC 94). And John Felstiner, after carefully examining Beerbohm's revisions to some of the *Caricatures of Twenty-Five Gentlemen,* concludes that "if we look at the jaw and the neck in paintings or photographs of Kipling, we can see that Beerbohm's judgment of the man determined his technique before the technique conveyed a judgment."[12] The fact is that even though there is an element of exaggeration in Beerbohm's drawings that is purely pictorial, one that never dies out and indeed keeps the best of those drawings from ever becoming less than caricatures, there is an equally strong literary-intellectual element, an appeal to memory and to words, that begins to manifest itself in *The Poets' Corner* and continues to assert itself throughout the remainder of his career even in drawings that do not have specifically literary subjects.

Before the publication of *The Poets' Corner* Beerbohm's caricatures were confined almost wholly to single figures in isolation, with only the barest of backgrounds. There is usually no pictorial or symbolic clue to the profession of the subject. The impression conveyed is a wholly pictorial one, and the apparent haste of composition suggests immediacy and the absence of premeditation. Yet even the sketchiest of these drawings does not fail to communicate a sense of personality through the distortion of physical detail. In what is probably Max's first professional caricature, the one of Oscar Wilde done in 1894 (HD 1779; BLC 54), there is nothing approaching a firm outline, yet the drawing exudes a distinct notion of porcine elegance, of a style of life that is at once fascinating and repellent, as though the altered portrait of Dorian Gray itself were to walk abroad quite unconscious of the effect it was producing. Another apparently hasty sketch, done of Swinburne in 1899 (HD 1642, pl. 44), probably after his first meeting with him, captures perfectly the curious posture and that quality of elfin old age described in "No. 2. The Pines." To a fellow professional caricaturist, this sketch of

> Swinburne is really exquisite. For the line of the great forehead — it is nearly a full face — the quill was deliberately left nearly empty of ink. So there is a perfectly firm, though faint, double line ex-

63

actly fulfilling the needs of the high light. The few remaining curls are sketched in with a full pen, and the clothes are lightly tinted with a wash. The left shoe is half off the foot — as ever in Max's caricatures of Swinburne. You feel, in looking at this drawing . . . that there could have been no preparation, no study on Max's part. He had, I imagine, an inspiration and transferred it to paper at once, without the slightest hesitation and without a false stroke. It is not the sort of thing that happens often.[13]

Indeed it does not happen often. For, however immediate the execution of a Beerbohm drawing — and they are very rarely elaborate compositions — they are almost invariably the product of reflection rather than the impression of the moment. No seaside artist of instant caricatures, Beerbohm disdained to draw from models, asserting that "it is only in recollection of his subject that the unconscious process of exaggeration begins to work."[14] In his political caricatures very often that exaggeration becomes purely lineal, conveying a sense of the subject's personality in only the most abstract way. Several of the *Caricatures of Twenty-Five Gentlemen* work in this fashion. Thus the profile of Joseph Chamberlain (HD 271) is reduced to a matter of three arcs that yield a pointed nose and a pointed brow; in the drawing of Sir George Lewis (HD 926) full rich curves in figures suggesting teardrops or chemical retorts predominate, forming the basis for not only the subject's hair, profile, fur collar and cuff but, altered to a pear, his encased body as well. In a more elongated and sinuous form the same shape is used in Beerbohm's 1903 drawing of the dramatist Arthur Wing Pinero (HD 1164; BLC 21) to represent essentially the same features, but with one significant addition — the celebrated Pinero eyebrows, which Max once described as being like "the skins of some small mammal, don't you know — just not large enough to be used as mats."[15] Shallow scalloped edges are used to represent the jowls and multiple chins of Sir William Harcourt (HD 689); repeated more amply, the line becomes the basis for his protruding belly, and the motif is cleverly reasserted in the tufting of the parliamentary bench behind him. Military figures, on the other hand, are often depicted cubistically. The duke of York (later the Prince of Wales and still later King George V) is shown

Toward the Imaginary Reminiscence in Caricature

in an 1899 drawing (HD 573) in naval costume with a perfectly elliptical face and cylindrical arms; Lord Kitchener of Khartoum, done a year later (HD 865, pl. 17), stands as rigid as an automaton on legs nearly twice as long as the rest of his body, legs that are literally triangular prisms. Generally, though, the reduction through exaggeration of literary figures tends to be less geometric. Hall Caine's nervous-looking physiognomy — the vast worried brow beneath an umbrella of hair, the goggle-eyes, and the untrimmed moustache — seems to have been extruded through a long neck fixed into a mere jumble of lines that has no suggestion whatever of a human torso (HD 218). Together with the enormous feet on a pair of spindly legs, these features convey the image of some frightened, exotic, flightless bird. Another bird is suggested in the presentment of Frank Harris in the 1896 volume (HD 711; BLC 66), who, in Felstiner's words, is seen "preened and inflated like a fighting cock, as if to signify his sexual activity and self-confidence."[16] Yet another kind of stylized representation appears in the 1899 drawing of R. B. Cunninghame Graham (HD 624), where the attitude of defiance struck by the pose is enhanced by the hair, moustache, bow tie, and breast handkerchief, all of which curve upward, ending in flamelike tips, suggestive of a fiery radicalism. But whether the reduction is effected by geometry or stylization, the impact of these caricatures is wholly visual. They do not illustrate — they are.

The literary tendency mentioned earlier relies less exclusively on physical distortion. Any caricature that requires a caption, a legend, or dialogue departs from purely visual art and begins the journey down a road that passes through illustration and whose terminus is the comic strip. Nothing in Beerbohm's work is closer to the comic strip than the several series of drawings he sketched before the impulse was properly restrained in *The Poets' Corner*. If we except *The Second Childhood of John Bull* (drawn in 1901 but not brought out in book form until 1911) on the grounds that one cannot caricature an allegorical figure, then none of these series was published in Beerbohm's lifetime. The first, a group of eleven entitled "Mr. Gladstone Goes to Heaven" (HD 584–594), was probably occasioned by the death of the former prime minister in 1898 but was doubtless deemed too irreverent for publication. Executed in pencil and watercolor, this series is far more impressive visually than the line drawings of *Twenty-Five Gentlemen,* as Osbert Lancaster observes.[17] But the humor is fairly sophomoric as Gladstone, never far from his umbrella and top hat, trudges from one celestial encounter to another: he picks up a fallen angel, avoids General Gordon, expostulates with Parnell, incurs the wrath of Homer and Horace for his translations, and finally departs for Hell, but not before having observed that one of the principal thoroughfares of Heaven is named Disraeli Avenue. More amusing is Beerbohm's Homeric travesty "The Edwardyssey" (HD 486–494), a group of nine drawings inspired by King Edward's European tour in the spring of 1903.[18] More ingenuity is manifested here as Max fits the epic to the circumstances of a less heroic royal hero. Calypso is Marianne herself, the symbol of France, the Syrens are a group of singing nuns whose convent Edward visited, the Cyclops is the Portuguese King Carlos, and Circe is Pope Leo XIII. Edwardysseus' mother, Pallas Victoria, appears to him in the guise of a Highland shepherd. Two drawings, the feeblest of the series, constitute the recognition scene, and two more involve the vanquishing of the suitors of Penelope-Alexandra — a crew that includes, among others, Joseph Chamberlain, Lord Rosebery, Winston Churchill, and the ever-present Hall Caine — by their inability to smoke the cigar of Edwardysseus. The effect is still one of cleverness rather than of penetration, but this series, like the earlier one, shows Beerbohm beginning to subject portrait caricature to dramatic fancy. He drew two other sets of drawings in 1903, both of his friend G. S. Street (HD 1611–1616, 1617–1623), the first of which burlesquely illustrates a quotation from an article Street had recently published in defense of an intellectual and cultured life lived away from the capital.[19] These series are symptomatic of a growing tendency in Beerbohm's caricature toward illustration. What he had not quite discovered in 1903 was a way of using physical caricature to illustrate his own private fantasies, themes, and variations about real people.

That tentative state, the not-quite-effected fusion of portrait and illustration, is perfectly exemplified by a drawing of Kipling that almost looks as if it came from *The Poets' Corner* (HD 854;

BLC 69). Indeed the rays of light pouring through the Gothic windows, the stylized posture of poetic inspiration assumed by the subject, and the title of the drawing itself — "Scenes from the Lives of the Poets. Mr. Rudyard Kipling composing 'The Absent-Minded Beggar'" — would all seem to make it a natural candidate for inclusion in that volume.[20] Possibly it was so intended, displaced in the end by the more biting caricature of Kipling and Britannia (HD 855; BLC 70). The physical exaggeration of Kipling is almost identical in the two drawings: the same protruding jaw, the same "back of his neck, the thick back, . . . receding forehead, the regular pushing face, like a battering ram, of the man who means to succeed."[21] But there is nothing essentially comic in the representation of a figure so drawn in the pose in which he is seen. With the head of a Spenser or a Milton the drawing would not be funny at all. It is only when the identification with Rudyard Kipling is made that the satire becomes apparent — the viewer is expected to know beforehand that Kipling's pretensions to poetry are as ill-founded as Shadwell's in *MacFlecknoe*. But the drawing does not convey this knowledge visually. If it works at all, it does so like an editorial cartoon. There is not the union of pictorial and literary elements that we find in Beerbohm's maturest work. That union is perfected, of course, in *Rossetti and His Circle*, where Beerbohm transfers the insights of his experiments in prose into graphic form, achieving the imaginary reminiscence in caricature. Before that transfer could take place, however, both the pictorial and the literary formulas for generating caricatures had to become considerably more complex.

On first consideration it would appear that very little complication is possible in pictorial caricature. A long nose or a peculiar pair of eyebrows can be taken only so far. But Max never ceased to be fascinated by details of this kind even after the nineties. The way A. J. Balfour held himself seems to have been for Max his most singular physical characteristic, and he is almost invariably depicted in full length to show this singularity, whether before, during, or after the time he was prime minister. Other qualities — his frailty, his philosophical detachment, or his indecisiveness — are depicted from time to time, but Balfour's carriage is a constant. As one of the *Twenty-Five Gentle-*

men (HD 60), he is shown with his body describing Hogarth's line of beauty, though the effect is anything but beautiful. His abnormally thin left arm, swung straight back, holds a dispatch box, which looks as though it is throwing him off balance. The effect is that of a grotesque discobolus. In the 1913 album, *Fifty Caricatures,* that characteristic posture has become wholly stylized in "Mr. Balfour — a Frieze" (HD 75), described by Hart-Davis as "Five full-length drawings of A.J.B. leaning further and further back until his top hat falls off." A pair of drawings done about 1901 show the progression of the figure in profile of James McNeill Whistler into an extinguished candle in a candlestick (HD 1769, 1774, pls. 57–58). Rarely does Beerbohm venture his exaggeration this far into abstraction, however. It is true that the high collar of the lord chamberlain, Earl Spencer, which rests just under his moustache and ears in 1907 (HD 1578), has grown so enormous by 1912 that it reaches the top of his head and is provided with eyeholes through which he can see (HD 1580). But the more usual form of exaggeration is less drastic — though possibly more devastating — as in the 1912 drawing of G. K. Chesterton giving an after-dinner speech (HD 312; BLC 39). Not only does the table seem to be supporting the speaker's ample girth but a segment of its full rotundity is cut off by the right-hand edge of the paper on which it is drawn, implying that the subject is too enormous to be encompassed.

Very early, Beerbohm learned that the effect of physical caricature could be multiplied by bringing in additional figures. In "Celtades Ambo" ("Both of them Celts") of 1899 (HD 1825; BLC 31) the familiar spindly shape of Yeats with his long delicate fingers, legs that look almost intertwined, and ungovernable locks of dark hair is constrasted strongly with that of his fellow-dramatist in the Irish Literary Theater, Edward Martyn, who is portrayed as balding, short and dumpy and very much this-worldly, with hands thrust in his pockets and feet firmly planted apart. Less polar is the opposition of Swinburne and Watts-Dunton in the undated drawing "At the Pines" (HD 1647; BLC 50), which looks as though it might have been done at about the time of the 1899 Swinburne sketch discussed earlier in this chapter. If Swinburne looks a little less elfin, Watts-Dunton certainly looks gnomelike as they are observed by the

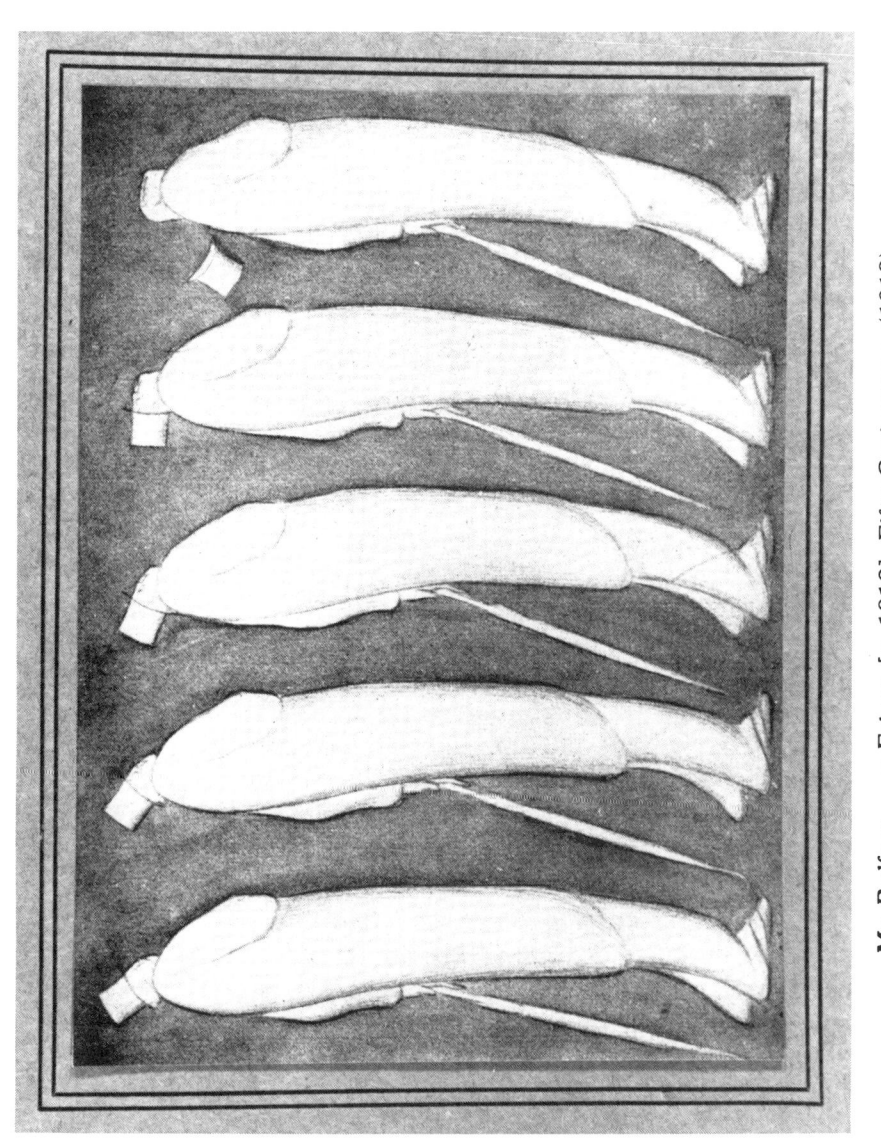

Mr. Balfour — a Frieze. [c. 1912]. *Fifty Caricatures.* (1913).

"stunner" in the Rossetti portrait hanging above them. The more usual group portrait, however, involves a crowded scene, whose figures do not always make contact with one another. In such instances it is not so much contrast as diversity that is apparent. "Dante Gabriel Rossetti, in his back garden" (HD 1268; BLC 49), drawn for *The Poets' Corner,* certainly looks forward in its choice of subject to the later great volume that will take up again all the people caricatured in the earlier one. But the treatment and attitude there will be wholly different. For in this early drawing we have a menagerie pure and simple. There is no central action, though nominally Rossetti is seen sketching a live model, indifferent to everything else going on around him. A diminutive Whistler, quite self-satisfied, is striking a pose while from the wall above, Swinburne is twirling the distinctive single white lock of Whistler's hair, Watts-Dunton looking on admonishingly. Meredith gazes heavenward, his chin resting on a hand supported by the wall. Beneath him Burne-Jones is contemplating a flower, though it is possible that eye contact has been established between him and the kangaroo. Further to the right, William Morris is declaiming his verses while a pelican reads over his shoulder and a snake coils at his foot. Holman Hunt and John Ruskin are disapproving spectators at the same time as Hall Caine peers over from the other side of the wall, wearing an expression of consternation or fear or both. We do not have to know who the figures are to appreciate the confusion and eccentricity depicted. But it is also very clear that in 1904 Beerbohm had not considered very deeply what these Pre-Raphaelites and their friends may have meant to one another or what they signified to Beerbohm himself.

His drawing "Some Members of the New English Art Club" (HD 1586), executed in 1906 and printed a year later in *A Book of Caricatures,* presents an even greater diversity of physical types and approaches classical composition in the disposition of the figures. The center of the drawing is dominated by the ungainly seated figure of Wilson Steer, who looks like an upright turtle, a tiny head surmounting a thick rubber neck. Arching above and behind him on the left are the two parallel sinuous shapes of D. S. MacColl and Henry Tonks while to the right the massive forefinger and jaw of a diminutive Will Rothenstein, who is standing tiptoe on a table, are thrust under his chin. A tiny Albert Rutherston sits tailor-fashion beneath the table, balanced on the left by an only slightly larger William Orpen. Three other figures appear on each side of the triangle thus formed.

In 1908 Max drew three group pictures, none of which was ever reproduced in his lifetime. One of these has a Cambridge setting — "Mid-Term Tea at Mr. Oscar Browning's" (HD 186, pl. 24) — and in it Beerbohm creates an unusual effect by interspersing the carefully detailed heads of nine reigning European monarchs among the characterless and ill-defined faces of the undergraduates who are serving them. The second takes us to Oxford, where Max envisions the "Encaenia of 1908, being an humble hint to the Chancellor, based on the Encaenia of 1907, whereby so many idols of the market-place were cheerily set up in the groves of the Benign Mother" (HD 386). It is unnecessary to list the names of the unlikely candidates for honorary degrees that Beerbohm depicts all in academic regalia (Hall Caine is of course among them), but it is apparent that they have been chosen as much for their caricaturability as for the inappropriateness of their being awarded academic honors. In other words, Max's sense of humor overwhelms his sense of outrage. The scene of the last is a library, where "Mr. Max Beerbohm receives an influential, though biassed, deputation, urging him, in the cause of our common humanity, and of good taste, to give over" (HD 1423, pl. 6). Sixteen figures whom Max had frequently caricatured are massed on the right; some, like James, Moore, and Pinero, stand with heads inclined in apparent deference; others, generally larger men, like Shaw, Sargent, and Chesterton, seem more defiant. In the center their leader, the Marquis de Soveral, expostulates diplomatically with an innocent-looking Max seated at a table, who listens with great interest to their collective grievance. Although busts of Soveral, Hall Caine, and Chesterton adorn the bookcases, this drawing, like the Cambridge and Oxford ones just described, seems fairly free of statement or comment. Generally Beerbohm's group drawings have no greater purpose than the assembly of figures he happens to enjoy caricaturing. There is, however, one significant departure from this practice among the caricatures drawn before World War I. In "Revisiting the Glimpses" (1911) seventeen years after his death and as a shade from the other world, Robert Louis Stevenson has just been conducted by Edmund Gosse on a survey of the present state of literature (HD 1599). Stevenson says to Gosse, "And now that you have shown me the new preachers and politicians, show me some of the men of letters," to which Gosse replies, "But, my dear Louis, these *are* the men of letters." Hart-Davis's description of the drawing reads: "The authors, tub-thumping and orating in all directions, are Cunninghame Graham, Wells, Chesterton, Galsworthy, Shaw, Zangwill, Hewlett, Belloc, and Kipling." Here we have not merely an array of subjects that are good for caricature — Beerbohm once observed that "the very fact of a man being interesting gives some sharp turn to his features, and therefore makes him caricaturable"[22] — but they are disposed in exaggerated postures as well. And not only Beerbohm but Stevenson and, apologetically, Gosse as well, find the contemporary writers long in rhetoric but short in art. We are still considerably removed from the imaginary reminiscence in this drawing, but it is a memorable fancy nevertheless.

The group caricature, on the whole, did little to advance Beerbohm on the path to the imaginary reminiscence, for, like the single portrait, it appears posed rather than spontaneous. None of Beerbohm's group caricatures catches their subjects at unguarded moments, however typical their attitudes; and it is this quality, accompanied by the suggestion that the vision is uniquely Beerbohm's, that is required to produce something equivalent to "No. 2. The Pines" or "Enoch Soames." The start in that direction was effected, not by multiplying figures, but by showing them in hyperbolic action, as in "Lord Byron shaking the dust of England from his shoes" from *The Poets' Corner* (HD 210; BLC 8), where the theatricality of the poet's disdain is almost enhanced by the childish representation of the sun, the boat, and the very dust itself. From the same volume "Walt Whitman, inciting the bird of freedom to soar" (HD 1776; BLC 12) conveys the expansiveness and enthusiasm of Whitman by having his upraised hands and outstretched feet cut off by the edges of the paper. He literally cannot be contained, a suggestion enforced by his generally shaggy appearance, the absence of firm outline, and the exposure of a pair of suspenders. The

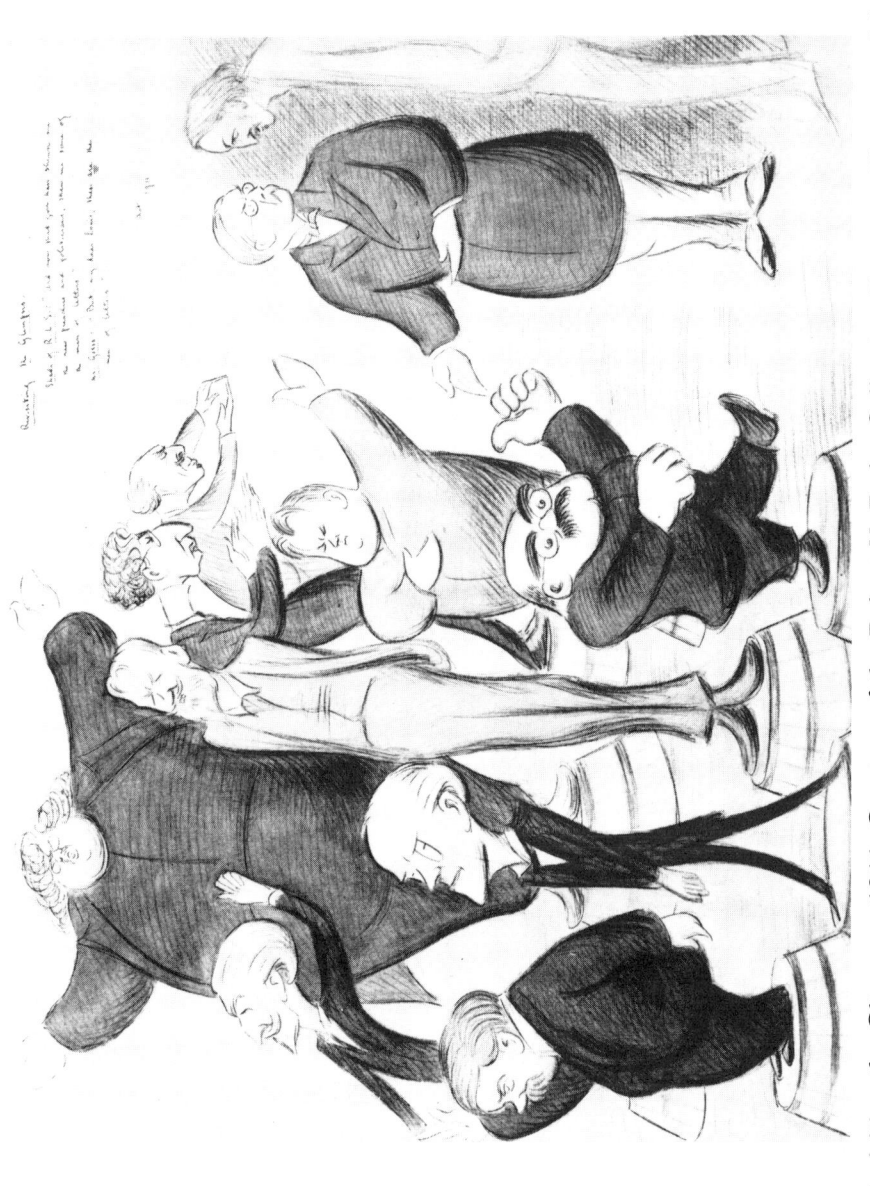

Revisiting the Glimpses. 1911. Courtesy of the Robert H. Taylor Collection, Princeton University Library.

bird of freedom, on the other hand, looking more like a crow than an eagle, perches sullenly in seeming indifference to Whitman's exhortations. Neither drawing conveys a particularly subtle attitude; yet in each of them caricature of action is added to caricature of person, which together constitute a unified reflection on the character and personality of the subject. And though the subjects are literary, the appeal of the drawings is wholly visual. One need never have heard either of Byron or of Whitman to appreciate them; from the drawings alone one can conjecture the kind of poetry that each wrote. The captions are a bonus to the literate. In "Mr. Sargent at Work" (HD 1365), the colored frontispiece to *A Book of Caricatures,* the American artist is charging at his canvas (shown on end) with a brush in each hand. Behind him on a platform is a richly clad aristocratic lady whose portrait is being painted while in the foreground a trio of string musicians is playing, each with a distinctive attitude of absorption. Curiously the cello has no neck and is being held upside down. It is impossible to say what "message" the drawing has to convey, but it is an excellent contrastive study of movements — Sargent's controlled frenzy and the more restrained, but no less expressive, actions of the musicians, all of them simultaneous.

The principle of contrast can be extended beyond casual and physical differences into the opposition of one figure or group to another. Conflict is not necessary, but the engagement, however slight, of one to the other is essential. That engagement is sufficient to invest the scene with dramatic force. Beerbohm first experimented with such confrontations in *The Poets' Corner,* and that volume contains some of the finest instances of the type before *Rossetti and His Circle.* In "Mr. Robert Browning, taking tea with the Browning Society" (HD 187; BLC 11), the seated poet is the only figure whose flesh is colored (his upholstered chair picks up the same tint); he is surrounded by earnest, dour, and drab admirers all craning for a glimpse of the presence, one old man straining to catch his words, a young one shyly fidgeting with an open book held behind his back, possibly intending to present it to the bard for inscription. There is certainly physical contrast here between the lionized and the lionizers. What lifts the drawing into confrontation is the irony of the situ-

Toward the Imaginary Reminiscence in Caricature

ation. "Beerbohm assumes, of course, that Browning's actual aversion to the formation of a Browning Society is known to the viewer of his drawing."[23] Indeed, most of the confrontation caricatures establish their points visually but clinch them by appealing to general knowledge. In "Mr. Tennyson, reading 'In Memoriam' to his Sovereign" (HD 1656; BLC 9), the joke is obvious enough. The immensity of the room and the distance between the two tiny black figures suggest just how little they can actually communicate with each other. Again the drawing is enhanced by the irony of the situation, for the lives of both the poet and the queen seem to have centered upon their bereavements. Hallam's death occasioned the poem Tennyson is declaiming; Prince Albert's framed portrait forms the apex of the triangular composition. Yet the two living figures are leagues apart. The most outstanding of the confrontations in *The Poets' Corner* is "Henrik Ibsen, receiving Mr. William Archer in audience" (HD 28; BLC 19). Archer, himself a distinguished critic, translator, and playwright, probably the greatest single force in popularizing Ibsen in England, is shown in total adoration of his idol, kneeling to kiss the toe of the gruff Norwegian. There is marked physical contrast between the two: Archer is well-groomed and lithe, with a supple neck and a graceful, delicate hand whereas Ibsen, whose white hair and side-whiskers stick out like the quills of a porcupine, appears to have no neck at all, for his head sits directly on top of a chunky body, his right arm dangling over the arm of the chair and terminating in a coarse and massive paw. We can read expressions on their faces as well. Archer's obeisance is matched by Ibsen's sullen imperiousness, which is further enhanced by the background. The gloomy egoist's state chamber is bare save for a chest of drawers on which stand a bottle of champagne and a single glass. His only decorations are a portrait of himself and his own visage repeated endlessly to form the pattern of the wallpaper. Beerbohm was to use the wallpaper trick in a number of other caricatures, but never so effectively as here.

Once established in *The Poets' Corner*, confrontation became for Beerbohm a significant device for generating caricatures. It was particularly useful in dealing with people whom he found enigmatic and elusive. George Bernard Shaw provides an excel-

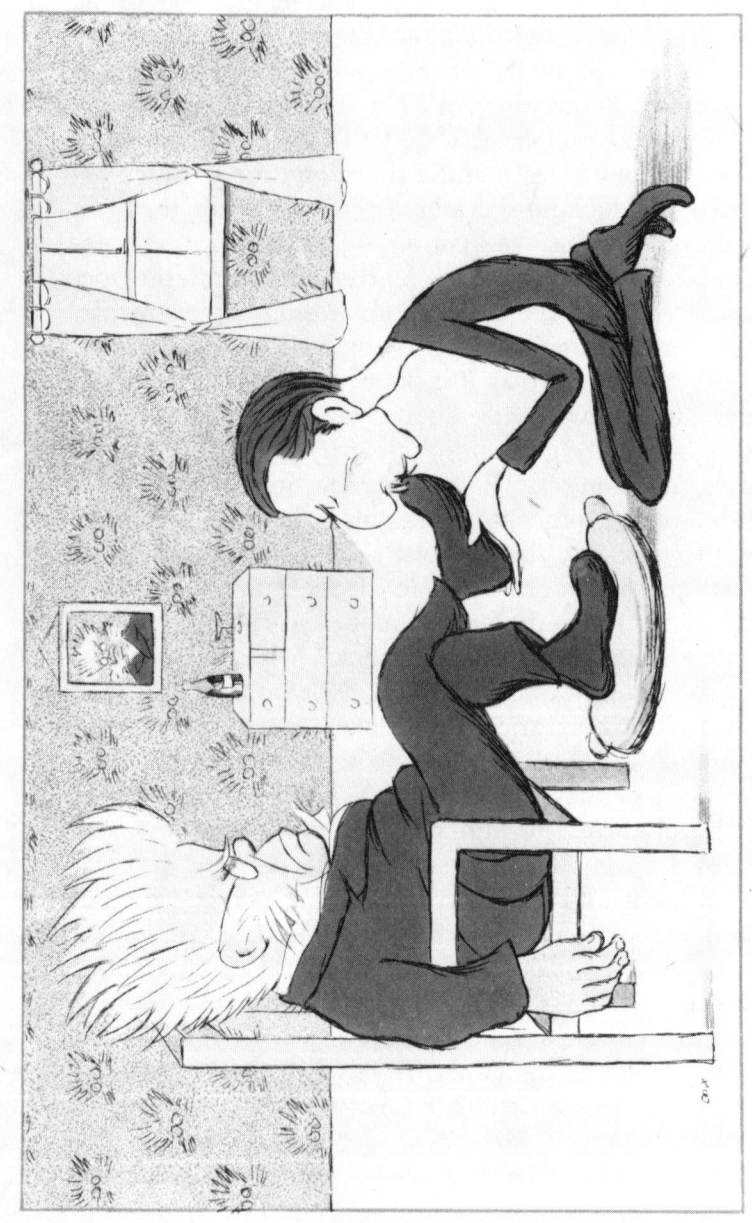

Henrik Ibsen, receiving Mr. William Archer in audience. [1904]. *The Poet's Corner,* (1904). Courtesy of the Municipal Gallery of Modern Art, Dublin.

Toward the Imaginary Reminiscence in Caricature

lent example. Beerbohm drew over forty caricatures of Shaw, not counting his appearances in groups. The most interesting of these involve confrontations of some kind. One of them, not particularly effective visually, has one Shaw dressed as Pantaloon encountering another Shaw clad as Mephistopheles (HD 1490, pl. 32). Although designed to "illustrate" a passage from Chesterton's biography of Shaw, the drawing really makes no sense unless it is understood in the light of Beerbohm's frequent assertions of wonder at Shaw's dual aspect — Shaw as clown and Shaw as propagandist. Beerbohm associated artistry with elegance, and in the Shaw drawing for *Fifty Caricatures* (HD 1499; BLC 23) he "refutes" the dramatist merely by placing himself alongside him. Shaw is depicted literally standing on his head, grimacing with strain, of course, suspenders exposed, baggy trousers slipping down to reveal his big, crudely shod feet and wrinkled socks. The posture is clumsy and undignified. Max, on the other hand, is neatly attired; his face, with its heavy-lidded eyes and carefully trimmed moustache, suggests the genial distress of a parent at the conduct of a clever but misbehaving child, and his feet taper away into points. The caption is as patronizing as the drawing: "Mild surprise of one who, revisiting England after long absence, finds that the dear fellow has not moved." In the following year Beerbohm challenged Shaw's originality as a thinker in a drawing entitled "Life Force, Woman-Set-Free, Superman, etc." (HD 1500; BLC 24). The scene is the pawn shop of Georg Brandes, the Danish literary critic, who is examining the old clothes Shaw has offered him for sale. "What'll you take for the lot?" Brandes asks. "Immortality," replies Shaw. Brandes: "Come, I've handled these goods before! Coat, Mr. Schopenhauer's; waistcoat, Mr. Ibsen's; Mr. Nietzsche's trousers — " Shaw: "Ah, but look at the patches!" Although it is true that the point of the drawing could not be made at all without the dialogue, the picture is no less important for all that: it is necessary to establish the notion that ideas are commodities that pass through many hands, that their worth, moreover, can be assayed, and that the seller is in no position to dictate the price. Shaw and Brandes are actually bargaining. Shaw's left hand is extended forward asserting the quality of the goods he has brought in; Brandes, holding a pair of tattered checked trousers in both hands, looks directly at Shaw with one eyebrow raised as if to say that Shaw's imposture may pass with others but not with him.

The pictorial element of Beerbohm's caricatures is subject to yet one more complication. If to a confrontation between two figures a third is added, a triangular configuration is generated in which relations and tensions are multiplied; for each figure thus responds to, not one, but two others. Since the most frequent social situation in which such arrangements occur is the introduction, I have used that word to designate these triangular relationships. Obviously, the more widely disparate the characters in temperament or appearance, the more potentially hilarious is the caricature. The introduction is utilized with the greatest sophistication in *Rossetti and His Circle,* where at least four of the twenty-three plates consist of formal introductions. But an early and classic manifestation of the type again appears in *The Poets' Corner* in what is probably Beerbohm's single best-known caricature — at least it is one of the most frequently reproduced — "Mr. W. B. Yeats, presenting Mr. George Moore to the Queen of the Fairies" (HD 1827; BLC 32). The familiar swaying figure of Yeats dominates the center of the picture, and the eye is drawn up to his elongated scholar's head by a series of apexes formed by his body — the slippered feet make a rather obtuse angle between them, but that of the legs before they come together at the bent knees is more acute. The major triangle is established by Yeats's two arms, the right one paternally encircling Moore's shoulder, the left dead straight, with fingers continuing the line, pointing to the Queen of the Fairies. Each arm, moreover, creates a smaller triangle in relation to the trunk of the body. Even the unruly forelock, an essential characteristic in all of Beerbohm's drawings of Yeats, has in this instance a pronounced bifurcation. As in a number of Max's drawings of tall men, there is the impression here that if Yeats were to straighten up, his head would go through the top of the picture. But frail and grotesque as he appears, he is physically imposing. He seems to be imposing as well his vision upon the embarrassed Moore, who has doffed his hat and brought the knob of his walking stick to his lip as though in wonder whether he is seeing anything at all. The Queen of the Fairies herself is hastily

Toward the Imaginary Reminiscence in Caricature

sketched in a few lines such as a child might draw. What overwhelms the viewer is the utter conviction of Yeats, whose sinuosity is relieved only by the straightness of that arm pointing so directly and confidently to the palpable spirit that he doesn't even have to look himself. Is she really there, is Yeats self-deluded or is he a charlatan? The titles on the book-shelf — *Realism: Its Cause and Cure, Half Hours with the Symbols, Erse without Tears, Songs of Innocence, Murray's Guide to Ireland,* and *Short Cuts to Mysticism* — cannot be assumed to settle the issue, for Moore is hardly to be accepted, whatever his commitment to naturalism, as the representative of common sense. No less than Yeats, Moore was to be the subject of one of Max's "remembering" essays, from which he emerges, like Yeats, as a very distinctive yet ambiguous character. The joy of this introduction scene lies in the visualization of the unlikely meeting, as in the drawing Beerbohm exhibited in his 1911 show: "Mr. Henry James making a match between Mona Lisa and the Man in the Iron Mask" (HD 809). The Queen of the Fairies may be Beerbohm's hyperbolic invention, but she stands as a representative of the Irish Literary Theatre into which Moore had been lured. By creating a situation and providing us with an actual scene, Beerbohm can suggest deeper contrasts between the two Celts Yeats and Moore than he was able to in "Celtades Ambo" five years earlier.

The introduction is Beerbohm's most sophisticated pictorial device for generating a caricature. No comparable hierarchy exists on the literary side, for a simple literary idea can be executed with great pictorial effectiveness and, as frequently happens, a fairly complex one may elude representation altogether. We can, nevertheless, speak of a range of impulses to caricature that are primarily literary or intellectual, impulses that must then seek pictorial rather than verbal means for their expression. This range extends, not from the simple to the complex, but from references to general ideas to references to specific ones. At one end of the spectrum is the editorial cartoon where, shorn of ambiguity and personal distinctiveness, the human form is reduced to symbol. At the other end is illustration, where a specific text not only provides the occasion and inspiration for a drawing but is also itself the subject of the distortion. Between these two lie intermediate gradations of allegory, allusion, and parody. Given the proper pictorial handling, any of these impulses can be realized in a brilliant caricature. What must be remembered, however, is that these caricatures distort ideas, facts, and memories rather than persons. However well drawn, these caricatures are subject to failure from the obviousness or the obscurity of the intellectual conceptions that underlie them.

Although Beerbohm drew a fair number of editorial and allegorical cartoons, they are not among his most representative work; the best of them were done in the twenties, during the decline from the intensity of *Rossetti and His Circle*. It may well be that he came to do more drawing of this kind because he had exhausted his stock of visual memories or because the keenest of them were of personages no longer eminent in the eyes of the public. Under such circumstances it is understandable that Beerbohm's drawings might become peopled by Dame Europa and Brother Jonathan (HD 2006) in *Things Old and New* (1923) or by Civilisation and the Industrial System (HD 2028) in *Observations* (1925). Because there is no exaggeration in such drawings of actual identifiable persons, their qualification as caricatures has been brought into question. Accomplished satirists long before Beerbohm, however, had created or appropriated fictional types compounded out of figures of the day. One thinks of Daumier's Robert Macaire and Ratapoil. Beerbohm's invention does not operate in this way. He prefers, on the whole, to incorporate the standard representations of capitalists and workers, intellectuals and generals, and relies heavily on captions to make his points. What really unfits Beerbohm for the role of editorial cartoonist is his judicious and nonpartisan stance. Essentially nonpolitical himself, Beerbohm subjected national and international events and the statesmen of the day to the same ironic treatment he applied to Henry James or Rossetti. These drawings, when they touched sensitive nerves, were treated as political statements and objected to as such. In the early twenties Beerbohm called down upon his head the ire of both the liberal and the conservative press.[24] Politics had become less good-humored after the war. Just as the Liberal party itself had become virtually extinguished in the polar division between the Establishment and labor, so there was no longer a place for the

Toward the Imaginary Reminiscence in Caricature

detached and uncommitted political observer. But before the Great War Beerbohm's generally bland comments on large issues provoked no resentment. In "A Study in Democratic Assimilation" (HD 1962), the Scions of Nobility and Proletariat appear indistinguishably dressed in 1908 whereas a companion drawing presenting them forty years earlier shows them suitably differentiated. In "And Only Just Thirteen" (HD 1976), drawn in 1913, we are shown "the Grave Misgivings of the Nineteenth Century, and the Wicked Amusement of the Eighteenth, in watching the Progress (or whatever it is) of the Twentieth." The demonstration is effected through costume more than through action or situation: Beerbohm clearly delights in showing us what has been discarded — the starched shirt front as the only bit of white in the uniformly black and austere garb of the Victorian, the frock coat and knee breeches of the bewigged and snuff-taking paleo-Georgian — for the one-piece jump suit of the feverishly racing modern man. Both of these drawings appear in *Fifty Caricatures;* both of them, like the caricatures of real men that outnumber them, are essentially comments on *style.*

The literary subject matter proclaimed in the title of *The Poets' Corner* allowed Beerbohm to tap another source of ideas for caricatures, that of allusion. By confidently relying on the viewers' familiarity with the works and personalities of men of letters, Beerbohm was able to project his exaggerations from a platform higher than that afforded by mere physical distortion while flattering the knowledgeable and enlightening the uninformed. The great danger of allusion as a source of caricature is the danger of allusion generally; that is, references to the past may tend to be so familiar as to be commonplace, and references to the present may be so detailed and particular as to be obscure to all but a very few. *The Poets' Corner* illustrates both tendencies. The point of the drawing "Homer, going his round" (HD 766; BLC 1) depends on the viewer's awareness of but two bits of lore, neither requiring a knowledge of Greek: (1) that the epithet "many-headed" had been applied to Homer originally to signify the copiousness of his wisdom and imagination but latterly perhaps to suggest the multiple authorship of the epics attributed to a single man, and (2) that Homer is traditionally said to have been blind. Thus armed, the viewer may enjoy the joke of the drawing of a many-headed man singing to his own accompaniment on the lyre. For those who have not Greek enough to understand that the sign across the man's chest, ΤΥΦΛΟΣ, means "blind," there is a little dog with a tin cup in its mouth. Far more labored is the joke of the drawing "Mr. William Watson, secretly ceded by the British Government to Abdul Hamid, but, in the nick of time, saved from the trap-door to the Bosphorus by the passionate intercession of Mr. John Lane" (HD 1740). The drawing itself is crude and distracting — visually the most arresting figure is that of the swarthy slave conveying his bundle to the trapdoor — and would be totally incomprehensible without the caption, itself requiring annotation, which Max himself supplied for the 1943 edition: "At the time of the Armenian atrocities in 1896, William Watson wrote several sonnets denouncing the Sultan, Abdul Hamid. One of them ended with the words 'Abdul the damned, on his infernal throne'. John Lane, his publisher, is interceding."[25] In both of these instances the accomplishment of the drawing itself, because it has so little to say visually, does not seem worth the unraveling.

That is Beerbohm at his allusive worst. For his best in this vein, that is, in the creation of caricatures whose visual humor is fortified by the viewer's possession of special information, we must often turn to lesser-known drawings whose appeal was to an audience even smaller than usual. One such drawing, "A quiet morning in the Tate Gallery" (HD 995), occasioned by the presentation to the gallery in 1907 of the oil painting by William Rothenstein entitled *Jews Mourning in a Synagogue,* actually incorporated Max's version of that painting in the background. Rothenstein wrote facetiously to Beerbohm that his brother Albert "has told me of the moving character of your latest religious picture — I burn to see it,"[26] but the composition, in the careful style of pencil and wash he adopted after *The Poets' Corner,* using ink only for highlights, is a beautiful arrangement of blue, pink, and gold. Before the painting stand two men, "the Curator [D. S. MacColl] trying to expound to one of the Trustees the spiritual fineness" of it. The caption raises in the mind the possibility that this trustee may require special instruction in the merits of the painting, that he has perhaps objected to the subject, or that for some other reason he has personally to be per-

A quiet morning in the Tate Gallery. 1907. Courtesy of the Tate Gallery, London.

suaded. The irony is not apparent until one recognizes the trustee as Alfred de Rothschild. Among the drawings exhibited in the winter show of the New English Art Club in 1911, where the people depicted were sure to be not only spectators but fellow-exhibitors, Beerbohm proposed "An Illustration for 'Hail and Farewell'. Mr. Moore under the influence of the Boer War" (HD 1054). The first volume of that autobiography had appeared earlier in the year; in it Moore described how a decade before, returning to London from Ireland, whither he had gone to launch the Irish Literary Theatre with Yeats and Edward Martyn, he suddenly underwent a mystical conversion — almost like that of St. Paul — and in his obsession with the outrage of the Boer War conceived a detestation of all things English. In this state, in which he confessed that "art and literature had ceased to interest me," Moore consulted his portrait painters, not for the convivial aesthetic discussions of old, but to discover whether

> the great spiritual changes that were happening in me were recognizable upon my face. . . . And that night at Steer's, after a passionate protest against the wickedness and stupidity of the Boer War delivered across his dining-table, I got up and walked round the room, feeling myself to be unlike the portraits they had painted of me, every one of which had been done before the war. The external appearance no doubt remained, but the acquisition of a moral conscience must have modified it. . . . I could see that [Tonks] sympathized with the Boer women and children dying in concentration camps, and that Steer was thinking of the pictures he had brought home from the country. It was shameful that anyone should be able to think of pictures at such a time, but Steer takes no interest in morals.[27]

Beerbohm's "illustration" is just that. The inconsolable George Moore, his eyes drooping at the same angle as his walrus moustache, is depicted seated on a chair surrounded by his artist friends as comforters. The elongated figure of Henry Tonks, haloed by a symbolic convex mirror, must be bent in order to fit into the picture. With both arms touching Moore, he is trying vainly to bring him round. The ungainly Wilson Steer has dropped to his knees and is proffering a covered china bowl to

An illustration for 'Hail and Farewell.' Mr. Moore under the influence of the Boer War. 1911. Courtesy of the Ashmolean Museum, Oxford.

Moore, which is likewise disdained. Walter Sickert looks on with sad concern. The postures of all three of the comforters, in line with Moore's assertion that all their former portraits of him were no longer true, suggest a Holy Family scene, perhaps even a Pietà. Moreover, the ensemble offers a perfect visual counterpart to the relation described in Beerbohm's essay between Moore and these artists. One is not quite sure of *their* response to his sorrow; do they see him as a child to be humored or as an extraordinarily sensitive human being grieving at the world's injustices? These two drawings are both fairly elaborate pictorially and demonstrate the considerable care Max could take to compose his caricatures. Far simpler is the drawing entitled "The Old Pilgrim Comes Home" (HD 810; BLC 83), drawn in 1913 but neither exhibited nor reproduced until 1921. The Old Pilgrim is Henry James, stick in hand, trudging up a long road leading to a celestial city whose skyline, appropriately enough, is a composite of the distinctive architectural monuments of Rome (Coliseum), Paris (Eiffel Tower), London (St. Paul's), and New York (a skyscraper). The simple point, readily apparent to those reasonably acquainted with James's canon but not to others, is that for this cosmopolitan novelist "home" as a geographical locus simply does not exist. Hence the visionary gaze in James's eye, the upraised hand of salute: he is returning to a city of his imagination. The drawing is at once a tribute to that imagination and a sadder reflection on the lot of the exile.

Allusion may extend beyond books to art itself. Occasionally Beerbohm parodies a familiar painting in a caricature; the burlesque, in these instances, mocks not the original artist (as in *A Christmas Garland*) but the person being caricatured, who appears literally in robes borrowed for the occasion. In the early sketch, "King Edward VII is duly apprised of his accession" (HD 478, pl. 21), a grumpy, stout man clad only in pajamas is descending a staircase to be hailed by a kneeling lord chancellor and archbishop of Canterbury. Hart-Davis notes that this is "a parody of the well-known scene of Queen Victoria's accession."[28] What the viewer supplies, of course, his memory having been prodded, is the disparity between the innocent and conscientious young girl and the sixty-year-old sybarite her son and heir had become. The biographer of Whistler, Joseph Pennell, is

Toward the Imaginary Reminiscence in Caricature

featured in 1913 in the pose of Whistler's two most famous sitters, his mother and Thomas Carlyle (HD 1149). The humor of such drawings is unachieved unless the viewer can supply the appropriate recollection. Closely related to the foregoing in providing an ironic version, yet not technically a parody because of the difference in medium, is Beerbohm's illustration of a text, his most famous being the first plate of *The Poets' Corner*, "Omar Khayyam" (HD 847; BLC 2). In this drawing small identifying numbers are tagged to the principal objects depicted. These are all explained in a key in the upper right-hand corner of the picture: "(1–Book of Verses; 2–Bough; 3–Loaf of Bread; 4–Jug of Wine; 5–Thou; 6–Wilderness)." Assembling all the parts will yield the most famous quatrain of Edward FitzGerald's *Rubaiyat:*

> A Book of Verses underneath the Bough,
> A Jug of Wine, a Loaf of Bread — and Thou
>   Beside me singing in the Wilderness —
> Oh, Wilderness were Paradise enow!

By dismembering the lines of poetry into its constituents and labeling each one; by representing Omar as a paunchy self-indulgent layabout and Thou as a shrieking harridan, Beerbohm deflates the romantic sentiment and suburbanizes it. The caricature becomes an ironic wish fulfillment.

The preceding survey of the kinds of caricatures that Beerbohm drew before World War I is certainly not intended to establish rigorous categories. Rather it demonstrates how the tendency to exaggerate features of the human form, which is the essence of caricature, became complicated by the introduction of other figures and dramatic situations. This complication is strongly manifested in *The Poets' Corner*, as is the more or less successful integration of the literary element into Beerbohm's drawings. Both of these developments are continued in *A Book of Caricatures* and *Fifty Caricatures*, albums that in their miscellaneous character are equivalents to the volumes of essays discussed in the last chapter. There is not a clear and inevitable progression from these books of caricatures to *Rossetti and His Circle;* yet it is possible to see the artistic characteristics emerging that encourage the inclination to imaginary reminiscence.

Sir Max Beerbohm

The first of these, the insistence on the actuality of the subject, was indeed present from the very outset. We do not generally designate comic drawings of imaginary people as caricatures, for, as characters from the start, they do not have to undergo the process of reduction. Yet there is a leap for an artist to make from working from his own memory or sketch pad to working from photographs or the drawings of others. The difference between them is analogous to that between primary and secondary sources in the writing of history. Beerbohm's willingness to make the venture in *The Poets' Corner* involved considerable risk: the fine edge of physical caricature was in danger of being dulled by anecdote. It must be admitted that as a group the drawings of contemporaries in *The Poets' Corner,* such as the Ibsen-Archer, Yeats-Moore, and Kipling-Britannia, work better as caricatures than the historical ones, such as the Shakespeare, Wordsworth, and Burns. Costume may have something to do with it, but generally it is more difficult to read any expression into the faces of the historical figures. Thus *The Poets' Corner* simultaneously opened up a new area for Beerbohm to explore and revealed a potential weakness. If he was to engage in comic representation of historical personages, he would have to compensate for inauthenticity by care and the invention of probable fictions. Whistler might be depicted in 1898 crossing the English Channel on a broomstick (HD 1768) in a general spoof of the compositions he called "nocturnes," but the parody of Millais's painting (plate 3) in *Rossetti and His Circle* (HD 1039) is more carefully drawn; and although the prevision itself is not factually true, the substance of it is verifiable. Fortified by the presence among the illustrious dead of men whom Beerbohm had actually known and caricatured under other circumstances, such as Whistler, Swinburne, Meredith, Gosse, Watts-Dunton, Caine, and Wilde, *Rossetti and His Circle* works like *Seven Men* in persuading us of its general truth by mingling the real and the imaginary — caricatures drawn from the life with those drawn from pictures and photographs. To put it another way, for Beerbohm to take up caricaturing the dead at all meant a sacrifice of the more extravagant forms of physical distortion and a correspondingly greater reliance upon the intellect to illuminate the source of ludicrousness.

Toward the Imaginary Reminiscence in Caricature

A second characteristic, the presentation of a subject in action, in a dramatic situation or confrontation, may also have been stimulated by looking beyond the contemporary scene. Whereas a portrait caricature of a living person may amuse, flatter, wound, or shock the subject, his friends, acquaintances, and enemies, that of a dead one cannot arouse such feelings. The only justification for caricaturing the dead is to bring about a re-examination of our attitudes toward them, and to do so requires more than mere physical distortion can effect. And if the new interpretation is to pretend to any penetration at all, the caricature upon which it is based must catch the subject in an unposed and unguarded moment, in an attitude, however exaggerated, that is perceived to be characteristic of him, yet one that is not quite public: Byron shaking the dust of England off his shoes, Whitman inciting the bird of freedom to soar, Paul Verlaine as an usher in a private school in Bournemouth (HD 1723; BLC 14). The invention of such scenes, the creation of probable incidents, need not, of course, be restricted to the lives of those no longer living; and, as we have seen, many of Beerbohm's most accomplished likelihoods concern his contemporaries. But there are few instances of such caricature before *The Poets' Corner,* and it is reasonable to suggest that the incentive to examine his contemporaries through invented scenes arose from the necessity of examining historical personages in this way.

In our survey of Beerbohm's prose in the last chapter we saw in the growing personal involvement of the writer with his subject, in the absence of any pretense of objectivity, and in the frank delight of exploring his own responses rather than imagine those of others, that Beerbohm observed people with the eye of neither a dramatist, a novelist, a biographer, nor a historian, but with that of a remembrancer. And in that perspective lies the essence of the imaginary reminiscence. There is no exact equivalent for this authorial presence in Beerbohm's caricatures. It is true that Max puts in a personal appearance in a number of them, but that number is not that large, nor is he cast in those instances as one who is recollecting (and thereby reexperiencing) the past. Pressed to find an authorial presence in the drawings, one might say that the act of caricaturing itself constitutes a very personal recollection, mimesis being abandoned for a kind of impressionism. But to argue in this fashion would not only fail to distinguish Beerbohm from other caricaturists, it would obscure the conceptual differences between Beerbohm's early and late caricatures, thereby limiting discussion to matters of technique. If we lay aside, however, the issue of the physical presence of the artist in his work and consider instead the *quality* of the thing observed, we find an unusual correspondence between many of the essays and caricatures, a correspondence that allows us to designate them both as reminiscences. In his invention of private scenes from the lives of public figures, for example, Beerbohm chooses events commonplace in themselves, though revelatory, but not major incidents, nothing that might, if it had actually occurred, be of great biographical significance. The drama of his confrontations and introductions is modest. But above all, his pictorial anecdotes are open-ended: they invite viewers to interpret them; they present ambiguities and ironies. They are not illustrations of general truths or demonstrations of propositions.

In the drawings Beerbohm made before World War I, then, we can discern the presence and development of three characteristics necessary for the transformation of simple caricature into imaginary reminiscence: (1) the assertion of the veracity of the observation and the concomitant curb imposed on fancy, (2) an increasing reliance on scene or situation to carry the burden of exaggeration, and (3) the qualities of remembered rather than chronicled events: casualness, intimacy, familiarity. What had not yet been demonstrated by these drawings was any significant narrative consequence. Not that the drawings should tell a story as a comic strip does, each picture almost a frame in a movie film. But there is a sense in which a group of caricatures, particularly if they depict scenes rather than portraits, may cohere, may make considerably more sense as a group than as separate entities, as a poet's volume of poems is more than a printed portfolio. In his series drawings, particularly "Mr. Gladstone Goes to Heaven" and "The Edwardyssey," Beerbohm showed that he was aware of the advantages of extending a character and an angle of vision over more than a single caricature. But these are crude jokes in the light of the wit and sophistication exhibited in *A Book of Caricatures* and *Fifty Caricatures*. Even after *Rossetti and His Circle,* Beerbohm continued series drawings. *Things New and Old* (1923) contains two series — "Tales of Three Nations" and "Studies in the Eighteen-Seventies" — and *Observations* (1925) includes the admirable invention "The Old and the Young Self." All of these series are the product of greater care and study, both conceptual and technical, than those exhibited in Beerbohm's early work.

Finally, perhaps a word or two should be said about the media in which Beerbohm worked, for to some degree the ambitiousness of his projects is reflected by them. Reproduction, through which Beerbohm's caricatures essentially are viewed today, not only falsifies color and size but also obscures the artist's growing technical proficiency. Beerbohm's earliest drawings suffer least in this respect, for in the nineties, before his reputation as a caricaturist had been firmly established, he worked largely in black and white because his work was designed for publication in newspapers and magazines. A significant exception to this general tendency is his wistful *Vanity Fair* portrait of George Meredith (HD 1032), done in 1896 in the manner of Ape. Here we find him attempting effects of texture and shade that he could not achieve with pen and ink. The picture is drawn with pencil and crayon and given a pale blue wash. *The Poets' Corner* does indeed reproduce in color and does so fairly faithfully if we are to judge by the few originals to be found in public galleries. But it is obvious that the whole project was conceived with the limitations of technical reproduction in mind: the color is no more than tint, applied with uniform density as in a comic book, and the overall effect, with gray and olive predominating, is rather drab. Gradually, however, Beerbohm came to settle on pencil and wash as his preferred medium, inking in outlines with a fine pen at the beginning for emphasis but coming to abandon that practice as the first decade of the twentieth century wore on. What had happened, of course, was that the sale of the original drawings, not their reproductions, had come to constitute the principal source of his income derived from caricaturing. As in writing, so in his drawing, in leaving England and settling in Italy, Max was free to follow his artistic inclinations — to dictate the market for his works rather than be fashioned by it. At the height of his powers as an artist in 1910, his style having reached its maturity, Beerbohm needed only a grand theme that would fuse perfectly the pictorial and literary elements of his caricature.

CHAPTER IV

"The Mirror of the Past"

On 16 April 1910 there appeared in the *Saturday Review* Beerbohm's farewell article as a drama critic, appropriately entitled "Habit," in which he speaks generally of the security and oppression of fixed ways and familiar objects and particularly of his dread of Thursdays, the last day possible for the composition of his weekly reviews. He confesses that "writing has always been uphill work to me" and that "I do not recall that I have once sat down eager to write, or that I have once written with ease and delight."[1] After twelve years of doing his best, he felt that he had had enough. Less than three weeks later, on 4 May, in the Paddington Registry Office in the presence of his mother and Reggie Turner, he married Florence Kahn, an American actress whom he had known for six years and had been more or less engaged to for two. Beerbohm's earlier attachments to actresses, which by modern lights seem to have been so tenuous and unsubstantial as to be virtually nonexistent, had doubtless made him not only cautious in formulating his plans but secretive in revealing them as well. Yet despite the mystery to all but his most intimate acquaintances, Max's apparently sudden and impulsive decision was the result of long deliberation. His biographer, Lord David Cecil, citing the letters of courtship to Florence, demonstrates convincingly that Beerbohm's disaffection with the routines of his social and professional life was well established as early as 1907, though his determination to make Florence the partner of a new life was more ambiguous and tentative. However tortuous the road to resolution, at the age of thirty-eight Max decided to cultivate a new way of life and a new set of habits. Marriage and retirement from England were conceived of as but elements of a single change by which Max renounced simultaneously the freedom and bondage of the bachelor state and social life as well as the intellectual and artistic stimulation that life in London afforded. As if to punctuate the termination of that old life and to signal the domestication of the dandy, King Edward VII died two days after Beerbohm's marriage and was succeeded by George V, a monarch whose exemplary conduct made him virtually impervious to caricature.[2] After a honeymoon in Kent, the couple left for the Continent. By the end of August they had settled in the Villino Chiaro in Rapallo, which, except for brief visits to England on business and the longer stays during the two wars, was to remain their home until their deaths.

As a bachelor of not too expensive tastes and slender means, Max had lived decently but frugally on his earnings from the *Saturday Review*. But he had managed to do so only by living in the family home in Upper Berkeley Street. The cost of living on the Italian Riviera, particularly without the constant obligation of entertaining friends, was far lower than in London; yet without a steady income even a modest existence would have been precarious had he not financed the move with advances on future earnings. Specifically, he had arranged for an exhibition of caricatures for the following spring and was to write a one-act play, *A Social Success,* for the actor-manager George Alexander.[3] He had also brought with him the unfinished *Zuleika Dobson,* though she was forced "to stand aside for the caricatures."[4] But the novel was completed by the spring of 1911, and he was able to negotiate for its publication when he went to London for the exhibition of his drawings at the Leicester Galleries, which showing proved both an artistic and commercial success. When *Zuleika* did appear in the fall of the year, followed shortly by the publication of *The Second Childhood of John Bull* and the showing of additional drawings at the New English Art Club, Beerbohm's mastery of two means of expression and his ability to earn a livelihood from both on his own terms were assured. Delighted that the move to Italy had effected the very outcome he had sought — in 1907 he had written to his future wife, "I wish I could make my living by drawing"[5] — Beerbohm began planning for another exhibition in 1913, and by March of that year he had completed sixty-one unexhibited drawings.[6] As might have been expected, his pen lagged somewhat behind his pencil; he did indeed bring out *A Christmas Garland* in 1912 and *A Social Success* was produced in January 1913, but, as we have seen, these were works that were brought to completion rather than works initiated at Rapallo. Seven years were to elapse between the publication of *A Christmas Garland* and his next book of prose, seven years marked by considerable and often frustrating experimentation with literary forms — the years of the "remembering" essays, of "No. 2. The Pines," of the sketches that would eventually constitute *Seven Men*, and of that elusive scenario, fragment, and notes for a novel to be called "The Mirror of the Past."

Although the scholar may always find justification for the endeavor, the general question of the utility of describing and accounting for an unpublished work cannot be evaded. Why pore over what was not merely unfinished but also abandoned? The very existence of the work was not generally known during Beerbohm's lifetime. Riewald made no mention of it in his encyclopedic survey and bibliography;[7] and although Max spoke of it to Behrman in 1952, the distance of years had produced in his mind some confusion about just what was contained in the manuscript.[8] For his last radio broadcast, on Christmas Day 1955, Max drew together some of the anecdotes he had invented for the novel under the title "Hethway Speaking,"[9] but they provide little indication of the original intent of the work. Not until the sale of his literary effects in 1960 did the elaborateness of the original design, as it reveals itself in over one hundred folio pages, come to light.[10] That light is still somewhat obscure, and the manuscript, most of it notes and jottings, remains not only unpublished but unpublishable.[11] That Max did not destroy these papers and that he chose to return to them at the end of his life furnish sufficient evidence that, though the project had become unmanageable to him, he was far from repudiating it. It had cost him considerable pains and had, moreover, as I shall try to demonstrate, provided a passage to works of greater maturity that followed it — both sufficient reasons for regarding it as more than a curiosity. And, one feels, given Max's fascination with unfinished works of art, he would not have disapproved of the close study of "The Mirror." "There is a peculiar charm for all of us," he wrote, "in that which was still in the making when its maker died, or in that which he laid aside because he was tired of it, or didn't see his way to the end of it, or wanted to go on to something else."[12]

Before turning to the actual manuscript itself, it may be worth risking a few conjectures about the place that "The Mirror of the Past" was to occupy in Beerbohm's canon. By 1913, as we have seen, he had more than justified his move to Rapallo by the productions of his drawing board alone. The two exhibitions of 1911 and 1913 comprised nearly two hundred caricatures; and even though the earlier show contained many that had been executed before leaving England (quite a number of them untraced), there can be no question that as a visual artist he thrived in retirement. The completion of *Zuleika Dobson,* particularly after an interruption of so many years, may have left him, however, with a desire to compose a *chef d'oeuvre,* a literary work of some substance that would further explore his notions of storytelling, one that would, moreover, in its leisurely unfolding obliterate those traces of journalism still recognizable in *A Christmas Garland* yet not wholly efface the presence of the essayist, the self-conscious recorder of his own impressions. He had, he confessed to Behrman, since early manhood been struck with peculiar wonder by a piece of household furniture, a convex mirror:

> There is no poetry in a straight mirror — just a reproduction of life. But what one sees in a convex mirror is a complete picture, a composition, an *intérieur.* By miniaturizing, it concentrates and essentializes. It hung in my nursery, this mirror. Then, when as a young man, I occupied rooms on the top floor of my mother's house, I had it moved up there. It has been with me ever since. My father bought it at the Paris International Exhibition of 1867. It seems to me that during my childhood I was half asleep, but as I grew a bit older, this mirror began to fascinate me. I began to think of all that it had seen since my father bought it; he used to have it in his rooms. And then, when I reached the age of twenty-one — the age of reminiscence, of *seasoned* reminiscence — I began to see this mirror as a collaborator, with memories of its

"The Mirror of the Past"

> own, a *temps perdu* of its own. I began to write a novel about it, an autobiographical novel called *The Mirror of the Past*. I wanted to corporealize all the backs the mirror had seen leaving my room.[13]

Although the convex mirror and its yielding up of visual memories lie at the heart of the projected novel, the memories conjured up are not actually of events that took place in Max's room. They date from a time before his birth and a place more than two miles away. Max records these memories on paper and responds to them, memories wholly of his own invention of both real and imaginary persons. The fragment of the novel as we have it began taking shape in 1913 at about the same time that Max was composing the "remembering" essays. The convex mirror served the function of extending reminiscence further into the past at a time when Max was near to exhausting his own stock of recollections and when his self-imposed exile had cut him off from a fresh supply for the future. As a narrative device the mirror invites comparison to the experiments of eighteenth-century novelists, such as that of Charles Johnstone in *The Adventures of a Guinea* (1760). But as a fantasist himself, quite apart from the successful introduction of implausibility in the fiction of Stevenson and Wilde, two writers he particularly admired, Beerbohm would have been attracted to the challenge of converting the metaphor into a mechanism. He may also have been stimulated to do so by his dabbling in photography: "The whole fun of photographing is the developing and printing — this is really exciting, every time. . . . I have now become quite expert on my own account."[14] With the outbreak of war the following year, there seemed little likelihood of success for another exhibition of caricatures. Beerbohm was thus under less pressure to draw and could devote more of his energies to writing.

If, as Beerbohm's biographer observes, "it is not possible to date the composition of these stories [in *Seven Men*] exactly,"[15] it is even more difficult to date a composition that was never fully composed, especially one that caused him so much difficulty. Beerbohm does not appear to have mentioned it in any of his personal letters. Nor did he persist for any length of time in keeping a diary of his activities or works in progress. We cannot know, therefore, how long it was before contemplation succeeded to execution. But in the preliminary pencil draft of the beginning of the novel, which opens with Max the narrator recounting his receipt of a letter from the fictional Sylvester Herringham in 1896, the reader is asked rhetorically, "To how many people in 1913 is that signature significant of anything, I wonder?"[16] In the fair manuscript in ink, which contains instructions to the printer and runs unfortunately to only three pages, the same question appears, but the last digit in the year "1913" has been crossed out, with no other supplied in its place. At the head of the papers relating to the novel is a twelve-page letter addressed to the editor of *Century*, the American magazine that had already published or was to publish four of the five stories in *Seven Men*. This letter, marked "private and confidential," bearing neither a conventional heading nor complimentary close, carries the designation: *"A very brief and arbitrary account of a book I am writing, entitled 'The Mirror of the Past.'"* Although it may never actually have been sent, this letter constitutes a fairly extensive scenario of the projected work in a form that, unlike the working notes themselves, is fully explanatory of its design. This document, though not specifically dated, contains at one point the expression, "And now in 1916...."[17] Conventionally this has been taken as the terminal year of Beerbohm's active involvement with the project. One writer goes so far as to suggest that the work was abandoned because of lack of encouragement: "But the *Century* people were not interested, and so the work was never completed."[18] Yet there is reason to believe that "The Mirror of the Past" continued to occupy Beerbohm well after 1916. On the verso of the last sheet of the pencil draft (he usually wrote on only one side, though he would occasionally sketch on the other), there is in Max's handwriting in ink a sentence describing Sir Herbert Beerbohm Tree's "Impressions of America" of 1916 and 1917, a sentence later to appear in the volume of tributes to his half-brother (who died in July 1917), which volume Max edited.[19] This note would suggest that, whether actually working on it or not, Beerbohm had the manuscript by him in Sussex in the summer of 1919 when he was getting the book together for publication. Back in Rapallo after the war, Beerbohm resumed a diary he had begun in 1911

"The Mirror of the Past"

in a dummy copy of *Zuleika Dobson*.[20] On 16, 19, and 22 of October 1921 he noted that Florence had typed up passages that appear in the manuscript of "The Mirror." Significantly, Herringham had by this time been transformed to Hethway, perhaps an indication that the novel that had become unworkable was being mined for what it would yield. Yet in the preface to *Rossetti and His Circle* (in which a convex mirror figures prominently in one of the plates), written in 1922, Beerbohm coyly hints at the unusual assistance afforded him by the mirror in summoning up the presences of those dead before he was born: "Old drawings and paintings, early photographs, and the accounts of eye-witnesses, have not, however, been my only aids. I have had another and surer aid, of the most curious kind imaginable. And some day I will tell you all about it, if you would care to hear."[21] This statement alone establishes beyond question the firm link between "The Mirror of the Past" and *Rossetti and His Circle*, for which the manuscript itself gives further ample proof. But the real significance in the consideration of all these dates lies in the revelation that "The Mirror of the Past" is not only a bulky mass of papers that Beerbohm could never put into shape but was an enterprise that occupied his attention over a long period, a work begun in Italy, brought with him to England, and carried back again to Italy, a work he was involved with before, during, and after the composition of the stories that would constitute *Seven Men* and the drawings that would constitute *Rossetti and His Circle*.

The scenario letter, far better than the manuscript itself, reveals that at the heart of the work lay Beerbohm's fascination with the mirror as a collaborator in reminiscence. Conceived as a visual palimpsest, the mirror stacks up on its surface successive images of all things that come before it and replays them, or unpeels them, in the reverse order of their impression, the latest ones being given off first. As a convex mirror, moreover, it is capable of picking up images from all corners of the room, not merely those of objects placed directly in front of it. With a little practice the spectator, Max himself, learns to adjust to the peculiarity of seeing people walk backwards into a room when they are actually leaving it and candles bursting into flame after their wicks have been pinched. These conventions mastered, such a spectator actually becomes an unseen witness of history and is, moreover, free to respond to the scenes reenacted before him, unlike the historian or the novelist, without excuse or embarrassment. With a moderately plausible pseudoscientific explanation of how the mirror became endowed with such peculiar properties, Max might have then proceeded to record the past as it unreeled before him. He chose, however, a more oblique tactic, inventing an elderly friend, Sylvester Herringham, a kind of Bunbury of reminiscence, who is not only the mirror's owner, bequeathing it to Max upon his death, but also the scientist whose abstruse experiments have conferred upon it its singular capacity. By this expedient Max converted a curiosity into a plot device, for Herringham's researches had been undertaken with no other end but that of seeing once more the wife of whose betrayal he believes (quite wrongly, it turns out) himself to have been the cause. Herringham, a man who had entertained George Meredith in his home, labors under Meredith's sense of guilt, a guilt he feels can be expiated only by summoning up in the mirror the presence of his dead wife, Mildred. But in 1897, the year in which Max becomes acquainted with him, Herringham is sixty-seven years old; and fearing that he may not live until Mildred reappears, an event not scheduled to occur until 1911, he confides in the younger man, making him his surrogate in the rendezvous that is to take place.

Quite apart from furnishing greater credibility to Max's extension of memory, Herringham was intended also to bring to the tale a personal element that would have been absent if only the comings and goings of celebrities were to figure in the images cast back by the mirror. His domestic and emotional turmoil amid the glitter of mid-Victorian society was to provide pathos, as the later unraveling of the truth behind these crises was to provide suspense. As well as bequeathing to Max a magical mirror, Herringham was to be a mine of recollections in his own right. For in his attempt to distract himself from brooding over his lonely plight after Mildred's elopement, Herringham devoted himself not only to scientific study but also to the establishment of a salon where his personal friends among the poets and artists of the day could mingle with statesmen and noblemen in elegant surroundings. Despite the obliquity of the angle of vision,

"The Mirror of the Past"

Max persisted in seeing the novel as autobiographical, as his own encounter with the personages and events of the past, a past communicated to him and refined in three distinct stages. There was first the public past, available to him through published books and memoirs, the stories of distinguished men and women transmitted from mouth to mouth, and the gossip overheard in childhood. Max's childhood, it must be remembered, was passed in a household where distinguished visitors were quite frequent. Such stuff, uniquely interpreted, of course, was the material of Beerbohm's early essays, like "1880," the piece that first drew Herringham's attention to Max as a *laudator temporis acti*. Herringham conveyed to him a second past of a more intimate kind, anecdotes and recollections precious not merely for their being not generally known but also for their randomness, their unselectiveness. To Herringham, Whistler was not a legend, but a puzzling, indefinable presence. "One often didn't know what he was talking about, but the ejaculations held one.... Rather like a summer night in Italy, with fireflies sailing and darting, not casting much light — but very 'amazing.'"[22] For some offense he never actually understood, he had incurred the painter's ire, which Max documents by reproducing the Whistler-Herringham correspondence, complete with butterfly signature.[23] In instances such as these Herringham serves as an intelligent, well-educated foil to eccentric genius, a touchstone against which the myths of celebrity may be struck. The final vision of the past was the record of the mirror itself, made meaningful precisely because it was transmitted backwards and as a supplement and corrective to the other forms of truth. Herringham's wife, for example, had been painted by Rossetti, which portrait her husband destroyed in the fury of his first outrage and sorrow at her abandonment. That act of destruction, recalling as it does Rossetti's own renunciation in grief — the burial of his poems with his dead wife, Elizabeth Siddal — occasions a dialogue and scene between the dilettante scientist and the artist, a scene that serves to heighten Max's desire to see both the painting and its sitter in the mirror. For Rossetti, Herringham has assured Max, however he may have painted his other models, had not idealized Mildred. When through the agency of the mirror the portrait is miraculously restored to view for a few minutes years later in Italy, Max is struck by its rare and haunting beauty. The subsequent appearance of Mildred herself is a distinct disappointment. Unlike that of Lucian or Swift, however, Beerbohm's ironic demythologizing is not undertaken to destroy illusion; rather it serves to expose how all men — Rossetti, Herringham, and Max himself — can interpret nothing without the aid of imagination.

Such is the apparent intent of "The Mirror of the Past" as revealed by the scenario letter. But the letter also indicates that Beerbohm had not as yet found an appropriate way to conclude the novel. Mildred's reappearance was to have been for Herringham the climax. Yet Max not only records that event but continues peering into the mirror long afterward, observing as well her marriage to Herringham in 1914 (that is, 1863) and her subsequent disappearance forever. Herringham himself seems to be forgotten as the mirror shifts its place from the wall of his drawing room to that of a bachelor's apartment: "There it is, strangely far away from our modern world. Rossetti is very often there — and oh if I could but hear what he says as he lounges there on the sofa! And there is little tiny young Swinburne, with his flaming hair, reading aloud a manuscript — aloud, yes, for his lips are moving, but I, alas, am not of the audience."[24] "Oh" and "alas" are exclamations not generally encountered in the letters of authors to their prospective publishers, and Beerbohm later compensated, at least partially, for his poignant sense of auditory loss when he depicted visually the very scene he here describes in the drawing entitled "The Small Hours in the 'Sixties at 16, Cheyne Walk" in *Rossetti and His Circle* (HD 1275; BLC 44). It is likely that with the evocation of Rossetti and his friends, Max's interest in the earlier life of Herringham, or in that of his father, a Royal Academician with many a large historical canvas to his credit, effectively ceased. Although the letter goes on to sketch in some of the scenes the mirror may have witnessed in France, the place of its manufacture in 1743, it is abundantly clear from the manuscript notes that Max's active collaboration with the mirror extends back in time no further than the 1850s. But in regard to bringing his narrative to a close, Beerbohm can suggest nothing more satisfactory than the following:

> In December, 2051, all the stacked films will have been shed forth, and at the shedding of the last of them the mirror will resume its normal function of reflecting the present. In my will, therefore, I shall bequeathe the mirror to (say) the South Kensington Museum — the locked case that will contain it to be opened in January 2052, and to reflect thenceforth the mildly interested faces of posterity.[25]

In all likelihood the basic design of the projected work was conceived in Rapallo during or shortly after the time Beerbohm was preparing *A Christmas Garland* for the press. The first pages of the rough (pencil) draft and the three pages of fair copy bear, as has been noted, the date 1913. These fairly finished fragments do not actually bring Herringham on to the scene, but they prepare the reader for his entrance. Herringham's was the only letter of response, Max tells us, occasioned by the publication in *Works* of his essay "1880." The letter is reproduced in its entirety. Although Herringham betrays in it an unconsciousness of the irony of what Max refers to as his "mock-archaeological discourse,"[26] the letter contains a gracious invitation for Max to visit and interview a survivor of the period of social history that had so obviously fascinated him as an essayist. Max then heightens the suspense of the impending meeting by reflecting on how Sylvester Herringham's famous Monday-evening salon had figured in the imaginative fantasies of his childhood. He is certain that Herringham in the flesh will sustain his romantic attraction to a past he has been born too late to experience. "Always I have deemed an old man in a work-house richer, really, than a young Vanderbilt. Of course a vast inheritance of dollars or pounds inspired in me, against my will, a certain cold respect for the inheritor. But the red glow of reverence was kindled rather by one who had accumulated for himself a fortune not in coins but in years."[27] After a brief résumé of the artistic and financial career of Sylvester's father, the mystery of the son's marriage and the disappearance of his wife's portrait (said here to have been painted by Frederick Sandys) are casually mentioned. Although the fragment of the pencil draft breaks off at this point, the manuscript notes carry us a good deal further. Max finds Herringham himself rather shy and reclusive, considerably less impressive than his expectation of him. He is, moreover, for reasons that become apparent to Beerbohm much later, unusually apprehensive about the state of his health. Gradually he becomes more confidential, revealing to Max that he had met his wife through Rossetti, that she had, indeed, been one of his models, the sitter for the celebrated painting *Lilies That Fester,* and that it was largely through Rossetti's influence that Herringham had come to despise the marriageable women of his own class — "'J. Leech's dolls' — 'Bread and butter misses' — *thin slices* — swallow a dozen of them, unsatisfied," had been the artist's characterization of them ("Mirror," p. 25) — and had contracted the misalliance that had ended so unhappily. In subsequent interviews Sylvester speaks to Max more frankly of his wife, of her seduction and elopement with Lord Runcorn, and of her abandonment and death. Runcorn, meanwhile, was to make a satisfactory marriage and "afterwards became a famous Victorian and Edvardian statesman of the best and stodgiest and most admirable type."[28] The greatest and most dramatic revelation, of course, was to have been of the mirror itself, and Beerbohm filled several pages with notes and dialogue relating to that scene. There are also many pages of chronology relating the private events of Herringham's life to public happenings and to the careers of the poets and artists who figure prominently in Herringham's recollections. Especially indicative of Beerbohm's care to make his tale authentic are the elaborate diagrams he drew up for his own use to show the correspondences between actual time and that of the images being cast off by the mirror. As Herringham's experiment succeeded at 9:00 A.M. on 3 July 1889, all moments at equal temporal distances before and after that instant are paired. Beerbohm not only worked out these relationships to the year, day, and hour but noted as well the variations that would be introduced by leap years and the difference between Greenwich and Italian time. The papers also include a perpetual calendar from 1786 to 1950 executed on graph paper in splendid calligraphy.

The bright Italian sunlight was hospitable to the reception of these ideas for a novel, a grand work that in a circumstantial and leisurely way would celebrate the past; and it was probably no mere accident that Max scheduled his meeting with Mildred Crump, the "stunner" who had so captured the imaginations of the Pre-Raphaelites as well as awakening passion in the epicene Sylvester Herringham, for October 1911, the very month in which he published to the world his fascination with that other and literal *femme fatale,* Zuleika Dobson. Yet although the large scenes could be plotted and the composition could move forward in the isolation of Rapallo, the meticulous detail of the projected work required factual research that could be undertaken only in England. Max's library, if we are to judge from the sale of his effects, was not particularly extensive, but no private collection of books could have supplied him with all the data of his notes: jottings on the careers of Rossetti, Morris, Whistler, and others, including the sizes of canvases and details of frames; observations on the fashions of the 1860s; and informed speculations on what Chelsea must have looked like when Rossetti and Herringham were neighbors in Cheyne Walk. One page of the manuscript (page 26) has a long list of items headed "To Look Up," a shorter one of places labeled "To Visit," and one of inquiries to be made of particular friends such as Edmund Gosse and D. S. MacColl. These researches could have been carried out early in 1914 when Max, who had stayed on in London after the Christmas holidays while Florence visited her family in America, was checking references in the British Museum for some other essays.[29] Certainly "Enoch Soames," which Lord David Cecil dates as having been written before Beerbohm's wartime sojourn in England, reveals an intimate familiarity with the ways of the Reading Room and the mysteries of its catalogue. But it is more likely, considering how much there was to consult and how little the work could advance without such consultation, that the bulk of it was carried out in 1916, the year of the scenario letter, at a time just when Beerbohm had resigned himself to sitting out the war in England and just before his investigations into the private lives of the Pre-Raphaelites took a more exclusively graphic turn.

His desire to invest his novel with authenticity had taken him to Bloomsbury and probably to galleries as well as to knowledgeable friends. But it must have become increasingly apparent to him, as it certainly does to one who works his way through the mass of notes, that Herringham's personal drama began to recede in significance as the artists whom he befriended came on the scene. In "Hethway Speaking," of course, which preserves many of the anecdotes Max actually managed to write up fully, we see but a ghost of a character in the presumed narrator. But Herringham's impalpability was inherent in his very conception. Max had summoned him into being to provide the mirror with an owner and with an explanation of its powers. He had neglected to endow him, however, with any strong characteristics of his own. He is not merely dwarfed by the stronger personalities with which he clashes — or, more properly, collides. Beerbohm shows little interest in documenting the scientific studies that Herringham is reputed to have engaged in: "It was said of him by Faraday, whom [Herringham] delighted to entertain, that were he not rich he might rise to high eminence."[30] But Faraday is the only scientist named in the whole manuscript of "The Mirror of the Past." Nor was the gentleman-scientist altogether the anomaly in the nineteenth century that Faraday is made here to suggest. The man who delighted to entertain Faraday would have had much more in common with a man like William Henry Fox Talbot (1800–1877), whose investigations into photography couched in the elegant language of *The Pencil of Nature* certainly bordered more nearly on those of Herringham's presumed researches. On one of the unnumbered pages of the manuscript there is a long list of names, thirty-six in number, of people who were to make an appearance before the mirror. They are all artists, writers, and actors. Below that there is a list of Royal Academicians in 1866. And far to the right is the notation "Scientists, rather boring." Whether this represents Herringham's opinion or Max's hardly matters. The fact remains that, although the materials for authenticating the parts of Herringham's life that were not purely social lay all about him, Beerbohm was less interested in Herringham than in his artistic friends. He made no attempt to see him from the inside out.

Beerbohm knew where his strength lay. In speaking of the projected work, he wrote "Purely apocryphal these memoirs are — founded only on my rather full knowledge of the *actual* memoirs of the period, on my instinct for character, and on my rather dreadful little talent for 'parody.'"[31] But he was not insensitive to the consequences of appearing to abandon Herringham: "These apocryphal memoirs are an integral and important part of this book about the past; but I must be careful that they don't overweigh the actual dramatic side of the story — the personal, sentimental side of Herringham's life." His method of avoiding this danger was to include Herringham in his imagined scenes wherever possible, even if only as a passive observer. Readers familiar with "Hethway Speaking" will recognize this method in the anecdote in which William Morris storms his way into the drawing room with grandiose schemes for its refurnishing and redecoration and retreats just as unceremoniously at the owner's feeble protest.[32] The manuscript contains a few more of such scenes which could not be as readily extracted for use in the radio broadcast. Mention has already been made of the Whistler-Herringham correspondence, which serves as a complement to the description of Carlyle's sittings to Whistler.[33] There is another excursion into "Scoto-Carlylean jargon"[34] in the venerable sage's commiseration with Herringham on the failure of his marriage. Meeting Carlyle in the street one evening, Herringham is offered the consolation of philosophy: "And so ye've lost y'r woman. . . . They're given to us, they're taken from us; that's the way of it. And we've to plod on as we may. . . . Come in and see me sometimes." But the sympathy and the extended friendship were apparently of short duration, for Max later discovers in a book that Carlyle spoke of "a feeble, pernickety, infinitesimal man — one H, a dabbler with numerals and the like, who comes and pesters me with his kickle-cackle" ("Mirror," p. 20). George Meredith is made to invent at Herringham's dinner table for the particular amusement of his wife an Eastern shaggy-dog story, recited in the extravagant language of *The Shaving of Shagpat* ("Mirror," p. 60). Beerbohm tried to remember that Herringham's associations would not be confined to the eminent, either real or imaginary; and he projected that the two of them, Max and Sylvester, would witness in the mirror a rerun of a servants' party originally held in the house when the master was abroad and that Sylvester's outrage at the liberty would mellow with the recognition that it had all really taken place a very long time ago ("Mirror," p. 31).

It was with Dante Gabriel Rossetti, however, that Herringham was to have established the most intimate tie of friendship, a connection not all that difficult to imagine in view of the variety of people whom the artist attracted. Their acquaintance was first struck up while Herringham was still an undergraduate at Oxford, when in 1857 Rossetti, Morris, Burne-Jones, and their friends undertook to decorate the walls of the Union (of which Sylvester, like Max, was a member) with murals depicting scenes of Arthurian legend. Herringham was to have stood gaping at the work in progress, as Jowett does in *Rossetti and His Circle* and, with the knowledge of painting derived from his father, would pronounce that "it can't last" ("Mirror," p. 36). This remark, which turned out to be prophetic, neither daunted the artists nor kept Herringham from visiting their residence in George Street, where they played whist together. Their friendship survived the frescoes, which had begun to perish almost as soon as the paint had been applied to the ill-prepared walls. We have already noted how instrumental Rossetti was in Herringham's marriage and how Herringham destroyed the Rossetti portrait of Mildred in his possession upon her elopement with Lord Runcorn. Beerbohm appears to have intended Herringham to play the role of one of Rossetti's numerous nurses and protectors — practical, level-headed men, who could look after the financial and physical well-being of the otherworldly genius. In this capacity he warns Rossetti about the dangerous influence of Charles Augustus Howell, the mysterious adventurer of obscure Portuguese origin, a constant intriguer, who acted for many years as Rossetti's agent and secretary. But in the dialogue that takes place between them, Rossetti overrides Herringham's caution by observing that, though he knows Howell to be unscrupulous, "a man who's got work to do, Sylvester, can't afford not to have amusing people about him. Charles Howell is the most amusing fellow I know. He *gives* me something all the time. As for the off-chance of his doing me a mischief round the corner — why, that's all the more reason for not letting him out of my sight. I must see more of Howell" ("Mirror," p. 51). The lives of Herringham and Rossetti were thus to interesect over a

"The Mirror of the Past"

period of twenty-five years, strangely paralleling each other as well in marriage, bereavement, remorse, and renewal through work. Rossetti's course, however, was to have run before Herringham completed that series of experiments that culminated in the mirror's yielding up its treasure of stacked images. Their last meeting, an almost wordless encounter, was to have taken place in November 1881, when Herringham, fully restored to an active social life, is returning home late from a party. He observes a now infirm and worn-out Rossetti leaning on the arm of a small red-haired man, whose pompous chatter about the "phenomenal public" and "sales" of the recently published *Ballads and Sonnets* identifies him to the alert reader as Hall Caine, though Herringham is unable to recollect his name. Despite the fact that Herringham and Rossetti have become somewhat estranged in recent years and though it is obvious that his dependence on Caine is not the least of the symptoms of Rossetti's decline, there is yet a bond between the two old friends. As Hall Caine chirps on about "'the heart of every man and every woman in the English-speaking world,' I caught Rossetti's eye, and I thought I saw there for an instant a gleam of the great old laughter" ("Mirror," p. 47).

That gleam of awareness that passes between Rossetti and Herringham, implying as it does the ironic perception of the lover of pure beauty destined to end his days under the solicitous attendance of one for whom art is mere commerce, is a sensation so characteristic of Beerbohm's own acuity of observation that it clinches for us what we have suspected all along — that Sylvester is but an extension of Max. Although Beerbohm went to great pains to give Herringham a story of his own and to differentiate him from himself by providing him with wealth, scientific interests, and a tragic passion, their fundamental ways of seeing are identical. Sylvester in Cheyne Walk and Max at the Café Royal are one and the same. As Sylvester is sympathetic witness to and survivor of the Pre-Raphaelite experiment, so Max is of the decadence of the *fin de siècle*. Like the messenger in the Book of Job they might both exclaim, "I only am escaped to tell thee." This function that Herringham shares with Max, far more than the fact that he is an invention of Max's, may perhaps explain why Beerbohm persisted in seeing the work as bas-

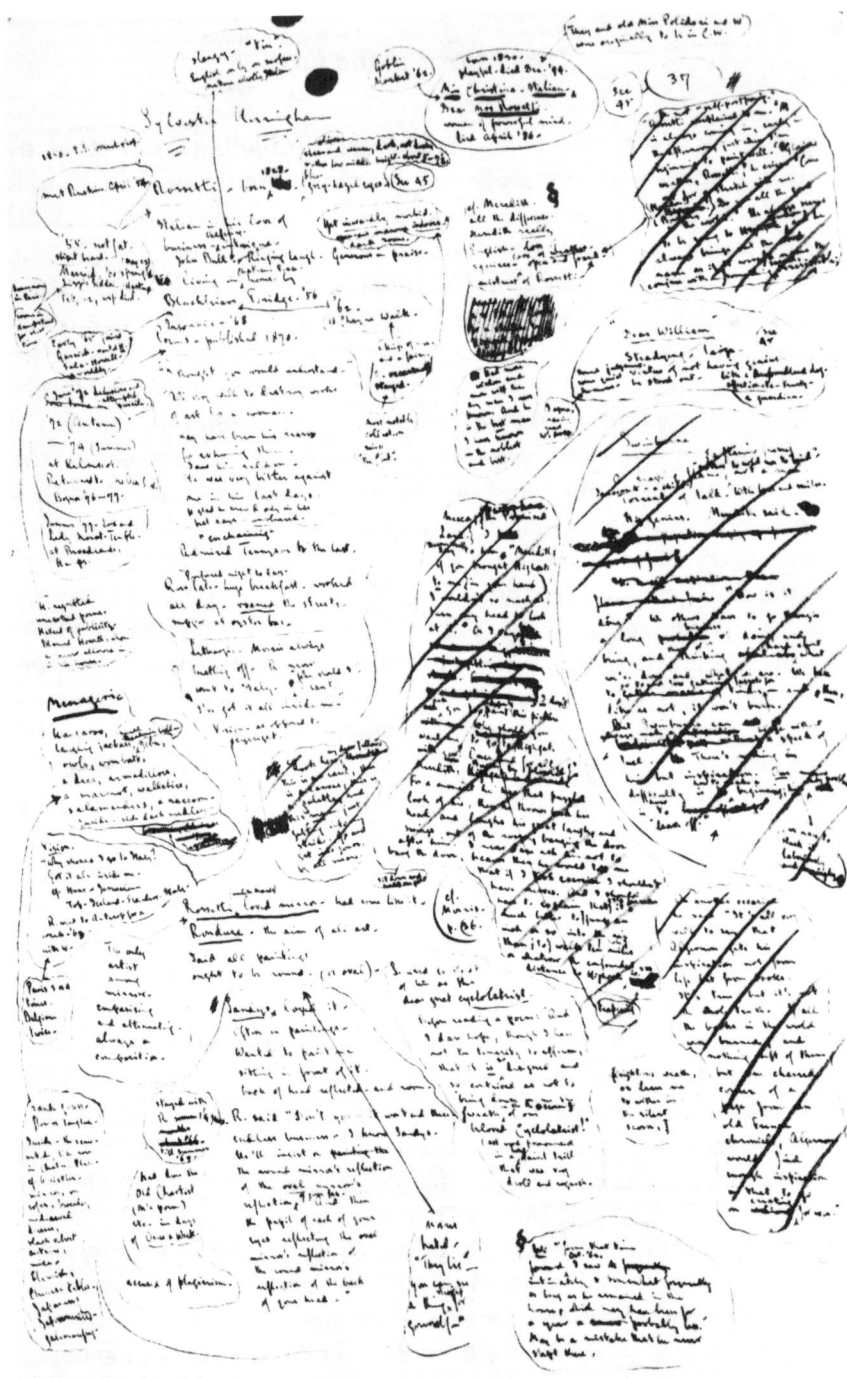

"The Mirror of the Past," msp. 37. Courtesy of the Robert H. Taylor Collection, Princeton University Library.

"The Mirror of the Past"

ically autobiographical, to be narrated in the first person and that first person to be unequivocably identified as the real Max Beerbohm, the lively wit of London and the recluse of Rapallo. It may explain, too, why he found it so easy to ascribe to Rossetti his own almost mystical fascination with the mirror ("Mirror," p. 37), why after the passage of years the contents of the papers relating to his unfinished novel and his "remembering" essays became fused in his mind, and why, upon broadcasting some of the imaginary reminiscences from "The Mirror" and publicly acknowledging their source, he was able to apologize to his listeners for the deception of the fictitious remembrancer: "Please don't be vexed with me for having let you suppose Sylvester was a real person. I thought that he as a real person would be likelier than I as a fabricator to impress and please you."[35]

It should by now be obvious that although "The Mirror of the Past" was to have been an extended work of fiction, by no reasonable definition could it have qualified as a conventional novel — or even an unconventional one. That core of general truth (not necessarily generally accepted truth) that underlies the novel from *Tom Jones* to *Ulysses,* whether reducible to neat formulation or not, which alone validates our troubling ourselves with the behavior and fortunes of invented beings, would have been absent from Beerbohm's *magnum opus.* Its justification would have resided in the savor of its individual scenes and in the coruscations of insight its narrative observers would have afforded us. It would have been to a far greater degree than *Zuleika Dobson* an essayistic work of fiction — not a work of fiction with essays embedded in it, like the novels of Thackeray and Trollope, but a riotous and unashamed extrapolation of an age of cultural history into verbal caricature. In the strong assertion of a personal and idiosyncratic view rather than a consensual, commonsensical one, Beerbohm's affinities are more with Carlyle and Disraeli than with any of the standard Victorian novelists, even novelists as diverse as Eliot and Dickens. The preservation of a scene together with an interpretation of it as performance was what Beerbohm was after. The invention of Herringham and the collaboration of the mirror were but devices contrived to bring immediacy and concentration to the memoirs and letters and photographs out of which "The Mirror of the Past" was to have been compounded. And let us not omit the reminiscences of old men. A passage from "No. 2. The Pines" is particularly relevant in this connection. Composed as it was during the gestation of "The Mirror of the Past," it virtually proclaims the challenge Beerbohm tried to take up:

> As he was to the outer world of his own day, so too to posterity Rossetti, the man, is conjectural and mysterious. We know that he was in his prime the most inspiring and splendid of companions. But we know this only by faith. The evidence is as vague as it is emphatic. Of the style and substance of not a few great talkers in the past we can piece together some more or less vivid and probably erroneous notion. But about Rossetti nothing has been recorded in such a way as to make him even faintly emerge. I suppose he had in him what reviewers seem to find so often in books: a quality that defies analysis. Listening to Watts-Dunton, I was always in hope that when next the long-lost turned up — for he was continually doing so — in the talk, I should *see* him, *hear* him, and share the rapture. But the revelation was not to be. You might think that to hear him called "Gabriel" would have given me a sense of propinquity. But I felt no nearer to him than you feel to the Archangel who bears the name and no surname.[36]

Beerbohm's real object in "The Mirror of the Past" was nothing less than to make up for the deficiencies of Rossetti's contemporaries, to supply the propinquity that they paradoxically could not, to compose reminiscences of a man he never knew as feelingly and precisely as he explored his impressions of those that he did know in his "remembering" essays.

Considering the ambitiousness of the enterprise, the long period that he labored over it, and the fact that he left so few of his projects unfinished, we may naturally wonder what caused Beerbohm to abandon "The Mirror of the Past." It seems unlikely that the want of encouragement, particularly from a commercial source, would have deflected Beerbohm from an artistic course to which he was committed. He was not indifferent to financial considerations, but few writers of this century have so deliberately scorned popular success. To S. N. Behrman, Max confided that the work "became too involved, you know, too complicated. I couldn't understand it myself."[37] And Lord Da-

"The Mirror of the Past"

vid Cecil records that "he explained later that he had come to the conclusion that to make the device of the mirror plausible to a reader required what he had not got, a science-fiction type of imagination like that of H. G. Wells."[38] There is no question that accounting for the mirror's unique properties caused Beerbohm considerable difficulty, for his draft never managed to arrive at the point where the subject was to have been introduced, though there are several preliminary explanations worked out in the manuscript.[39] The mirror was undoubtedly a stumbling block, perhaps the one Beerbohm *chose* to stumble over; yet it need not have proved an insuperable one. He who had managed fantasy so wittily in *The Happy Hypocrite* and so adroitly in *Zuleika Dobson,* who was to invoke the supernatural in realistic settings so masterfully in *Seven Men,* might have overcome or worked around the issue of plausibility in "The Mirror of the Past" had not the work been vexed by graver, more fundamental problems. All of these related to the unresolved question of whose story was ultimately to be the central one — Max's, Sylvester's, or the mirror's. From his notes it would appear that Beerbohm's original intent was to pursue the images in the mirror well back into the eighteenth century, long after (or before, depending upon how one looks at it) the real story behind Herringham's luckless marriage had been concluded. But it is hard to see what would have sustained the narrative interest. At any rate, Beerbohm's researches and invented episodes do not extend substantially beyond the career of Sylvester's father, Sir William "Apelles" Herringham, hints for which were culled from B. R. Haydon's *Journal.* Yet even if the original scenario had been revised to restrict the scope to Sylvester's life and times, there would have been a conflict between the two narrators. Even though Herringham, as we have noted, is possessed of many of Beerbohm's powers of observation, he is really no match for him. The pencil draft that continues the fair copy of the manuscript gives some indication of why Beerbohm may have had such difficulty in moving it forward. It is so heavily ironic in tone that it is hard to see how Herringham or his pathetic little tale could ever have gotten a judicious hearing. The fact of the matter is that Beerbohm was really more interested in Herringham's friends than in Herringham himself.

Sir Max Beerbohm

That interest drove Beerbohm to consult books of general reference as well as more particular ones. The notes do not often acknowledge his sources of information, though it is unlikely that he did not peruse extensively Holman Hunt's *Pre-Raphaelitism and the Pre-Raphaelite Brotherhood* (1905) and possibly, for the last years, Hall Caine's *Recollections of Dante Gabriel Rossetti* (1882). He must certainly have known well the papers edited by Dante Gabriel's younger brother, William Michael Rossetti — *Ruskin: Rossetti: Praeraphaelitism* (1899) and *Praeraphaelite Diaries and Letters* (1900) — for he speaks of him as "W.M.R., that dear character and good sound writer, that stable old rock on which so much of knowledge is founded."[40] These researches led to the invention of anecdotes and probable scenes, bits of likely dialogue from the lives of Rossetti and his friends. It is significant that Beerbohm began working up these sketches long before he had decided precisely how they would fit into the narrative, and significant too that at least one of them, preserved in "Hethway Speaking,"[41] an exchange between Meredith and Rossetti in which the former tries to lure the artist away from his easel and take exercise, is transformed into an actual picture in *Rossetti and His Circle,* where it bears the legend "Rossetti insistently exhorted by George Meredith to come forth into the glorious sun and wind for a walk to Hendon and beyond" (HD 1274; BLC 46). This is more than an anomalous instance, however. No sooner do the manuscript notes begin to focus on the activities of the Pre-Raphaelites than actual sketches of them begin to appear on the pages. There is a whole sheet of heads — drawn in the manner of Rossetti — of Swinburne, Ruskin, Rossetti, Rossetti's brother, Ford Madox Brown, William Bell Scott, and Elizabeth Siddal. There are also sketches of two of Rossetti's models, Fanny Cornforth and Alexa Wilding, as well as a crude sketch of "Lancelot's Dream," the subject of Rossetti's contribution to the walls of the Oxford Union. It may certainly be argued that these sketches, obviously copied from books, may have been drawn as visual aids to verbal description rather than as proposed illustrations. Somewhat more puzzling, however, is the unmistakable presence, amid the pages, of connected discourse or random notes of the heads of Beerbohm's own contemporaries, faces made so familiar to us

"The Mirror of the Past"

by the frequency of his caricaturing them that they are immediately recognizable. In the middle of one of Beerbohm's involved explanations of the phenomenon of the mirror a profile of Winston Churchill looks away from the text. Several pages later, on the verso of a sheet headed "*Whistler*," near a full-length sketch of Pablo de Sarasate (copied from a painting by Whistler), there is the fainter puzzled visage of George Moore. Pinero's huge beak and weasellike eyebrows peer forth from the page that outlines the numbered forward and reverse sequences of events in the scene of dramatic confrontation in which Sylvester learns of Mildred's infidelity. And both a worried Lord Rosebery and a flat-domed Henry James adorn the pencil draft. As the former of these is drawn in ink, we may assume that it was done when Beerbohm was preparing the fair copy from the rough one. Drawing faces was, we know, Beerbohm's favorite form of doodling, and we ought not to attach too much significance to the fact that in moments of weariness or distraction he might have shifted his attention from the remote to the nearer past. Yet one cannot avoid the impression that the further the manuscript advances from outline and preliminary planning toward actual execution, the more "graphic" it becomes.

Beerbohm's laconic references to his major unfinished work may be augmented by the following conjecture. Having outlined the basic design of the novel and performed some preliminary research, he began to founder when it came to the actual writing. For one thing, accounting for the mirror was proving an obstacle; for another, the vitality of his secondary narrator, Herringham, began to wane as his studies gave him sufficient confidence and authority to envision scenes and incidents from the lives of Rossetti and others. The caricatures, whose appearance was not always restricted to the margins, were symptomatic of a general restlessness, though he had made it plain on many occasions that he regarded writing as work and drawing as pleasure. Slowly it must have occurred to him, perhaps while copying out some of Rossetti's sketches — ostensibly work, but increasingly a pleasure — that the difficulties of narration and explanation might fall away completely without loss of the immediacy of the scene if only the medium of expression were changed from words to drawings. The drawings, to be sure, would be more "literary" than his usual caricatures, would involve far less physical distortion than they. But although one of the narrators would have to disappear, the ironic presence of the other, Max himself, would be abundantly manifested in the contrivance of scenes and in the legends that would accompany them. As a trial, perhaps, the Meredith-Rossetti dialogue was translated from prose to picture even though the notes abound with suggestions for many of the other drawings that would constitute the developing series. Once the process had begun, however, "The Mirror of the Past" effectively ceased as a literary project: Max's drawings, whose unconscious origin had been as illustrations, no longer required a text. "The Mirror of the Past" was the chrysalis out of which *Rossetti and His Circle* emerged.

This conjecture seems even more reasonable in view of the fact that 1916, the latest that we hear of any very active work's being done on "The Mirror of the Past," is also the year in which the first drawings of the Rossetti series were executed. It is probably true to say that "The Mirror of the Past" was not so much abandoned as superseded. An interesting drawing of Beerbohm's, first exhibited in the posthumous show of 1957, provides a perfect link between the pseudo-history of "The Mirror" and the equally strong impulse to caricature. The drawing, entitled "Princeps Triplumiferus" (HD 502), dates from 1916, the year of the transition, yet purports to be "A little-known portrait in oils of Edward VII (then Prince of Wales) by D. G. Rossetti. Circa 1873." Combining his close study of the actual paintings of Rossetti with his merciless mockery of the late king's foibles, Beerbohm probably intended it purely for his own amusement and for that of his friends.[42] The drawing depicts a bull-necked Albert Edward in evening clothes, seated with his elbow on a table, contemplating with all the astigmatic intensity of Rossetti's women in the symbolic portraits the three white feathers, heraldic emblem of the Prince of Wales, he holds in his delicate left hand. Although less crowded round with things than most of Rossetti's subjects, the "painting" is more than usually detailed for a Beerbohm: two vases, one large and one small, a burning oil lamp, an ornate finial on the prince's chair, and behind him — most symbolic of all — a richly framed convex mirror. Entertaining enough as a parody of Rossetti's last artistic phase,

"The Mirror of the Past"

"Princeps Triplumiferus" is accompanied by a six-hundred-word legend, the longest text Beerbohm ever wrote for a drawing, composed as though for a catalogue or for one of the many slender illustrated volumes of appreciation of Rossetti. The description ends with the apology that "much of the beauty of the work is, alas, lost here through the limitations of the three-colour process." But most of the description is anecdotal, detailing how the enterprising Howell attempted to procure His Royal Highness as Rossetti's patron and how H.R.H. condescended to sit for a portrait on the understanding that Howell was to procure Jane Morris for him. There are also specimens of the inane interrogations that characterized the prince's conversation.

"Princeps Triplumiferus" was, we may be sure, never intended for public exhibition — certainly not with its accompanying description. Like the "Edwardyssey" (not shown until 1945) and the "Proposed Illustrations for Sir Sidney Lee's forthcoming Biography" of Edward VII (some of which illustrations had given such offense when they were shown in 1923 that they were hastily withdrawn), it is a lighthearted, but not particularly good-natured, lampoon of the late king's self-indulgence. As such, it might have been more appreciated in the court of Charles II than in that of George V. But the drawing does raise the question of the uses to which Beerbohm's research into the Pre-Raphaelites was to be put. What, in short, would have been the tone of "The Mirror of the Past"? The scenario letter would seem to suggest a nostalgic reverence enlivened by the humor of slightly exaggerated incidents like that of the Whistler-Herringham correspondence or the examples of Meredith's table talk. The bits preserved in "Hethway Speaking" are characteristic of the not too serious cast of the projected anecdotes in the manuscript. But how would Beerbohm have handled, in a work that aspired to intimacy, the growing estrangement of Mildred to her husband or alluded to what was hardly concealed even in the discreet biographies of the day, Rossetti's increasing addiction to chloral, which certainly hastened his death? Perhaps the awareness that writing a novel, as opposed to reminiscences, would restrict his liberty about the kind of scenes to be included made the switch from words to pictures that much easier. From every aspect, therefore, it appeared preferable to

Princeps Triplumiferus, 1916.

D. G. Rossetti, *La Bella Mano*. 1875. Courtesy of the Delaware Art Museum, Samuel and Mary R. Bancroft, Jr. Memorial.

publish the images of the mirror as a series of slides rather than as a talking motion picture.

The absorption with Rossetti affected Beerbohm's approach not only to his caricatures, as evidenced by "Princeps Triplumiferus," but also to his parodies. In 1917 John, Viscount Morley of Blackburn, the grand old Liberal statesman and biographer, published two volumes of *Recollections*. To Max the work must have been a mine of inspiration, doubtless suggesting the introductory scene in *Rossetti and His Circle* where Morley brings together John Stuart Mill and Dante Gabriel Rossetti in the assurance that each man's admiration of women will lead both to a gratifying intellectual collaboration (HD 1280; BLC 60). Max could not fail to have been amused by the Utilitarian blinders Morley seems to have worn all his life. But his reaction to Morley as a stylist must have been particularly vigorous, for in the unconsciousness of his pomposity Morley himself verges on self-parody. The following passage from the *Recollections*, describing a volume of Matthew Arnold in his possession, is a fair sample:

> As it happens, I find written on the fly-leaf of this small treasure some words I had inscribed at what was to prove a memorable date: *Read with much fortifying quietude of mind on the forenoon of our departure, on the matchless terrace at Beatenberg*, June 12, 1914. In a few weeks, hardly more than a few days, the blunders and precipitancy of folly-smitten rulers let loose a fierce hurricane of destruction and hate that swept quietude out of the world for a long span of time to come.[43]

Beerbohm's response was as immediate as it was characteristic: he produced "Further Recollections by Viscount M., O.M.," a four-page parody that captures with deadly accuracy the self-importance, the garrulity, and the opaqueness of Morley's memoirs.[44] The piece purports to be an omitted chapter describing his first meeting with Dante Gabriel Rossetti, whose article Morley, as editor of the *Fortnightly Review*, had commissioned but not yet received. His errand is, of course, forgotten when the two come together, and Morley's "recollection" consists almost wholly of name dropping and self-aggrandizing digressions interspersed with fragments of their cross-purposed conversa-

Lord Morley of Blackburn. 1911. Courtesy of the Ashmolean Museum, Oxford.

tion. So self-absorbed is he that he can describe the twilight in Cheyne Walk as he leaves the house only by making himself the vehicle of the simile: "The lamps along the embankment were already lit, gleaming pale and ineffective like the ideas of some great statesman in an age not ready for them." Like the spurious portrait of Edward VII, the spurious recollection of Viscount Morley not only illustrates Beerbohm's "rather dreadful little talent for parody" but suggests as well just how difficult it would have been for Max to sustain a posture of serious irony through a long prose work without breaking up with laughter.

One other artifact related to "The Mirror of the Past" should be mentioned here. An oil painting doubtfully attributed to Max, a canvas about four times as large as the largest of the watercolor originals of *Rossetti and His Circle,* may now be seen in the Beerbohm Room that adjoins the library of Merton College, Oxford. It depicts a Rossetti, younger than he appears in most of Max's drawings, walking along the riverside in the company of another man originally thought to have been Swinburne but bearing no resemblance whatever to Beerbohm's presentments of that poet. If any Beerbohm figure is suggested at all, it is more likely to be that of Sylvester Herringham. In his *Catalogue* Sir Rupert Hart-Davis has reproduced a sketch representing two men in virtually the same attitudes as in the painting (HD 1284, pl. 56) and has taken its title from a Leicester Galleries list of Max's drawings: "S.H. vainly endeavouring to enlist D.G.R.'s interest in some singularly interesting experiment." That experiment doubtless concerns his researches into the mysteries of the convex mirror. The detail of the sketch is quite crude, though sufficient to indicate that the two men are strolling along the Embankment. But the painting is lovingly detailed, and the location is more clearly defined as Cheyne Walk by the bend in the river, the dim outline of a bridge joining the two banks in the distance. In the right foreground the furled sails of ships moored to the embankment jut above the stone railing while from the further shore smoke curls from the industrial stacks that, like the distinctly recognizable spire of Battersea Old Church, cast reflections in the water. Whether Beerbohm actually painted the picture (if so, it would constitute his only venture into oils) or merely acquired it, its presence among his possessions may be

Oil painting attributed to Walter Greaves. Courtesy of the Warden and Fellows of Merton College, Oxford.

regarded as a symptom of his "Rossettitis." It almost seems to have been designed for the purpose of authenticating Herringham's existence. There is no hint of imposture in the painting itself, but there may be in the signature, "W. Greaves." Walter Greaves had been a pupil of Whistler's and contended that he had been made to promise not to exhibit his own pictures without Whistler's permission. Providing the art world with a sensation when it broke in 1911,[45] the story was apparently still current enough in 1920 for Beerbohm to allude to it in a caricature (HD 1770). We have no proof that he did so, but if he did, it would have delighted Max to sign a painting that would document the friendship of Rossetti and Herringham with a signature that just *might* hint that it had actually been painted by Whistler.

The visible residue of "The Mirror of the Past" is not very grand: apart from the bundle of unpublished papers itself, there are the pieces assembled for "Hethway Speaking," which amount to little more than ten printed pages; and there are the two parodies and a possible forgery, all of them private jokes — not a very impressive array for all that labor. But, as we have seen, "The Mirror of the Past" was the scaffolding for *Rossetti and His Circle,* the source not merely of the information and the point of view that suffuse that album but also of the invention and the fable, if one may use the word, which so distinguish it from all the other books of Beerbohm's caricatures. In "The Mirror of the Past" Beerbohm fashioned a new realm of existence to explore, a realm halfway between the actual world of history and the imaginary world of fiction — the world of the likely, in which real people mingle with imaginary ones and perform acts characteristic of themselves, a world whose intensity is conveyed by the careful observation of a sensitive witness. The path to that world, the world of the imaginary reminiscence, explored in *Seven Men* no less than in *Rossetti and His Circle,* lay through the looking glass.

CHAPTER V

Seven Men

Ever since it achieved literary respectability in the eighteenth century, the novel has been the most favored fiction form in the English language. With an occasional notable exception our literature can boast of few writers of fiction of any stature, however eminent their achievements in the short story or novella, who have not graduated to the longer form or at least attempted to do so. No small part of the explanation is commercial: a virtually insatiable market for novels exists, whether they appear serially, as in the last century, or hurtle precipitously onto the wire-rack displays of drugstores, as in this. Short stories have usually made their initial appearance in magazines (a market fast disappearing), generally as a writer's apprentice work. If they are later collected into book form, it is almost invariably because the writer has established a reputation through more substantial composition; if they are anthologized with the work of other writers, as often as not the book is destined for a readership of college freshmen. The advocacy of Poe notwithstanding, most readers prefer their fiction long and their poetry short. There are, to be sure, other causes for the preference for long fiction, a preference that appears less pronounced in other national literatures. For the exploration of character or the conflict between the individual and his society, nothing less than the novel will really do, and such concerns have come to be identified with the aims of fiction generally. A writer like Beerbohm, who has other themes to advance, undertakes the novel at a great disadvantage. Although the impulse toward extensiveness may be as strong in them as in conventional novelists, the weight of tradition is against them. Even if Beerbohm had carried "The Mirror of the Past" beyond its fragmental state, the result would have been a literary stillbirth.

Beerbohm's second attempt at a novel had aimed to surmount the limitations of the first. Admitting that his own presence, both as witness and as stylist, was essential to any prose he might pen, he determined to provide a justification in "The Mirror" for what had appeared as self-indulgence in *Zuleika Dobson*. Ironic though the utterance might be, Max designed to keep an absolutely straight face in "The Mirror of the Past"; this novel would be suffused with the same intensity that pervades the "remembering" essays, the fugitive and casual nature of whose reminiscences would yield to the gravity of a longer work invested with sustained narrative consequence. Because he could neither keep himself out of it nor limit his responses to beings wholly of his own creation, Beerbohm conceived the world of "The Mirror of the Past" from the very outset as one in which fact and fiction might mingle freely. Had it succeeded, the work would have been a significant instance of the early-twentieth-century novel's transcending the conventions of realism. As it now stands, "The Mirror of the Past" is a failure that instructs us both of Beerbohm's intentions and of his achievements. For in attempting a novel on his own terms, Beerbohm came to understand better what he could and what he could not accomplish. He learned, for example, that to observe character externally, however sensitively and acutely, is not quite the same thing as accounting for motive. Sympathetic though he might be, Max could not identify with a fictional character — he could only respond to one. It was equally futile to expect that the fortunes or misfortunes of such characters considered independently of Max's responses to them could constitute a thread strong enough for a long work. A "remembering" essay could simply not be stretched to the length of a novel. It would snap for want of an overall vision. On the other hand, his struggle with "The Mirror" probably did serve to instruct Beerbohm about which of his essayistic propensities *were* adaptable to the writing of fiction. His taste for the fabulous and fantastic, a characteristic of his earlier tales (though it complicated "The Mirror of the Past" almost to bedevilment), had nevertheless proven itself effective in *Zuleika Dobson* and was not to be abandoned, however unwieldy its manifestations might threaten to become. Parody, which in *A Christmas Garland* had confined itself to a form of literary criticism, became in "The Mirror of the Past" a means of generating character: Rossetti, Morris, Meredith, and Whistler become known to us essentially not through their actions but through Max's attribution to them of utterances wholly of his own invention, utterances held, moreover, to be quintessentially characteristic of those who speak them. Even Herringham is first introduced to us through a letter, whose style and content Max takes great pains to analyze as an index of what we may expect of Sylvester. In *Seven Men,* as we shall see, a man's character is virtually determined by the quality of his literary creations; and in the case of one of them, Beerbohm actually wrote the play attributed to "Savonarola" Brown before he conceived of the character of the author.

Beerbohm's work on "The Mirror of the Past" thus served to isolate and to identify his strengths and weaknesses as a writer of fiction, a precondition for embarkation on *Seven Men,* his most artful and complex literary enterprise. The most significant advance Beerbohm made through his engagement with "The Mirror" was to learn to rely more extensively upon "found" than upon "invented" characters. A "found" character is one who originates essentially from actual life — exaggerated perhaps, colored more strongly by imagination, simplified, reduced. Such characters may be historical personages or eminent contemporaries, or else they may derive from obscure and even fleeting acquaintances. The important thing about them is not their identification with real people, which in many instances cannot even be established, but the fact that they are uncompounded. They are drawn into literature behaving substantially as they did in life, undergoing adventures comparable to the ones they experienced in life. Only the arrangement, the intensity, the interpretation are supplied by the writer. An "invented" character, on the other hand, derives from no unique prototype; he comes into being as a blend of traits drawn from myriad sources; his fate may have been determined by history, but his plight has been wholly imagined; his motives are perfectly understood by his creator because he has been completely fashioned by him. All of Shakespeare's characters are invented — it is the essence of dramatic characterization — whether they derive nominally from Plutarch, Holinshed, or Italian romances, because they are more than externally observed. In his first novel Beerbohm had invented Zuleika and the duke but had persisted in treating them as found characters; in "The Mirror of the Past" he invented only Herringham, who, as we have seen, was soon overwhelmed by the found characters. In *Seven Men* we encounter only found characters: the real persons, Will Rothenstein and A. J. Balfour, to name only two, are obviously not invented; the eponymous heroes of these sketches are just as obviously fictional because their lives (despite Max's efforts to persuade us otherwise) are undocumented outside of Beerbohm's work, but they are manifestly caricatures of observed human beings. Even Brown, who is begotten by his own artistic offspring, is not so much invented as discovered — an hypothesis confirmed. By means of an exclusive reliance on such found characters to people his fiction, Beerbohm effectively managed the transition from "remembering" essay to "remembering" story.

That this may have been his inclination all along, that the extended work of fiction may have been totally alien to his genius, undertaken in response to some external imperative that bade him, now that he had the time for it, to engage in a more substantial literary composition than hitherto, may be suggested by the early date Lord David Cecil ascribes to the writing of "Enoch Soames" — 1914.[1] As in "The Mirror of the Past" itself, on which Beerbohm was working simultaneously, the author's recollection in "Enoch Soames" is touched off by a desire to complete the record, to fill in the omissions in a survey of the recent cultural past. In "The Mirror" it is Max's own essay "1880" that is the stimulus; in "Enoch Soames" it is Holbrook Jackson's work *The Eighteen Nineties* (1913), which Max, with characteristic modesty, neglects to note has been dedicated to him. Jackson's book demonstrated the truth that has become a commonplace in our century, that little more than a decade need elapse before the romantic revaluation of an age may commence. This popular work of nostalgia and criticism legitimated Max's eyewitness role assigned to Herringham, the survivor, a role he could now assume without the elaborate artifice of the mirror; having once assumed it, he could proceed to a narrative reminiscence of a found character. The ease and success he experienced in doing so may have made it more difficult to carry on with "The Mirror of the Past" as he had originally conceived it. As sketch followed sketch, though initially with little thought of the volume they would ultimately compose and with the Rossetti material finding its expression in pencil and water color, Beerbohm would hardly have felt frustrated because "The Mirror of the Past," his intended *magnum opus,* had stalled. The intent of the work, as well as most of its content, was being realized in other forms.

It is very likely that among external stimuli Jackson's book was the most significant releasing mechanism for the flow of reminiscential sketches that were collected in 1919 as *Seven Men,* but it is by no means certain that "Enoch Soames," though it stands first in the volume, was the first of the pieces conceived. The dating of each of the compositions, however, does not appear a particularly rewarding enterprise because they do not present us with a developing, maturing vision so much as a set of variations on a theme. (The exception, of course, is "Argallo and Ledgett," not written until 1927 and not included in editions of *Seven Men* until 1950. Although conformable to the original sketches in surface characteristics, "Argallo and Ledgett" is markedly different from them in tone and does reflect an altered conception of reminiscence brought about by the passage of time.) What is significant is that, like "The Mirror of the Past," *Seven Men* was essentially a war work — all of the sketches were either composed or first published between 1914 and 1918. Beerbohm returned to the desk from the drawing board because he reasoned that the times were hardly auspicious for the reception of his caricatures. But he was celebrating as well the more self-conscious and less complex era that had come to an end with the death of Edward VII. Hearing English spoken all about him once more and living in the company of Rothenstein, whose friendship dated from the period he was recalling, Max could work on what would become *Seven Men* with greater enthusiasm than he could muster for "The Mirror of the Past."

Sir Max Beerbohm

Even though the individual sketches that came to constitute *Seven Men* seem a natural consequence of Beerbohm's artistic growth and his experimentation with form, particularly as they have been traced through his drawing and writing, nevertheless the appearance of a major work that represents the writer at the height of his powers demands that someone investigate the possibility of significant external influences. If such an investigation yields no sources, it may perhaps produce a few instructive analogues. It is particularly tempting in this instance, for *Seven Men* occupies a halfway position between memoir and fiction, and the redefinition of genres that the work implies is of considerable interest to students of modern literature. Of writers who imposed imaginary conversation and activity upon historical personages or who attributed significant historical activity to imaginary ones there is no dearth of names that spring to mind. Since the time of Lucian, dialogues of great men and women have been the sounding boards for the satirical and philosophical judgments of their inventors. Acting on the assumption that no major influence would go unchronicled in Beerbohm's essays or correspondence, we can reduce the number considerably. The most notable nineteenth-century practitioner of the fictitious dialogue of real people is Walter Savage Landor (1775–1864), to whom Max alludes once in a letter, actually signing himself with that appellation.[2] It is uncertain, however, whether in doing so Max means to identify himself with Landor's *Imaginary Conversations* or to refer to his self-imposed Italian exile. There is little similarity between the work of the two men. Landor's conversations are just that; though many are not without poignancy, none are narrative or reflective of the processes of thought and feeling. Frederic Manning's *Scenes and Portraits* (1909), on the other hand, does indeed attempt to reproduce those processes, and we know it to be one of Beerbohm's favorite books.[3] But Manning, too, is more concerned with ideas than with personalities, and in this regard his method and his intent are considerably removed from those of Beerbohm. He projects his own views through his fictionalized characters, to be sure, but not as the stage ventriloquist that Beerbohm depicts; rather he is a marionettist. Quite apart from the fact that none of his pieces deals with contemporary or recollected figures, Manning's ironic de-

Seven Men

tachment conveys no clear impression of his own self actually in confrontation with his creations. Manning's work might serve as an illustration and a confirmation of the liberties that wit might take with history, but it could hardly provide Max with a model.

Indeed, the uniqueness of *Seven Men* baffles our search for a single influential source. The name of one writer, however, does suggest itself as a possible stimulus to Beerbohm's invention — Walter Pater. Although the direct contact between Pater and Beerbohm could hardly have been more than brief (Pater died in the summer of 1894), Max does record in an early essay his distinct disillusion upon accidentally encountering the illustrious Oxford don in a bookshop.[4] Significantly, Max drew but a single portrait caricature of him (HD 1146), so the visual impression Pater left upon him cannot have been very strong. But as a literary force, particularly one who claimed such disciples among Max's acquaintance as Oscar Wilde and Richard LeGallienne, Pater must have appeared formidable to the young man. There is frequent mention of Pater in Beerbohm's early collections of essays, and the references are as frequently to the latest and now forgotten works as to the anthology pieces.[5] It is not to the purpose here to inquire into the extent to which Pater's habits of style influenced Beerbohm. But it is apparent from the foregoing evidence that Beerbohm was neither unaware nor indifferent to Pater's impact on late-Victorian prose. Half in imitation, half in mockery Max wrote of him, "I was angry that he should treat English as a dead language, bored by that sedulous ritual wherewith he laid out every sentence as in a shroud — hanging, like a widower, long over its marmoreal beauty or ever he could lay it at length in his book, its sepulchre."[6] And perhaps impudence as much as anything else led the twenty-three-year-old Max to publish his slender volume of *Works* in 1896, one year after the ten-volume posthumous edition of Pater's *Works* had collected the books, the fugitive pieces, and the unpublished fragments together with a bibliography.

Whether reverentially or skeptically, as an Oxford undergraduate in the early nineties, Beerbohm was the inheritor of a number of attitudes concerning writing that can only be called Paterian. Foremost among these was the meticulous attention to style, to the beauty of literary expression. Concomitant to this was the imposition of aesthetic rather than moral criteria upon human actions and creations. Taken together, these attitudes produced an allusive, impressionistic criticism, a highly sensitive but also highly unscholarly and idiosyncratic approach to art, and an almost casual indifference to the conditions of real life. This statement is, of course, a vast oversimplification and damns Pater for the excesses of his followers. Yet in one particular way Pater's practice may have exerted a specific influence — namely, in his use of fiction to expound a personal vision that purports to have historical validity. Like Pater, Max lived in a narrow world of literature and art; like him he attempted to use narrative as a mode of critical discourse. Pater's example was more cautionary than instructive, however. Max knew exactly how bloodless and rarefied were Pater's creations. Although he observed facetiously that he had read *Marius the Epicurean* as a schoolboy "mainly as a tale of adventure,"[7] his judgment was not always so oblique: "Life was too harsh, chaotic an affair for the timid and exacting soul of Pater. He could not relish or digest it till art had minced it for him. He seldom mentioned it directly. When he cast his criticism in the form of fiction, it was always some antique or very cloistral phase of life that he handled, some secretive and remote soul that he dared finger."[8] Perhaps it was the recognition of his own affinity to Pater in his preference of art to life that made Beerbohm so conscious of his limitations and so determined that, modest though his experience in the great world might be, his fictions would never be deficient in vitality. *Zuleika Dobson* makes no pretense to realism; yet it is suffused with the spirit of Oxford. From Pater's Oxford study, however, issued forth the summonings rather than the achieved evocations of earlier cultural epochs — second-century Rome in *Marius the Epicurean* or the dawning of the Renaissance in *Imaginary Portraits*. Choosing a far less comprehensive range than Pater and revealing character through detail and anecdote rather than through thought and reflection, Beerbohm in his studies of the Pre-Raphaelites and the Decadents seems more "authentic" not only in fact but in feeling. Beerbohm's purpose in *Rossetti and His Circle* and *Seven Men*, however, was not so much one of critical elucidation as one of irony, if not satire. And although I do not propose to read *Seven Men* as a parody of *Imaginary Portraits*, it is difficult not to feel that we are in the presence of burlesque when the self-deprecating narrator holds up for our esteem such preposterous would-be artists as Soames, Maltby, and Brown. Against the dreamy and romantic idealism of Watteau, Denys L'Auxerrois, Sebastian van Storck, and Duke Carl of Rosenmold conjured up by Pater, men passionately driven by noble and selfless impulses, we juxtapose the eccentric and perverse monomania of *bourgeois manqués,* whose very aspiration merits not tragedy but bathos. As in all mock-heroic, the mockery is aimed at two objects — most immediately at the subjects being derided, particularly the vanity of their pretensions, and at the society that, however passively, allows them to sustain these pretensions. Somewhat less directly the very notion of the aesthete as hero is under attack. We know the grimness and sordidness of the Victorian Age; it was capable of producing a few flawed and unhappy geniuses like Rossetti and Swinburne and a host of unimaginative and banal imitators. Have we any reason to believe, asks the satirist, that other ages were any different? Quite apart from its other characteristics, *Seven Men* not only demolishes the literary fads and posturings of the recent past, it also punctures the romantic aesthetic myth of the artist that was so assiduously nurtured by the nineteenth century.

Even though the outward appearance of the work would seem to suggest parallels to other imaginary portraits and a large part of the content deals with the clash of commercial and aesthetic attitudes in a particular age, rendering it a rich primary document for the literary historian, *Seven Men* is best interpreted as the culmination of Beerbohm's quest for form — the mature manifestation of the imaginary reminiscence, a complex and ingenious vehicle for the conveyance of Beerbohm's irony. That the work was not originally planned as a whole, even that the parts are not uniformly masterful, merely confirms the fact that Beerbohm was primarily a miniaturist, that his works are essentially collections of short pieces. *Seven Men,* however, obviously possesses greater unity than the usual periodic gathering up of otherwise fugitive pieces, like *Works, More,* and *Yet Again.* It also possesses greater unity than the collections of specialized pieces, the parodies of *A Christmas Garland* and the selected drama reviews of *Around Theatres*. Conceived initially as separate sketches of a lightly fictional cast, taken together the pieces constitute a set of variations on the encounters of the literary imagination, in its manifold forms, with the world of actuality.

Before proceeding to examine these variations singly, it may be well to speak of their properties collectively as imaginary reminiscences. Foremost among these is the insistence that the narration is veracious. Beerbohm was particularly energetic on this point. Not only does the text consistently uphold the truth of these fictional recollections, Beerbohm determined as well that the very physical appearance of the book should sustain that illusion. In a letter offering the American publication rights of *Seven Men* to the Century Company, Max specified that "the book's format should be unlike that of ordinary fiction."[9] When the book was finally brought out in America, he provided a set of antedated caricatures of the subjects of the stories by way of further authentication, caricatures that were to be incorporated into the book not as interleaved illustrations but as an appendix. These caricatures were to be documents verifying the existence of Beerbohm's imaginary beings (can one exaggerate what has never been seen?), and he went so far as to draw the hasty portrait of A. V. Laider, complete with ink blots on paper worn at the fold, on stationery he had specially printed up to bear the letterhead of a fictitious hotel.[10] In every way, therefore, the reader is to be persuaded that he is dealing with a work of fact rather than one of imagination.

Unlike the earlier "remembering" essays, however, these mature imaginary reminiscences do not confine themselves to the impressions of a moment or their recollection in later years. Although they do not abound in external incident, they convey a greater sense of action and analyzable plot than do the essays. This is perhaps to say no more than that they are recognizably stories where the pure reminiscences are not. And being stories, they have narrative consequence; that is, the reader is led to a conclusion for which he has been carefully prepared, a conclusion that invites him to interpret the entire experience, perhaps to apply it to other circumstances, whereas in ordinary reminiscences there is a sealing off of the revelation: it illuminates only the "reminiscer" and the "reminisced." When we read mem-

SEVEN MEN

For Jack Lynch, with all
best wishes from

Hilary Maltby.

J. Braxton

Jas. Pethel

A. V. Laider

Ladbroke Brown

Max Beerbohm

Half-title page of presentation copy of *Seven Men*. Courtesy of the Warden and Fellows of Merton College, Oxford.

oirs, whatever artistry appears is usually secondary; we are conditioned to read for information.

A third essential characteristic of the imaginary reminiscence is the presence of the narrator as a character, not merely as the storyteller. First-person narrators have traditionally been either protagonists or raconteurs. Conrad, it is true, had made familiar to the English public the introspective narrator, whose interpretation of the actions of the more vigorous characters did much to reshape the modern reader's expectations of fiction. But Beerbohm as author clearly means us to think of himself as one of his seven inventions, and he defines his own character indirectly through his definition of the characters of the others. A consistent character emerges from the five original sketches, but in each the narrator seems to be possessed of a negative, though not vicious, quality that makes him appear, initially at any rate, to some disadvantage. In "Enoch Soames" he is callow; in "Hilary Maltby and Stephen Braxton," gossipy; in "James Pethel," timorous; in "A. V. Laider," credulous; and in "'Savonarola' Brown," obtuse. All of these Boswellian postures, we realize much later, are the masks of the *eiron*. In "Felix Argallo and Walter Ledgett," added to the 1950 edition, Max has grown considerably in self-confidence and as an assessor of literary worth. The naiveté appropriate to the recollections of a journeyman writer has been replaced by the shrewd manipulativeness of one whose own position in the republic of letters is fairly well assured. The posture is no less ironic, but it is no longer self-deprecating. The purpose, we come to understand, of emphasizing the truthfulness of these narrations is to allow the author to speak in his own person without being an intruder. Unlike the novelist or the dramatist, the essayist never permits the disembodiment of his personality in his work. Beerbohm creates fables but insists upon being the hero of them.

By transforming memoirs and biography into the stuff of fiction, moreover, Beerbohm succeeds in investing the everyday world of the sojourner in imagination — the practical world in which he either makes or does not make a living by his craft and in which he worries about the reception of his work — with a sense of adventure and moral consequence. Instead of indisputable facts, we are confronted with mean and noble deeds, with opportunities taken and missed, and with complex judgments implied but not stated. We are shifted from the plane of knowledge to the plane of interpretation. But our interpretation, we come to realize, constitutes our only knowledge: Beerbohm's imaginary reminiscences do not provide us in the end with the clarifying, definitive visions for which we generally turn to fiction. They insist upon the irreducible mystery of human behavior, on the disparity between motive and act and between the image of the self projected and the image of the self received. Ultimately we must settle, not for the truth, but for the most sensitive interpretation available, which is, of course, that of the author. We can easily understand Beerbohm's admiration for the work of Lytton Strachey, who was virtually the only writer younger than himself for whom he expressed unqualified enthusiasm. Strachey's relentless irony, his distinctive style, and his pervasive presence in all that he wrote, more than his debunking of Victorian respectability, were the qualities that most attracted Beerbohm to him. That Strachey's subject happened to be biography is not insignificant but is clearly of less importance to him than the artistry of Strachey's prose. In his 1943 Rede Lecture at Cambridge, Beerbohm said of him: "If I were asked what seemed to me the paramount quality of Lytton Strachey's prose, I should reply, in one word, Beauty."[11] In *Seven Men*, although Beerbohm had finally settled upon a manageable and congenial subject, the achievement lies in the cunning workmanship.

"Enoch Soames" stands first in the volume and is probably the best known individual sketch. Frequently anthologized as a tale of the supernatural or of a voyage through time, this reminiscence appears to possess the greatest resemblance to conventional stories. The central character is very distinctly portrayed, and the action seems far more physical than mental. It is worth noting, however, that the character of Soames is established as much through dialogue and quotation from his works — that is to say, through parody — as it is through physical description and events and that the drama of the piece does not actually begin until the Devil makes his appearance, which happens halfway through the story. Beerbohm thus accommodates himself only partially to the conventions of fiction. He allows himself a leisurely, apparently desultory, exposition in which he modestly sets forth his own qualifications as a man of letters against the feeble flamboyance of Soames. Like all of the pieces in *Seven Men*, "Enoch Soames" purports to owe its genesis as a recorded reminiscence to a stimulus administered by the world of hard facts — in this instance by the omission of Soames's name from Holbrook Jackson's book, a compendious survey of the writers of the *fin de siècle* subtitled "A Review of Art and Ideas at the Close of the Nineteenth Century." Jackson not only had dedicated the book to Max but had devoted a whole chapter to him as well. Max's magnanimity in preserving his friend Soames from oblivion is thus made all the more striking; as he commences the narrative, the reader is disarmed of the least suspicion that he is to be hoaxed.

The events of the tale are simply outlined. While yet an undergraduate Max is introduced by the artist Will Rothenstein into the dazzling literary and artistic world of London, to whose fringes clings Soames, a would-be poet of Bohemian persuasion. Max's unformed taste and judgment, his literary innocence, lead him to take Soames's pretensions more seriously than his friends do, and he assiduously follows the man's unpromising career over the next four years — a period, incidentally, during which Beerbohm himself acquired considerable literary celebrity. Max dutifully buys and attempts to read Soames's books as they appear. The generous extracts that Beerbohm makes of the archetypally Decadent verse, together with his earnest attempts to wrest meaning from them, are hilarious reading. As regards the man himself, Soames's pompous attitudinizing and his farrago of absurd notions strike the reader as comic rather than pathetic. Max himself, however, refuses to pass judgment and continues to marvel at Soames's imperviousness to discouragement. That apparent indifference is shown to be a façade when Soames confesses to Max that failure has indeed been bitter to him but that it might more easily be borne were he to be assured of the acclaim of future generations. At this point a Mephistophelian figure who has overheard their conversation interrupts them and offers the distraught poet a severely modified version of the Faust bargain. In exchange for a five-hour projection into the British Museum Reading Room of a hundred years hence, where he may regale himself with the "endless editions, commentaries, prolegomena, biographies" that he envisions he will find listed in the catalogue under his name, and against Max's strenuous advice Soames consents to sell his soul to the Devil. He is whisked away in an instant only to return from his research expedition even gloomier than before. Querying him about the future, Max finds that his own worst apprehensions will have been realized: men and women all regimented with identification numbers and uniforms, reformed phonetic spelling, and the organization of the literary profession into a government service. Poor Soames's expectations have been utterly dashed, moreover. Not only does he find no elaborate critical edifice raised to his honor but the only reference to himself that he can find at all is the discovery, in a volume entitled *Inglish Littracher 1890–1900,* to be published in 1992, that he is no more than a character in a story written by Max Beerbohm, an example of "hou seriusli the yung men ov the aiteen-ninetiz took themselvz."[12]

Beerbohm's ingenious way of mending the omission in Holbrook Jackson's book turns out to be by inventing a character who will be mentioned in a future literary history. Both in plot and in genre what begins as memoir ends up as fiction, though Max protests to Soames, by way of exculpation, that "I don't write stories: I'm an essayist, an observer, a recorder" (p. 40). This assertion seems to be upheld by the fact that the narrative does not end with the Devil's dragging the poet off to Hell. Rather the author continues his imaginative reflections on the locale in Soho Square in which the abduction, which appears to have stirred no one's interest but his own, took place and on the flaw whereby the literary historian of the future will mistake a work of fact for one of fiction. The final passage of the sketch, which would strike the reader as anticlimactic or inept at best if the fortunes of Enoch Soames really lay at the heart of the piece, enforces the belief that the whole invention has concerned itself with imagination and reality. Encountering the overdressed and overbearing Devil on a Paris street, out of an automatic politeness Max smiles in recognition, only to be cut by him. Max fumes at the insult of being snubbed by such a vulgarian. But the reader, now alert to the intricacies of Beerbohm's narrative, can supply at least two interpretations of the incident: either Max only *imagines* him to be the Devil, in which case they have never actually met before, or he is indeed the Devil, only their first meeting in the company of Soames hasn't taken place yet because their present encounter antedates the composition of the story, which alone can actualize it. From the first to the last paragraph we have been so teased that we are no longer certain of what is real and what is imaginary.

Beerbohm knew well the operatic potentiality of his material — the narrator as tragic witness to the perdition of a soul whose thirst for fame caused him to overstep human limitations — for he indicates as much in the bit of literary history ascribed to T. K. Nupton that Soames copies out in the Reading Room. But he knew as well that writers in stories never undergo any serious criticism of their compositions as they would in real life. They thus enjoy an undiminished heroism, either as romantic geniuses whose gifts are recognized or as romantic geniuses whose gifts are not recognized. The unromantic possibility of their having dedication but no talent is one simply not explored. Yet that is just the one possibility that fascinates Max. Enoch Soames's performance as an artist is subjected to the same scrutiny as those of "Romeo" Coates, Moore, Swinburne, and Yeats (to whom he bears some superficial resemblance). He takes his place in Beerbohm's portrait gallery of worthies along with others. This statement is literally true, for Soames even appears in a group caricature "Some Persons of 'the Nineties'" published in the 1925 album *Observations* (HD 1650; BLC 51). The implications of this comic hoax, however, are quite serious and emphasize the meaninglessness of the distinction between fact and fiction for the artist. By first establishing the actuality of Soames's existence through a meticulous verisimilitude that involves minute detail, the enlistment of real people as characters, and the elaborate reconstruction of the narrator's own responses to imaginary events and then deliberately demolishing it with the conventionally obvious fictions of the Faust legend and the journey into the future, Beerbohm drives home the fundamental truth that an imaginary man becomes real when imaginatively written about — and conversely that a real man can be made to appear unreal when he is written about without imagination.

In "Enoch Soames" we have an account of an unimaginative man whose only reality lies in the imagination of another man. In "Hilary Maltby and Stephen Braxton," Beerbohm gives the effect another turn of the screw. Not only is reminiscence embedded in reminiscence but Beerbohm also presents us with *two* imaginary authors, one of whom additionally haunts the imagination of the other. Elsewhere I have considered fairly extensively the biographical and thematic implications of this story and how the archetype of the "double" may lurk behind the hallucinatory presences conjured up by Maltby's guilty conscience.[13] At present I mean to consider "Maltby and Braxton" essentially as an imaginary reminiscence. Cecil observes of *Seven Men* that "each story is inspired by some phase of its author's history, and involves a description of places and people he had known and lived among."[14] Yet there is another kind of comprehensiveness about the work that belies the casualness implied by Lord David's statement. Soames is a *soi-disant* poet; Maltby and Braxton are fashionable novelists who quickly fall out of fashion; Brown is a closet dramatist. Even Laider has literary pretensions, inventing tales of excruciating suspense whereas both Argallo and Ledgett are miscellaneous writers whose letters and diaries come under scrutiny. All provinces of the republic of letters are thus represented, almost as though Beerbohm had consciously planned a satirical survey of the late-Victorian and Edwardian literary scene.

Certainly "Maltby and Braxton" begins as though it means to recall an era, one in which the billowy sleeves of women and the craze for bicycling were fads no more lasting than the reputations of popular writers in whom celebrity passes for merit. Like Soames, both Maltby and Braxton are presented as characteristic of their times. These two novelists of fantasy seem to divide the territory between them — Maltby, urbane and witty; Braxton, earthy and straightforward — and have both come into public notice at about the same time. Consequently their books and their persons are forever being compared and contrasted. Their rivalry, moreover, appears to be the only memorable thing about them, and indeed the narrator cannot identify Maltby in his later self-imposed Italian exile without immediately recollecting Braxton as well. From Maltby Max learns of the fateful debacle in the spring of 1895 that preceded the flight into oblivion. So systematically had the publication of their books, their interviews with the press, and their social engagements been matched, that even a casual scanner of newspapers could hardly observe the competition of Maltby and Braxton other than as a sporting event. Max was, of course, more assiduous than the casual scanner. For him in Braxton's apparent failure to equal or surpass Maltby's triumph in being invited to spend a weekend at Keeb Hall, home of the lionizing duchess of Hertfordshire, lay a deep mystery, one unravelled only by Maltby's confession seventeen years later. Maltby confides to Max that it had been the duchess's intention to invite Braxton down as well, but that he, Maltby, succeeded in persuading her that owing to his inordinate shyness Braxton would have difficulty in refusing her even though he had a horror of leaving London overnight. The ruse was successful and Maltby was thus assured that he would be the sole and uncontested representative of literature among the dignitaries and aristocrats assembled at Keeb. Maltby is an unbelievable snob: he defines his personal and professional success in terms of being taken up by the privileged class. But he is punished for his self-serving lie in a manner particularly appropriate. An apparition of Braxton, impalpable and invisible to all except Maltby, comes to haunt him at Keeb. Although he knows the insubstantiality of the specter, as a man who traffics in fancifulness, he cannot avoid being affected by it. In his novel *Ariel in Mayfair* Maltby had told, Max informs us, "how Ariel reembodied himself from thin air, leased a small house in Chesterfield Street, was presented at a Levee, played the part of good fairy in a matter of true love not running smooth, and worked meanwhile all manner of amusing changes among the aristocracy before he vanished again."[15] Behind the sentimentalization and trivialization of fancy — the trashing of Shakespeare — implied by the invocation of Ariel, lie instances more immediate and painful to Beerbohm of the inartistic use of supernatural agency to reform character, of works such as Jerome K. Jerome's *The Passing of the Third Floor Back*, a dramatization of which he excoriated in a review as "twaddle and vulgarity."[16]

Maltby is punished not merely for his snobbishness, opportunism, and mendacity but for his misuse of the gift of imagination as well. For not only does Braxton's ghost discompose Maltby, it prevents him from "shining" in the august assembly to which he has been summoned. In a series of manifestations graduated in their demoralizing effect, Braxton causes Maltby to retreat from the garden party, to cut himself so severely while shaving that he must descend to dinner scarred with sticking plaster on his cheek, and to overturn a bowl of beet soup on his dinner clothes. When he retires early to avoid further embarrassment (Maltby ironically fails to note that the company he so wishes to impress is rather dull), he finds Braxton occupying his bed and must spend the night sleeping fitfully on a chair. In the morning Braxton takes possession of the bath, forcing Maltby to an early breakfast. Maltby's fortunes seem to repair when he enters into conversation with Lady Rodfitten. While the two of them are bicycling round the terrace, Maltby dreams of becoming her protégé and begins mentally composing the dedication of his next book to her. Suddenly he swerves into her bicycle, bringing them both down with a crash. It is of course useless to protest that he was trying to avoid the figure of Braxton that loomed in front of him. Lady Rodfitten withdraws, unhurt but furious. Braxton even pursues Maltby into church, where the terror climaxes with Maltby's rushing out in the middle of the service. He flees not only the church, not only Keeb Hall, not only London but England itself. As he tells Max, "I leapt straight from Ryder Street into Vaule-la-Rochette, a place of which I once heard that it was the least frequented seaside-resort in Europe. I leapt leaving no address" (p. 101). Exaggerating the impact of his bizarre behavior on his betters, Maltby seeks out obscurity and renounces high society. Or not quite. The elderly woman in a wheelchair whom Maltby accompanies on a daily promenade in Lucca had formerly been his landlady and is now his wife. "'She was the Contessa Adriano-Rizzoli, the last of her line. She is the Contessa Adriano-Rizzoli-Maltby. We have been married fifteen years. . . . She is a lineal descendant,' he said, 'of the Emperor Hadrian'" (p. 104).

Hilary Maltby is probably the most richly observed fictional character in all of Beerbohm's work. His attitudes and responses are carefully delineated, and he is allowed the rare privileges of telling his own story and of actually having the last word. Braxton, on the other hand, seems quite shadowy (which is perhaps as he should be, since his appearance is essentially that of a ghost), a mere intellectual projection of a polar antithesis to Maltby. The reason for Maltby's fullness of characterization may be that, caricature though he is, he was "found" at no great distance from Beerbohm himself. The fastidious dandiacal temperament, the physical appearance as evidenced in drawings,[17] and the common circumstances of their leaving England in the middle of their careers to settle modestly in Italy are similarities too numerous to be passed off as accidental. Whether he intended it or not, Beerbohm created Maltby by exaggerating aspects of himself.[18] Specifically, he fashions Maltby as an uncritical worshiper of the upper classes, one who "knew his aristocrats only through Thackeray, through the photographs and paragraphs in the newspapers, and through those passionate excursions of his to Rotten Row" (p. 57). A man so constituted would be dazzled by his admittance to the purlieus of the artistocracy, and it might well take him seventeen years to realize that his dinner companion that evening at Keeb Hall, though *Lady* Thisbe Crowborough, had been "an abysmal fool." A man so constituted would also resent to the point of obsession that equal regard was about to be lavished upon Braxton, not merely a rival, but a coarse vulgarian who wore pepper-and-salt suits. As a fantasist, Maltby would embody that obsession, even while knowing it to be a product of imagination. As a snob, he could convince himself that his conduct was unpardonable and that he could maintain no standing among the aristocracy once the story got out.

Despite the intense vividness of both Maltby's character and Maltby's plight, the resolution of the tale strikes us as rather feeble. To end the account with the revelation that Maltby has abandoned literature to become the consort of a decayed Italian noblewoman is to terminate suspense with mere anecdote and to vindicate the criticism of those who found Beerbohm deficient as a writer of short stories.[19] But the fact is that "Maltby and Braxton" is not a short story, nor is Maltby's confession to Max simply an interior narration. In "Enoch Soames" what appears to be a real person turns out to be an imaginary character. In "Maltby and Braxton," using the same devices of authenticity — the casual presence of actual people in fictional circumstances, the citation of newspapers and reviews, the evocation of a certifiable ambiance — Beerbohm carries the imaginary reminiscence a step further: not only does the real character turn out to be imaginary himself but his own imaginings are proved to be determined as well by his author. Just as Soames exists only because he has been conceived in Beerbohm's mind, so Maltby cannot exist without his opposite Braxton because Beerbohm has originally conceived them as a pair. Maltby's attempt to behave autonomously, to break out of that conceptualization, is doomed. In the very moment of exultation when he enters the railway train compartment reserved for visitors to Keeb, he cannot forbear reflecting on Braxton's envy of his success. Denied a physical presence as a guest of the duchess of Hertfordshire, however, Braxton takes on a ghostly one. Beerbohm's exposition has defined each character in terms of the other: "Dapper little Maltby — blond, bland, diminutive Maltby, with his monocle and his gardenia; big black Braxton, with his lanky hair and his square blue jaw and his square sallow forehead. Canary and crow" (p. 55). Maltby can no more violate the conditions of his conception as a character than Soames can become anything other than "dim," the *mot juste* Beerbohm has applied to him. And when Maltby decamps, refusing to endure the rivalry that his own duplicity has now internalized, he occasions not only his own death as an artist but that of Braxton as well. The pair are resurrected, rescued from utter oblivion, only when Beerbohm brings them together through the outer reminiscence. Far from relinquishing his essayistic control, even to a narrator to whom he exhibits a striking affinity, Beerbohm is firmly in command from beginning to end.

If there were any strenuous contention that Beerbohm was conscientiously attempting to write conventional fiction in *Seven Men* (and not quite achieving it), then "'Savonarola' Brown" provides an easy refutation. Nearly three-fourths of this sketch is taken up with the four acts of the historical verse drama Brown lived to complete and with the scenario for the fifth that Max, as Brown's literary executor, briefly projects. Whereas the quality of the failed artist is conveyed in earlier pieces by quotation — Soames's poetry, for example, or extracts from reviews of the novels of Maltby and Braxton — nothing less than the reproduction of the whole play (or what exists of it, for it is an *unfinished* masterpiece) will do for the illumination of Brown. Although the last of the original group to be composed and placed last in all editions of *Seven Men*, "'Savonarola' Brown" may appropriately be discussed out of order because of its close thematic relation to the first two. Unlike the other sketches, however, it was not originally conceived as a reminiscence at all. Manuscript evidence definitely establishes that the Shakespearean (or pseudo-Shakespearean) parody was composed first and that the narrative and expository portions were later additions.[20] It is quite likely that the success of his other imaginary portraits led Beerbohm to adapt this extensive parody to the form. Brown's play is "found" — a distortion, a caricature of blank-verse drama; Brown, on the contrary, is invented: he is the kind of man who would write such a play as a serious undertaking, never perceiving its ludicrousness. It is convenient, therefore, to speak of the play first and of its narrative enclosure second.

What strikes one immediately on confronting "Savonarola," the tragedy purportedly written by Ladbroke Brown, is the elaborateness of the spoof. To be sure, the four acts are not full ones by conventional dramatic standards, yet Beerbohm has allowed Brown to compose nearly four hundred lines of blank verse, of which he says, "I have searched vainly for one line that does not scan."[21] This count is exclusive of the idiotic quibbles and inane ditties of the Fool, who, upon leaving his original post and becoming the Gaoler, undergoes a change of speech as well:

> Unfortunately I have been discharg'd
> For my betrayal of Lucrezia,
> So that I have to speak like other men —
> Decasyllabically, and with sense. (P. 210)

And not least of the fun are the elaborate stage directions, more Shaw than Shakespeare. Clearly the parody was not simply tossed off. In the collected edition of Beerbohm's works (1922–1928) the play takes up more than twice the number of pages of the longest of the parodies in *A Christmas Garland*.

Seven Men

Set in fifteenth-century Florence, the play is fraught with anachronisms and written in a kind of artificial language that aspires to Elizabethan eloquence but descends as often to modern colloquialism. Brown appears to have studied early plays carefully, however, for his is replete with their characteristics and conventions in ludicrous guise. Specifically, there are involuted constructions, lengthy similes, and irrelevant "poetic" flights, all designed here to conceal poverty of meaning. Stichomythia, aposiopesis, and even the parceling out of a single line of verse among as many as four speeches, devices that could be employed as manifestations of passion, are trivialized into instances of mere technical virtuosity. Language apart, Brown has also compounded a potpourri of characters and scenes. The *dramatis personae,* beside Savonarola and Lucrezia Borgia, the two principal characters — here portrayed as helpless lovers — include in speaking roles St. Francis of Assisi, Leonardo da Vinci, Dante, Lorenzo and Cosimo de Medici, Pope Julius II, and Cesare Borgia, as well as the afore-mentioned Fool-Gaoler, a sacristan, a friar, and two apprentices. Needless to say, their numerousness does not allow for much character development. There are a number of nonspeaking roles as well. Acts I and III both end with the entrance of *"Guelfs and Ghibellines fighting."* Act III concludes with an additional crescendo in its stage direction:

> *Enter* MICHAEL ANGELO. ANDREA DEL SARTO *appears for a moment at a window.* PIPPA *passes. Brothers of the Miscericordia go by, singing a Requiem for Francesca da Rimini. Enter* BOCCACCIO, BENVENUTO CELLINI, *and many others, making remarks highly characteristic of themselves but scarcely audible through the terrific thunderstorm which now bursts over Florence and is at its loudest and darkest crisis as the Curtain falls.* (P. 207)

"Savonarola" is not merely a compendium of the literary and political figures of the Italian Renaissance; it is also a compendium of the types of scenes sure to please audiences of the English Renaissance. Soliloquies, of course, abound; there is, in addition, a mob scene reminiscent of *Julius Caesar* in which the crowds are swayed back and forth by rival speakers who harangue them in language they cannot possibly understand. There is a jail scene, a mad scene, and a scene in which a foe magnanimously eulogizes his fallen enemy, ordering pompous obsequies for him. (This speech has to be repeated a second time, as the corpse has been mistakenly identified.) The hilarity resides in the extraordinary compression of it all. Whatever has struck us as unnatural or unlikely in form or convention in a Shakespearean play is here rendered absurd by exaggeration and reduction — as though the greatness of Shakespeare resided in these externals and not in his breadth of vision, his psychological penetration, and the richness of his imagination. Imagination is the key word. Brown's play is utterly devoid of it. Even if we did not know that Brown had chosen his hero, not out of any fundamental sympathy for him or interest in his plight, but because "the name was in itself a great incentive to blank-verse" (p. 178), it is fairly obvious that the play is funny not because it is inept — that would simply make it a bad play — but because it *pretends* to be art whereas in fact it does nothing more than imitate the appearance of art. Brown's characters are without motive, his plot without design, his whole endeavor without purpose. Like Soames and Maltby, Brown is more interested in being thought a writer than in writing. He has nothing to express, only a set of borrowed formulas with which to dabble.

It has always been tempting to read *Seven Men* as a series of *contes à clef,* and in the case of "'Savonarola' Brown" the temptation is almost irresistible. Although Beerbohm's invention of Brown subsequent to the composition of the play may tend to deflect the search for a specific victim of his satire, the play itself seems too lovingly lingered over not to have been inspired by abuses of a particular kind. The man most frequently suggested as Ladbroke Brown's prototype is Stephen Phillips (1864–1915), an identification all too easily made, "Mr. Phillips," as Max observed, "being the only dramatic poet we have."[22] Beerbohm was puzzled by the extraordinary acclaim that attended *Paolo and Francesca,* Phillips's most popular play, which seemed to him devoid of genius, "very delicate, very smooth, wholly derivative. It might have been the work of a beautiful, etherialised sixth-form boy with an instinct for the stage."[23] Max suspected that the Phillips phenomenon would "blow over,"[24] as indeed it did, but he was not regardless of Phillips's merits, as the generally appreciative reviews of his other plays reveal.[25] The real issue for Beerbohm was not whether Phillips was talented, but whether the stuff he was writing had any essential vitality, whether it reflected or illuminated the concerns of contemporary men and women. Reflecting in the century year on the current state of the theater, Beerbohm wrote: "In these times, poetic drama can be but a happy survival, a beautiful little backwater remote from the main current of the stream. That main current . . . is of realistic modern comedy and tragedy. Regret it as you may, modern realism is the only direction in which our drama can really progress."[26] To the extent, then, that Stephen Phillips was an atavism in the history of modern drama, he may be said to resemble Brown. But although they quickly fell out of fashion, his plays are by no means foolish. Nor are they fragmental or unactable. Phillips achieved, moreover, in his brief heyday a considerable measure of success. In the final analysis the only real point of comparison between Phillips and Brown is that they both wrote dramas in blank verse.

The fact that Phillips was able to provide a commercially successful alternative to the standard theatrical fare of the Edwardian stage may have been inspirational to other would-be dramatic poets, of whom Brown is a fictional instance. Among the nonfictional ones may perhaps be reckoned Newman Howard (1861–1929), a London accountant who published three verse tragedies in the first decade of the twentieth century.[27] The second of these, *Savonarola*, bears something more than a casual resemblance to Ladbroke Brown's play of the same name. Apart from the coincidence of title and hero, the two plays are almost equally awkward in their attempts to practice some modulation between exalted flights and colloquial speech in blank verse. The language of Howard's play, like that of Brown's, serves to obscure the characters' motivation without offering the reader any compensation. Like Brown, too, Howard seems to have had little regard for the possibilities of actual production: his stage directions, particularly in crowd scenes, seem especially ludicrous, as in the following examples:

Four barrels are rolled in, marked severally "Pitch," "Oil," "Resin," "Gunpowder."

Sir Max Beerbohm

The murmur of the crowd is suddenly checked by a clap of thunder, whereat the Monks look up as if in appeal to Heaven.[28]

In such instances, and in a few others — such as the extraordinary reversal of passions within a single scene, the interjection of foolish songs to heighten dramatic tension, and the gratuitous allusion to well-known historic personages (Lapo, the pragmatic philosophic villain is made the teacher of Machiavelli, for example) — Howard's play is virtually indistinguishable from Beerbohm's parody. There is, however, no evidence to suggest that Beerbohm either knew of Howard or was acquainted with his play. It is not unreasonable to suppose that he may have come across the title or even the book itself, for *Savonarola* was published during Beerbohm's tenure as drama critic for the *Saturday Review*. And it would be altogether in keeping with the play of Beerbohm's fancy for him to immortalize the imaginary author of a caricature of verse drama while the real author of a seriously intended play of the same name fell into obscurity.

Fortunately our delight in Beerbohm's invention does not depend on our being able to point to a specific original. Any verse play, whether by Shakespeare, Browning, Howard, or Phillips, will do for a reference. Brown's play amuses us in its badness because it is so inert, so wholly the product of imitation and formula. The narrative envelope that surrounds the play, the slenderest of all of the fictions in *Seven Men*, is essential for revealing how inartistic, not merely how inept, Brown's great labor has been. Max practically admits that the reminiscence is but a pretext for printing the unfinished play, but it also provides an explanation of how the play has come into his possession. Max first knew Brown at school, where, tormented for his peculiar Christian name — Ladbroke — chosen by his unimaginative parents from the street on which they lived, he withdrew from the society of his schoolmates to the solitary consolations of literature. Years later Max again encounters him as a confirmed "second-nighter" at London theaters and gradually wins his confidence. Brown has apparently not overcome his isolation. He has become, however, not merely an appreciator but a creator of literature. Over a period of nine years he has labored upon his verse drama, keeping Max abreast of the latest developments — for the play seems to have a life of its own independent of its author — and engaging him in discussions of dramaturgy. When Brown is suddenly knocked down and killed by a passing omnibus, Max finds that he has been named as his friend's literary executor. He has the problem of marketing an unfinished play. After attempting a crude scenario for a fifth act, Max challenges his readers near the end of the narrative to provide a better conclusion: "The writer of the best Fifth Act sent to me shall have his work tacked on to Brown's; and I suppose I could get him a free pass for the second night" (p. 219). Max's ironic suggestion, therefore, is that almost *anyone* can complete Brown's play. Undertaken without a plan, Brown's "Savonarola" is as arbitrary and capricious as Brown's own accidental death. Unlike life, however, true art is purposive. The victim of modern theories, Brown had resigned the authorial function of control: "I gave up my notion of inventing a plot in advance. I thought it would be a mistake. I don't want puppets on wires. I want Savonarola to work out his destiny in his own way" (p. 180). But the more traditional Max finds that the characters, of whose autonomy Brown had assured him, simply will not perform for him. Thus Brown, who has attempted to breathe life into the real but dead personages of history by formula without vision, not only fails to accomplish this task but also exemplifies the futility in his own death. Beerbohm, on the other hand, the practical journalist, given to no high-flown notions about rivaling the Elizabethan masters of poetic drama, succeeds in inventing a memorable personage out of ludicrous fragments. Once again caricature is incarnated by virtue of powerful imagination.

Alone among the fictional heroes of *Seven Men*, James Pethel has no literary propensities whatever. This fact has perhaps contributed to the relatively low regard in which his sketch is held. It is rarely mentioned independently of the others and then only in passing. For the fact of the matter is that literature and the circumstances of its creation are the most congenial and successful of Beerbohm's subjects. As one critic observes: "When [Beerbohm] writes of men of letters — especially of the exquisitely minor men of letters — he is like a man speaking his own language in his own country. When he wanders outside the world of authors he writes under a sense of limitations, like a man venturing into a foreign tongue."[29] But although the portrait is of a nonliterary figure and although it is the earliest and least confident of the sketches, "James Pethel" is of considerable interest as an imaginary reminiscence. For in this narrative, which literally fashions a palpable fiction out of the dry and artless facts of an obituary notice, Beerbohm not only investigates the workings of the nonliterary imagination but also concludes with a triumphant vindication of the literary imagination as the only instrument that can render Pethel intelligible. Max begins the piece as a shy vacationer in Dieppe, awed, as only a man of letters can be, by acquaintance with a man of action. Unlike Soames, Brown, Maltby, or Braxton, Pethel wears no external signs of singularity. "Everything about him, except the amount of money he had been winning, seemed moderate."[30] Yet his extraordinary wealth and luck in investments and gambling have made him into a legend, "a great character." Beerbohm's portrait is an investigation of that character, a substitution of the more rigorous and judicious standards of art in evaluating a life for those that equate greatness with mere celebrity.

Max first notices Pethel at the baccarat table in the casino, into which he has drifted one evening, and is introduced to him through a friend. Although disposed to dislike him for the effortlessness and undemonstrativeness with which he wagers and wins large sums at cards, Max is momentarily beguiled by Pethel's admission that he is a great admirer of Max's work. The reader is at some loss to understand the direction of the narrative, so unlike Beerbohm's other characters is this impassive gambler, unendowed with an apparent *idée fixe*. Indeed, Beerbohm seems conscious of the absence of any strong involvement with his character and floats a hypothetical fiction before us only to burst it before it has traveled very far.

> It flashed across my mind that yonder on the terrace he might suddenly blurt out, "I say, look here, don't think me awfully impertinent, but this money's no earthly use to me: I do wish you'd accept it, as a very small return for all the pleasure your work has given me, and . . . *There!* PLEASE! Not another word!" — all with such candour, delicacy, and genuine zeal that I should be unable

to refuse. But I must not raise false hopes in my reader. Nothing of the sort happened. Nothing of that sort ever does happen. (P. 113)

From their evening's conversation, however, we learn that Pethel is a habitual risk taker, that his pleasure consists in experiencing danger and hazard deliberately and directly, not vicariously. Unlike Max, he employs his imagination to heighten exciting experiences, not to substitute for them or to interpret them. Also unlike Max, Pethel is essentially inarticulate and incommunicative. He represents, therefore, an anti-Max, a being with whom Beerbohm would understandably be fascinated. Invited for a drive and luncheon in Rouen the next day with the Pethels, Max eagerly accepts, ready to penetrate further into the gambler's "character," to learn more of his motivation. He discovers that Pethel's love for his daughter has manifested itself in his encouragement in her of his own traits — she shares his intrepidity and his love of adventure — whereas Mrs. Pethel, with whom Max has no difficulty in identifying, is the most prudent and cautious member of the family. For Max the motoring trip is a series of hairsbreadth escapes from collision, during which he comes to realize that fast driving is for Pethel the equivalent of gambling, with his passengers serving as additional stakes. Having pierced the mystery of the man, Max feels no compunction in refusing to join the Pethels on their motoring tour through France and Switzerland.

At this point Max's active involvement with Pethel breaks off even though the account continues for another two paragraphs, projecting us forward seven years to return to the present time and quoting Pethel's obituary in full. Like that of all of Beerbohm's "heroes," Pethel's demise takes place discreetly, almost anticlimactically, lest attention be diverted from the main concern, Max's interpretation of the event. The conventional expectation is that Pethel, who has lived recklessly, will meet a sudden and violent end. Sudden his end certainly is: the obituary reports the cause of death as apparent heart failure, but the attack ironically is suffered after Pethel has made a successful descent in his airplane following a short but hazardous flight in which he was accompanied by his married daughter and her infant son. It is further reported that Pethel had had a history of heart disease, which Max takes to be the consequence rather than the cause of his behavior.[31] Max's quotation of the obituary notice in its entirety serves three purposes: (1) it provides full information, (2) it serves, he points out in "Pethel" itself, "as an echo and an amplification" of his own remembrance (p. 135), and (3) it underscores the discrepancy between the journalistic and the imaginative responses to a man's life. The last calls for some clarification. We have already noted that Pethel's wealth, his cool-headedness, and his daring had acquired for him considerable celebrity. To his friend Grierson and others Pethel was "a great character," though the case had not been proved to Max's "slower, more literary intelligence" (p. 111). That literary intelligence, too, must have been offended by the application in the obituary notice of the adjective "tragic" to describe Pethel's death. Such indiscriminate use of literary terms obscures rather than clarifies. Only the sensitive imagination, rejecting conventional designations and conventional plots, can provide truly satisfying, revealing, and vivid representations of life. Max's experiences of only one day with him validate James Pethel's existence where the obituary, though it may be filled with more information, does not. Furthermore, the imaginative account, while not shrilly condemnatory, is nevertheless judicial: it suggests that men are responsible for their deeds and that Pethel, in whom imagination served no communicable purpose whatever, grew to depend on it less and less and then employed it only to augment the thrill of risk. Without didacticism Beerbohm causes us to recognize that it is precisely this failure of imagination that leads Pethel from speculation and gambling (in investments and in love, as well as in games at the casino) to motoring and flying, venturing for the greater excitement not only his own life but the lives of others. Pethel is thus denied a heroic death and is shown to be morally reprehensible; his timorous and unadventurous remembrancer survives, converting anecdote into triumph.

In "A. V. Laider" we again return to the issues of "Enoch Soames" — the imposition of vivid, imaginative fabrications for truth, the experience of outrage at the discovering of the fraud, and the sense of one's powerlessness to resist such deception. A significant difference here is that Max allows himself to be the dupe: unwittingly he succumbs to an imagination that he has endowed with force stronger than his own. The story begins with Max's return in midwinter to a rather unfashionable seaside resort hotel, to which he has come, as he did a year before, to convalesce after a bout of influenza. To pass the time before luncheon he peruses the letterboard in the lobby, on which have been posted the unclaimed or otherwise undeliverable letters addressed to patrons of the hotel. He fantasizes a dialogue between a very old and a very young envelope, each vying with the other in its claim to enclose the more poignant and stirring contents. Not only does this dialogue signal us that Max is prepared to entertain some romantic fiction, it also heightens our suspense when he discovers a letter of his own affixed to the board, a letter addressed to Laider. Called to luncheon, Max is unable to retrieve his missive from its frustrating and ignominious captivity. The stage has thus been set for the introduction of Laider as a memory of the past, a memory with a mystery. We have been psychologically conditioned for a fabulous yarn: we long to know what prompted Max to write a letter to a fellow guest at this sleepy hotel and why Laider never received it.

With a reserve typically English neither Beerbohm nor Laider had intruded on the other's privacy the year before even though they were the hotel's only guests. Only on the last evening of Beerbohm's stay, when he entered the smoking room after a late dinner to discover Laider reading a weekly review he had bought the day before, did they have any occasion to speak to each other. Assured by Max's projected departure the next morning that neither need fear any lasting involvement with the other, they fell into easy conversation, first discussing their common ailment and then drifting on to the controversy raging in the correspondence columns of the review, the controversy over the conflict between Faith and Reason. Although Laider handled it with some facility, Max did not feel at home with metaphysical speculation, and to illustrate the distinctness of faith and reason while moving their talk away from abstractions, he adduced palmistry as a science in which he vaguely believed without having any rational basis for his belief. Laider countered by suggesting that he had evidence for the truth of palmistry, however unflattering it might be to our notions of free will. Thus began his tale. As a young man of modest means and uncertain direction, he had made a fairly thorough study of palmistry. He had discovered in examining his own hand that he was to avert meeting a violent death at about the age of twenty-six. Against his better reason, which scoffed at his irrational belief, he became apprehensive as he approached the fateful age. On a railway journey back to town he was prevailed upon to read the palms of five other passengers, who had all been his fellow guests at his uncle's estate in Hampshire. In all of them he detected complete breaks in the lines of life and fate portending imminent disaster, though of course he withheld that information from them. To his horror he suddenly realized that they were all destined to perish in a railway accident from which he would be the lone survivor. Determined to pull the emergency cord, yet unable to do so, Laider next remembered waking up in a hospital, having suffered a concussion. He then learned what he had already foreseen, that the others had all died in the collision of their train with another. Laider then presented himself to Max as a man tormented by guilt: he felt himself a murderer because he had done nothing to prevent their deaths. That he had been *fated* to do nothing did not in any way lessen his feeling of guilt.

It was to allay that feeling that Max, curiously affected by Laider's narration, had written to him from London: "How was Laider to be sure that his brain, recovering from concussion, had *remembered* what happened in the course of that railway-journey? How was he to know that his brain hadn't simply, in its abeyance, *invented* all this for him? It might be that he had never seen those signs in those hands."[32] Such were the contents of the letter that now, after his meal, Max means to reclaim. Approaching the letterboard, however, he discovers the letter gone — picked up by Laider himself, whom Max sights walking along the beach. Like Beerbohm, Laider is again a convalescent from influenza. The letter, far from having the effect that Max had intended, has had just the opposite. Laider is now plunged into a guilt far more profound than before: he confesses to Max that the whole story was an invention — an improvisation at that — stimulated by nothing more than the random turns the conversation had taken at their last meeting. Laider is now ashamed and mortified by his deliberate deception, the product, he claims, of too strong an imagination. Normally his will can check the excesses of this faculty; but when his will is weakened, as it is by influenza, his imagination is unrestrained and he imposes the most preposterous tales on friends and acquaintances alike. He suggests to Max, therefore, that since he is still in a somewhat debilitated state, in order to avoid another manifestation of this tendency, they keep apart from each other, reinstituting their civil isolation of the year before. Although it momentarily occurs to Max that Laider's explanation and recommendation may be but an elaborate artifice for avoiding his company, he consents to the arrangement, proposing only that, as in the previous year, they converse on the last night. Once again their talk is desultory until Laider seizes upon a subject that Max has casually introduced — sea gulls. Slowly he begins the sinister incantation that promises a tale of terror. But this time we do not hear the story. Max breaks it off before it actually gets going, assuring us, "It was a very awful thing indeed" (p. 171).

Of all the seven men (and the two others as well), A. V. Laider is the least realized as a character. His propensity for inventing extraordinarily moving tales about himself is certainly well exemplified, but the reader develops only an intellectual, not a physical, perspective on him. This limitation was apparently true for Beerbohm himself, for the two caricatures he drew of Laider are greatly unlike each other.[33] We have in "A. V. Laider" less a portrait of a man than an occasion for the elucidation of what we have come to appreciate as one of Beerbohm's favorite themes. The sketch amounts to another consideration of the relationship between the actual world and the imaginative world. The debate in the weekly review, which "meant nothing whatsoever" to Beerbohm because of its abstraction, spills over into the talk of the two convalescents. Laider's tale, because of its vitality and its appeal to human emotions, concretizes the issues of free will and determinism and brings Max to serious reflection as no mere philosophical argument could. The power of imagination, both in Laider (who is practically a victim of his) and in Max (who responds sympathetically), is profound, transforming a dreary and deserted hotel in winter into a theater of thrills. The larger story reveals yet another characteristic of imagination; namely, it is unified and atemporal, indifferent to the categories by which the actual world distinguishes its manifestations. There is no substantial difference, Max's experience with Laider suggests, between reminiscence, prophecy, and invention. Vividness is all. Laider is therefore not a liar but another of Max's artists *manqués*. If "Savonarola" Brown's failure lay in the absence of imagination, Laider's lies in the superabundance of it, descending upon him unbidden, venting itself in undisciplined improvisations rather than in artistic compositions. As in the other sketches, it remains for Max to clean things up, to place a frame around the picture and to hang it, so to speak. Although he has been duped once, and nearly twice, Max has the last word.

Although Beerbohm authorized the inclusion of "Felix Argallo and Walter Ledgett" in the 1950 edition of *Seven Men*, strictly speaking to discuss it here is inappropriate. Composed ten years after the last of the original sketches, this piece not only falls outside the span of the golden decade (1911–1920) of Beerbohm's maturity but is also decidedly different in tone from the earlier portraits. The original title of the work, "Not That I Would Boast," conveys that tone far better than the present one, for the emphasis really is on Max here, a Max much more self-assured, proud, and cynical than we have known him, a magician of reminiscence who finally and rather unprofessionally reveals to his audience how he performs his tricks. Like Chaucer's Pardoner, he is a spellbinder — an imposer upon men's imaginations — who cannot refrain from congratulating himself on his own cleverness. Yet because "Argallo and Ledgett" conforms in its external characteristics to the earlier form and because it is studded with echoes and allusions to those earlier works, the portraits it contains are not really all that out of place as the "two others" among the original seven men. But clearly the composition itself must stand last among the sketches, the ultimate variation on the theme, for it impeaches the very genre of literary reminiscence.

Like the other double portrait in *Seven Men*, "Argallo and Ledgett" conjoins two antithetical literary types in an improbable relationship. In "Maltby and Braxton," however, it was the caprice of popular literary fashion that yoked together the dandy and the *enfant terrible*, yoked them together so forcibly that neither could survive without the other. In "Argallo and Ledgett" Max himself not only effects the association but is responsible as well for establishing the reputation of both writers, using the fame of one to launch that of the other. Felix Argallo, a novelist and translator of Spanish extraction, led a solitary and reclusive life until taken up by Max and his friends, whose public-relations efforts bring about Argallo's sudden burst into celebrity. Belying his Christian name, Argallo displays sadness as his prevailing emotion, pity as his ruling passion. Once elevated by the press to public acclaim, his somber works, like the fatal charms of Zuleika Dobson, drive hordes to suicide. The effect of this fame on Argallo himself is to convert his stoicism into self-pity. It is partially as a therapeutic act, to redirect Argallo's pity to a more appropriate object, that Max prevails upon him to write a series of letters that will have the effect of raising the esteem in which another of Max's literary acquaintances, Walter Ledgett, is held. Ledgett, a bubbly, affable *littérateur*, a writer of slight plays, novels, and literary journalism, in addition to being the constant victim of good-natured but nevertheless wounding hoaxes, had increasingly suffered the posthumous slights of the mighty. Year after year, as the inhumation of a literary giant was inevitably succeeded by the exhumation of his literary remains, Ledgett found himself depreciated in the published correspondence. Stevenson, Patmore, Henry Irving, Meredith — the death of each, Max came to feel, had merely become the occasion of another belittling reference to Ledgett. Beerbohm lovingly reproduces extracts from these letters, parodying the original writers as he had done in "The Mirror of the Past" when he allowed Herringham to become the butt of Carlyle and Whistler. Deploring the unfairness of these bolts hurled by the dead against the living and priding himself on his powers as a literary manipulator, Max conceives a bold plan to raise Ledgett's stature by having him extolled by the now eminent Argallo. That the two men do not actually know each other does not hinder the project — it is enough that each of them knows Max, who thereby becomes a credible recipient for Argallo's adulatory and solicitous references to Ledgett. Excited to pity Ledgett, Argallo not only writes the predated letters at Max's dictation (including one that hints at an unfortunate romantic attachment between Ledgett and a mysterious woman), he actually commits suicide in order to accelerate their publication and thus be of greater service to Ledgett. This unforeseen but not unwelcome development forces Max in turn to speed up the next phase of the plan, that of convincing Walter Ledgett that all the details of his meetings and conversations with Argallo that would appear in the letters were true but had been blotted out of his recollection by selective amnesia. And since it was ultimately to be made authoritative by appearing in print, Ledgett comes round to accepting Max's version of his life in preference to his own remembrance of it. It is more vivid and more interesting — "stranger," says Ledgett, "than anything I could have imagined."[34]

In due course, along with a collected edition of Argallo's *Works,* the *Life and Letters* is published; Max is delighted to find that "by several critics the four letters addressed to myself were singled out as among the most characteristic and the best" (p. 262; p. 188). As expected, Ledgett's reputation rises; honors accrue to him — and profits — although he appears to respond to them somewhat surlily, as if collecting wages long overdue rather than in gratitude for good fortune. Nor have Max's labors on Ledgett's behalf been altogether disinterested. Laying up in anticipation of the boom "two 'clean copies' of the first edition of everything he had proliferated" (pp. 264–265; p. 190), Max awaits the propitious moment to unload his wares. The Great War severely depresses the market for things of the mind, yet even after the armistice Max forebears. Ten years later, after attending a memorial service for Ledgett in Westminster Abbey, Beerbohm believes the time is right. He arranges to display his stock to a prominent American "magnoperator," an agent for collectors of first editions. Although somewhat disappointed that there no longer seems to be much call for Argallo firsts, or even for the autograph letters, Max gleefully accepts nine hundred pounds for his Ledgett collection, the scourings of Charing Cross Road, whose inflated value is wholly the product of his own manipulations. That the magnoperator might realize a profit of a like sum in the resale does not trouble Max: he trusts

Felix Argallo and Walter Ledgett. Courtesy of the William Andrews Clark Memorial Library, University of California, Los Angeles.

that the revelations in his pages will effect a suitable readjustment of the market price of Ledgett firsts. In this most sardonic of his ironies of the artist as a producer of marketable goods, Beerbohm demonstrates a practical application of the literary imagination.

To those moderately familiar with Beerbohm's career, "Argallo and Ledgett" reverberates with echoes from the past. Max's dutiful pilgrimages to Penge to visit the retiring Argallo remind one of his similar journeys to Putney to meet Swinburne. The crude hucksterism of George Batford, Argallo's nephew and executor, who rushes into print with his ill-composed *Life and Letters,* recalls Beerbohm's distaste for Hall Caine, who moved in on Rossetti in his last months and churned out his *Recollections of Dante Gabriel Rossetti* within a year of the artist-poet's death. A quotation illustrating Batford's graceless style, particularly with its reference to "the English-speaking public both of the British Empire and America," summons up Caine's appearance as Rossetti's companion in "The Mirror of the Past" (p. 262; p. 188; see above, Chapter 4). Similarly Ledgett's decline of an honorary degree from Oxford in 1907 brings to mind one of Beerbohm's most accomplished group caricatures. Outraged at what he considered the unworthiness of the degree recipients in 1907, Beerbohm envisioned the "Encaenia of 1908" (HD 386) as a convocation honoring a preposterous assortment of candidates, including the hapless Hall Caine, the constant butt of Beerbohm's ridicule. These enriching associations, however, cannot efface the mocking cynicism in Max's self-portrait here. Gone is the *eiron* of "Enoch Soames," "Maltby and Braxton," and "'Savonarola' Brown." In this sketch Max divests himself of any residual deference to his heroes, appearing instead as one coolly in control, a manager of literary reputations, a speculator in literary investments. To be sure, the figure of Max here is recognizably conformable to the naive and immature Max of the earlier sketches, but there is a coldness in Max's attitude toward both Felix Argallo and Walter Ledgett, almost a contempt for them, whereas toward the original six, however ludicrous their postures or absurd their pretensions, there had been a measure of compassion. That since 1917 Beerbohm himself had become a commodity on the literary stock market, that he was being collected as well as pirated, may extenuate somewhat the move from Soho to the Exchange, the displacement of the aesthetic by the commercial outlook. But to imply, as Beerbohm appears to, that the public acclaim accorded men of letters both during and after their lifetimes is a thing independent of true worth, wholly the consequence of fashion and manipulation, can only discredit the whole artistic enterprise. "Argallo and Ledgett" leaves us with a particularly nasty aftertaste.

Technically "Argallo and Ledgett" is an ingenious variation on the imaginary reminiscence, for Max succeeds not only in implanting reminiscences in others — by working upon Argallo's better nature and Ledgett's worse — but also in equipping them with a timed-release feature. Both physically and temporally he removes himself as the apparent agent in nothing less than the rewriting of biography and criticism. Thematically, too, in its examination of the nature of literary fame "Argallo and Ledgett" recalls the earlier tales of *Seven Men*. Yet the Beerbohm of later middle age has become more introspective, less observant of the performance of others. Soames and Brown were incarnated for us by their compositions, Maltby by his fastidious self-consciousness. But here we have no more basis for accepting Argallo's presumed merit than for Ledgett's supposedly obvious worthlessness. The plot is more masterfully contrived than anything else in *Seven Men;* yet there is a failure of real vision. The hollowness of reputation is asserted, but the demonstration is almost mathematical. The passage of years, his isolation from the contemporary literary scene, and his general disenchantment with what the world had become in the twentieth century had made of Beerbohm a spectator even more remote than hitherto. The conception in "Argallo and Ledgett" is as keen as ever; the intensity, however, is diminished.

In *Seven Men* Beerbohm perfected the imaginary reminiscence in prose, creating for himself a narrative vehicle for the realization of his satiric and ironic propensities, a vehicle, moreover, that would minimize or disguise his limitations. In it he could freely record his own responses to his characters without apology and without elaborate artifice. He could write about the only world of affairs he ever really knew, the literary world (a world virtually without women), and could do so without the appearance of narrowness or parochialism. He could deal in caricatures without being frivolous, could push parody beyond facetiousness, and could invest his fantasies with earnestness. The accomplishment, however, is worthy of study in a larger context. Beerbohm's imaginary reminiscences constitute a series of experiments in the fusion and confusion of real and imaginary worlds. Long regarded as a pleasant and diverting backwater to the mainstream of literature flowing through the works of Woolf and Joyce, Beerbohm's channel can now be seen to run parallel to the course of such writers as Nabokov and Borges. And, in an ironic way, T. K. Nupton's judgment of Beerbohm is correct: beneath the immediate satire there is a residue of sensitive social observation. Few writers have explored as penetratingly as Beerbohm the conflicting roles of the writer in the modern world: the writer as artist, seer, celebrity, and producer of consumer goods.

CHAPTER VI

Rossetti and His Circle

The drawings that constitute *Rossetti and His Circle* developed, as we have seen, out of Beerbohm's intense research into the careers and personalities of the Pre-Raphaelites, an involvement necessitated by his work on "The Mirror of the Past." As that project became more and more unmanageable and as the impulse to draw manifested itself ever more strongly in the pages of the manuscript, Beerbohm began to transfer his invented anecdotes from one medium to another. This essentially literary rather than pictorial genesis of *Rossetti and His Circle* may occasionally overwhelm us, particularly when a drawing is accompanied by an elaborate caption, as in "George Meredith's Hortation" (pl. 13; HD 1274; BLC 46)[1] or "George Augustus Sala with Rossetti" (pl. 16; HD 1358); in such instances we recognize that the dialogue is far more incisive than the accompanying visual scene. For the most part, however, as with the best of Beerbohm's caricatures generally, drawing and caption reinforce each other. But the basic problem of "The Mirror of the Past," how to bring the fragments into some narrative coherence, though it might be mitigated by concentrating on the fictional adventures of actual people and by shearing away the less tractable parts — Herringham, the mirror, its images from the eighteenth and early nineteenth centuries — was not to be overcome by a mere switch from pen to pencil and brush. It is quite probable that, like *Seven Men, Rossetti and His Circle* was originally conceived in parts and only subsequently forged into a unified work. If Beerbohm initially thought of it as a book, it is

Sir Max Beerbohm

likely that he thought of it as resembling *The Poets' Corner,* unified by no more than its scrutiny of a group of artists but hardly a composition with a beginning, a middle, and an end, out of which one might educe a theme. As late as 1922, the very year of the publication of the reproductions in book form, the caricaturist Bohun Lynch, who wrote the first full-length study of Max, while recognizing that collectively the drawings are "a profound study of the period, the result of the most enthusiastic research, the 'finishing course' for any neophyte desiring initiation into the mysteries of Pre-Raphaelitism,"[2] still speaks of them as a series of discrete water colors on exhibition rather than as a single work.

There were in fact two exhibitions of these drawings before their publication in book form, one at a Modern Loan Exhibition at the Grosvenor Gallery in November 1917, where fifteen of them (all dated 1916) were shown, and another of the full set of twenty-three at the Leicester Galleries in September 1921.[3] The quality of the additional drawings (dated 1917) is not easily distinguishable from that of the original group — they fit in quite readily with the others — yet they seem to have been composed to fill out the design. Having drawn the original batch out of inspiration and the fullness of his Rossettian studies, Max may have felt the need for thematic, if not biographical, completeness in executing the later drawings. New and peripheral characters to the circle are delineated: Coventry Patmore, Thomas Woolner, John Morley, John Stuart Mill, and Christina Rossetti herself. We may even conjecture some other triggers for these drawings. In the scene, for example, of Gabriel exhorting Christina to adopt a livelier mode of dress (pl. 12; HD 1278; BLC 45), two gray figures amid a riot of colorful and patterned silks draped over chairs, Max alludes in the caption to "that new shop in Regent's Street." The theme of the drawing, of course, here reduced to a humorous domestic situation, is Rossetti's endeavor to realize in life the richness of his sister's poetic imagination. But the reference to the shop and the invention of the anecdotal scene itself may have been suggested to Max by notices of the death, in May 1917, of Sir Arthur Lasenby Liberty, the founder of the great emporium of oriental silks. Similarly, the inspired but wholly apocryphal introduction of Mill to Gabriel by

Morley (pl. 18; HD 1280; BLC 60) may have been touched off, as was the parody of Morley in another conjectural encounter with Rossetti, by the publication of his *Recollections* in the same year.[4] Less illustrative of the actual circumstances of Rossetti's life, these drawings tend to emphasize the significance of that life — in short, to convert visual anecdote into a form of interpretation. That Beerbohm recognized that he had, in fact, produced a volume rather than merely another album is evidenced by the section entitled "Note" that prefaces the book. In it he justifies his turning away from the present to caricature the men of the past, suggests the romantic appeal of his subject, and pleads that irreverence is not incompatible with admiration. Although not the only preface to a book of his caricatures (there is a mock apologetic "Epistle Dedicatory to Britannia" in *A Survey* and a lengthy dedication to Gosse in *Observations*), Max's prefatory note to *Rossetti and His Circle* is the clearest statement he ever wrote of the serious purpose of his art and a defense of his way of seeing as a way of knowing. Unlike the callow mocker of *The Poets' Corner*, Beerbohm presents himself in *Rossetti and His Circle* as a uniquely qualified biographer and cultural historian.

Whatever may have prompted the drawing of particular scenes, the entire series was executed in 1916–1917 while Max and Florence were staying at a cottage on the farm of Will Rothenstein in Gloucestershire. Both Will and his son have recorded their impressions of that time, particularly how Max, elegantly attired — though life in the country in wartime was rather informal — would trudge daintily through the snow to take his meals at the main house with his portfolio of drawings clutched tightly under his arm, so fearful was he of letting them out of his sight.[5] At this time Beerbohm was also working on "Maltby and Braxton" and "'Savonarola' Brown," and it is tempting to think that the extraordinary productivity of this period was due in no small measure to the wider and more critical response of the Rothensteins at Far Oakridge than the appreciative but limited audience of one at Rapallo. For Will and his wife Alice were not merely old friends but resources as well. Although no older than Max, Will had burst into prominence even earlier than he and had introduced him to the London art world of the nineties. Many of the friendships thus formed were of value to Max in gathering information about Rossetti. Will also offered him much technical advice and encouragement as an artist.[6] Alice Rothenstein, moreover, was the daughter of Walter John Knewstub, who had been Gabriel Rossetti's assistant in the sixties. Whether she was actually able to supply Max with anecdotal material to be transformed into caricature is unknown, but in her Max could find yet another link with the romantic past.

It would be a mistake, however, to suppose that *Rossetti and His Circle* was shaped by Max's unique access to intimate Rossettiana. The recollections of Watts-Dunton may have inspired him, as those of Gosse may have sustained him, and he acknowledged both by literally putting them in the picture.[7] For the most part, the apparently intimate glimpses in *Rossetti and His Circle* derive from his unconventional use of readily available materials. Out of Treffry Dunn's sketch of Gabriel's unfinished fresco at Oxford, Beerbohm creates a work in progress as background to a classic, though wholly imaginary, confrontation between Rossetti and Jowett (pl. 4; HD 837). Old photographs suggest not only features but postures, and the Pre-Raphaelite paintings themselves influence the hues of Beerbohm's water colors. Tedious and self-aggrandizing memoirs become for Beerbohm a source not merely of information but of attitude: "William Bell Scott wondering what it is those fellows seem to see in Gabriel" (p. 14; HD 1276) does not merely portray an onlooker but reveals a man disturbed by the undervaluation of himself implied by the adulation of Rossetti. And the large drawing entitled "Ford Madox Brown being patronised by Holman Hunt" (pl. 10; HD 185) probably derives less from a specific locus than from the general uneasiness these two artists felt toward each other as publicly revealed through books. Rossetti had applied to become a student to each of them, and the "PRB" designation clung to all three. When Gabriel passed into legend and the records of the middle decades of the nineteenth century came to be written up, the controversy over who influenced whom broke out in print, William Michael Rossetti, the historian of the Pre-Raphaelite Brotherhood, citing Brown's diaries and being challenged by Hunt in his *Pre-Raphaelitism and the Pre-Raphaelite Brotherhood*. Beerbohm has distilled the essence of the situation from its accidents: *amour propre* wounded by the lash of supposedly disinterested criticism.

The attraction that the figure of Rossetti exerted upon Beerbohm's imagination was generated from many sources. Beerbohm's isolation from the contemporary literary and art worlds, and particularly the stagnation of activity in those worlds during the war, made it quite reasonable for him to turn his glance backward in time. But it does not quite explain why he extended it so far back, nor why it lingered so searchingly on a single man. Part of the appeal of history for Max was that it was uncluttered by the superfluous and dull people that surround one in ordinary life. He did not doubt that such people existed in all times. But the historian, if he could not clarify the drama of events, could at least simplify the *dramatis personae,* reduce them to a manageable number. Something of this process takes place in Beerbohm's maturing vision of Rossetti. Max had demonstrated crude curiosity about the myth that had sprung up about the man in his depiction in *The Poets' Corner* of the menagerie of people and animals in the back garden of Tudor House, Rossetti's home in Chelsea for nearly twenty years (HD 1268; BLC 49). But in 1904 Max had seen only "the silver thread of lunacy"; by 1916 he saw it as part of "the rich golden fabric of 16 Cheyne Walk."[8]

Whatever Rossetti may have come to represent for Beerbohm, I think it likely that a measure of personal identification may have provided, if not the foundation, then the scaffolding of *Rossetti and His Circle*. Temperamentally, of course, the two men were leagues apart. Rossetti was a Braxton to Beerbohm's Maltby. Max could never inhabit the sensuous dream world of Gabriel. Yet in their artistic independence, their indifference to fashions and schools, and their single-minded devotion to the elucidation of a personal rather than a public vision (quite unlike Maltby and Braxton), one may discern a basic affinity. Gabriel, like Max, had alternated between visual and verbal art, achieving distinction in the former, despite severe technical limitations, almost wholly by the intensity of his vision. In each man the two careers were complementary; in each, too, the fame appears to reside less in the specific achievements in these media than in the general outlook those achievements convey. Rossetti was hardly an inspiration for Beerbohm or a model to emulate. But there was a fundamental sympathy between them. To Rossetti, moreover, Beerbohm ascribed some of his own almost mystical fascination with mirrors. In the manuscript notes to the hardly begun novel are the following jottings: "Rossetti (unlike Morris) *loved mirror* — had some like it — The only artist among mirrors — emphasizing and attenuating — always a composition — *Rondure* — the aim of all art — Said all paintings ought to be round — (or oval) — S. [winburne] used to speak of him as the dear great *cyclolatrist*."[9] Clearly Rossetti had become for Beerbohm something of a self-projection.

In another regard as well Beerbohm may have identified with Rossetti, whom he characterizes as an exotic alien, neither wholly foreign nor wholly assimilable. In origin three-quarters Italian, a translator of Dante and other Italian poets, Rossetti had never traveled on the Continent beyond France and the Low Countries. He regarded himself as a thorough Englishman, though it is obvious from his paintings that he inhabited a land quite removed from the Victorian London in which he lived. About Beerbohm too, apart from his parentage, there clung something ineradicably foreign. In attitude and demeanor no one could have been more British; yet he chose to live more than half his life outside England (in Italy, ironically enough, though he never learned the language, nor do the land and its people figure in his work), and neither of his Jewish wives were English. One feels that a very sensitive nerve has been touched in his drawing "British Stock and Alien Inspiration" (pl. 1; HD 776), one of the later drawings for the series. In terms of visual art it is one of Beerbohm's least inspired inventions, for it employs pictorial symmetry and similarity purely to make an explicit intellectual statement. But the statement is so cogent, so full of implication, that Max is to be forgiven for composing this editorial. The drawing consists of six male figures disposed as follows: four converse in pairs in the center background, the two larger ones in the foreground stand facing away from each other at the left and right of the picture. The foreground figures are readily identifiable as Disraeli (left) and Rossetti (right), though they have been depicted almost as mirror images. They are

Rossetti and His Circle

dressed similarly and each bears himself in a round-shouldered slouch, pensively resting his chin between thumb and index finger. Even their dark hair, though of different shades, is of the same shape and texture, and Disraeli's unruly forelock is duplicated by an equally unmanageable curl hanging over the nape of Rossetti's neck. Not only are the two comparable, they are markedly dissimilar from the erect, hands-behind-the-back, auburn-haired observers who are commenting upon them. One pair is facing each of the major figures and discoursing about him, though the comments, as the caption makes clear, are identical for each. The pair on the left scrutinizing Disraeli are top hatted and side whiskered, identified as First and Second County Members. The pair of artists on the right, mirroring the poses and garb of the politicians, differing from them only in their hatlessness and clean-shavenness (even the faces, though lightly sketched, are identical) are labeled Holman Hunt and John Millais. Their dialogue is represented as follows:

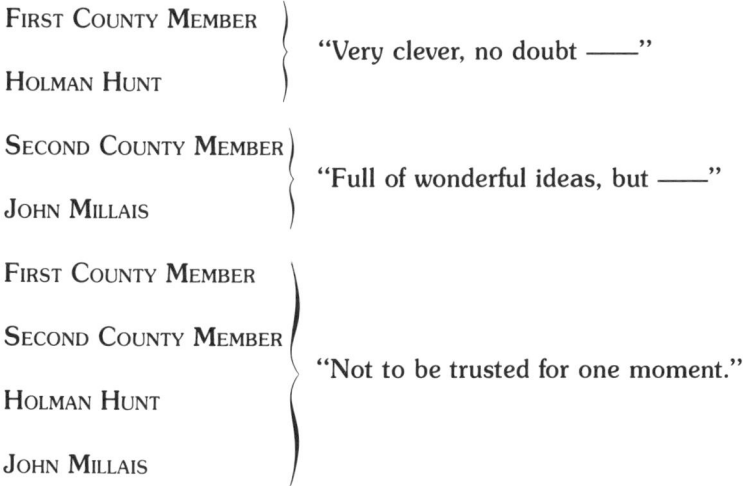

FIRST COUNTY MEMBER / HOLMAN HUNT } "Very clever, no doubt ——"

SECOND COUNTY MEMBER / JOHN MILLAIS } "Full of wonderful ideas, but ——"

FIRST COUNTY MEMBER / SECOND COUNTY MEMBER / HOLMAN HUNT / JOHN MILLAIS } "Not to be trusted for one moment."

Beerbohm's point is that the conservative establishment of the art world is no different from that of the political world. Both are suspicious of innovation, particularly if the source seems at all foreign. That Disraeli became prime minister and that Rossetti, in the public consciousness at any rate, came to be regarded as

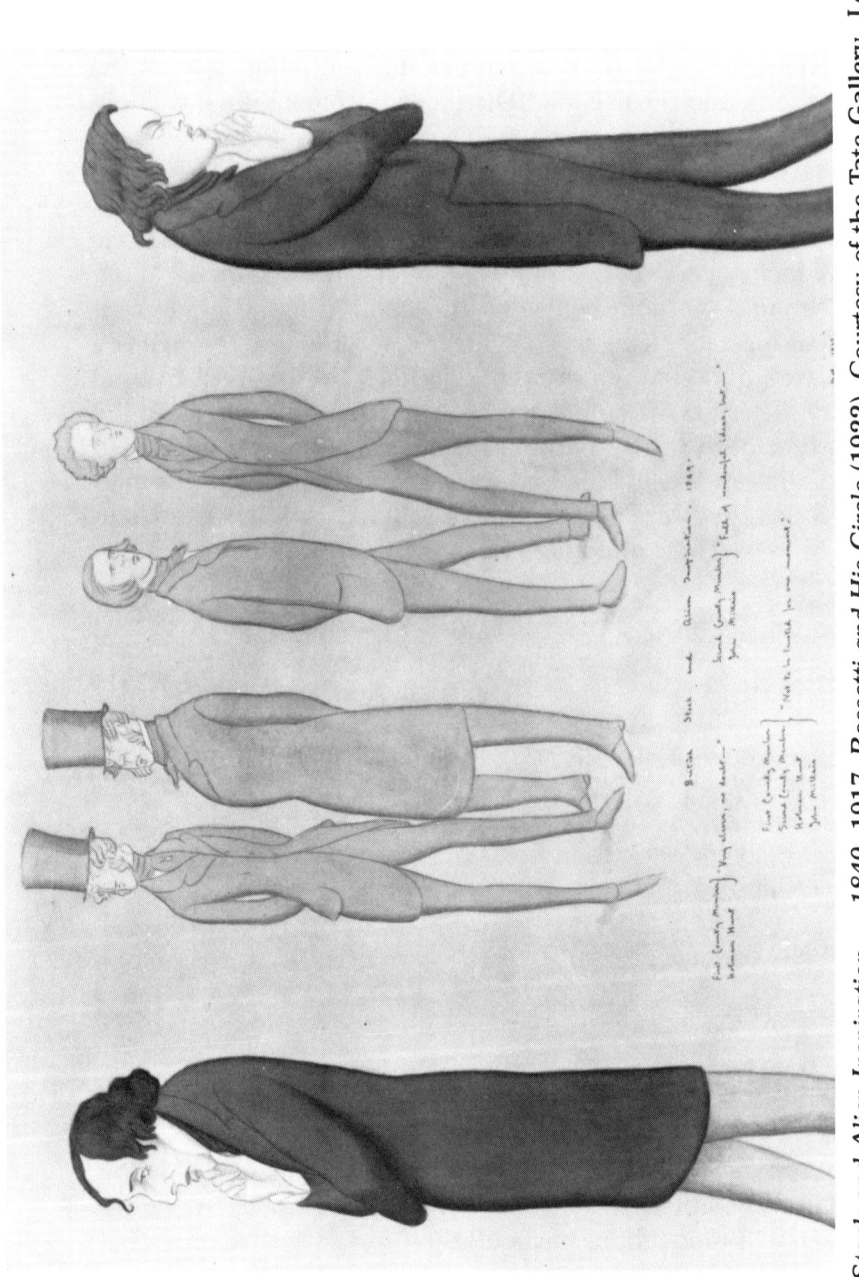

British Stock and Alien Inspiration — 1849. 1917. Rossetti and His Circle (1922). Courtesy of the Tate Gallery, London.

the leader of the Pre-Raphaelite Brotherhood in no way diminish the hostility of the native for the exotic. Grudging admiration rather than acceptance, even from those most closely associated with them, was the response of Victorian England to these flamboyant adventurers of self-expression.

"British Stock and Alien Inspiration" is too cerebral and abstract to be considered an imaginary reminiscence. It states rather than implies, presents a situation that is virtually allegorical rather than one that could conceivably have taken place in real life. As one of the additional drawings done in 1917 and placed first in the volume (after the frontispiece), however, it serves to integrate the more anecdotal members of the series and to alert the observer to the themes he may encounter in them. For however much *Rossetti and His Circle* may appear to address itself to the cognoscenti, providing them with hypothetical gossip about a legendary figure, its real subjects, like those of *Seven Men,* are the tensions between the artist and his society. By introducing Rossetti as he does, Beerbohm marks him for a particular role as a brilliant enchanter, subversive of the established order of things. In the subsequent drawings he will appear as either isolated from the concerns of the everyday world or resisting their allurements, constructing an alternative world of his imagination and drawing others (in both senses of the word) into it. Beerbohm's admiration for — or rather, wonder at — Rossetti resides less in what he actually accomplished than in what he signified both to his own and to later generations. A definition of that signification had never emerged from the mass of memoirs, biographies, and journals that had been compiled about Rossetti. In this most enterprising venture into imaginary reminiscence Beerbohm chose to illustrate a personal interpretation of the past. That his vision has imposed itself as memorable and "true" for over half a century is testimony to its vitality; Beerbohm accomplished what Watts-Dunton, who knew Rossetti intimately, had failed to do: he made Gabriel come alive.

Rossetti and His Circle is not only the most ambitious but also the most accomplished of Beerbohm's graphic works. Bohun Lynch writes glowingly of the maturation "in these caricatures [of] Max's technique in actual drawing, in composition, and in the use of colour."[10] Yet, however more elaborate and painstaking the design and execution of these pictures, and despite the fact that the set is a proud possession of the Tate Gallery (though not on permanent exhibition), it would be absurd to maintain that the appeal of the series is fundamentally aesthetic or that Beerbohm does or should occupy a significant place in the history of twentieth-century art. If in the following discussion there is some borrowing of the language of art critics and historians, then it is for a purely descriptive end, to demonstrate how a nonverbal medium is employed for purposes essentially literary. In *Rossetti and His Circle* Beerbohm tried to invest caricature with all the subtlety and nuance of his prose. One does indeed study these pictures more intently than his other drawings, but it is the intellect rather than the heart that responds to them.

The first thing that impresses the viewer of the originals of *Rossetti and His Circle* is their size. One expects, of course, that reproductions will be smaller, but one expects also that the scale of reduction will be more or less consistent. Reproduction has given all of them nearly the same dimensions, but the originals vary from two to three times the size of the reproduced plates. The largest of the pictures (15¾ inches by 14½ inches) is the last one in the volume (pl. 22; HD 1784; BLC 55), the one of Oscar Wilde uttering the name of Dante Gabriel Rossetti "for the first time in the United States of America," and it is more than twice the size of "Rossetti's Courtship" (pl. 2; HD 1270; BLC 41), which appears quite early in the sequence. No great principle seems to govern the variation in size, but in many instances considerable detail has been lost through reproduction, detail that contributes significantly to meaning. In all instances the diminution in size obscures Max's precision in drawing not caricatures but miniature portrait faces for his principal characters. Only through study of the originals can one appreciate fully how Beerbohm has transcended physiognomical distortion as a means of conveying his irony. The color of the originals is no less arresting. Rarely in Beerbohm's work is color applied with much greater attention to its overall effect than it is to a political map, but here, as Felstiner observes, "the complete watercoloring . . . romanticizes Rossetti's milieu. Two colors, gold and blue, suffuse these drawings with life. They were important in

Pre-Raphaelite painting, and predominate throughout *Rossetti and His Circle* almost as motifs for Arcadian vividness and innocence."[11] Green and russet also figure largely, the latter in varying intensity applied as the color of men's hair and beards, contrasting strongly with the drab aspect of their clothing. Rossetti's dress is generally nondescript, if not shabby, set off by the flashy vulgarity of George Augustus Sala (pl. 16; HD 1358) or the dapper elegance of Frederic Leighton, soon to be elected president of the Royal Academy (pl. 19; HD 919). Rossetti himself is colorless but is surrounded by worlds of brilliance, either that purchased by material success or that far grander one summoned into being by the imagination. Beerbohm conveys the sense of both by his use of color. Moreover, Beerbohm is more confident technically in these pictures: he avoids the ink highlighting of the quite successful water colors he executed earlier in the decade, relying here only on pencil and brush to achieve effects of texture and shading. The result is a more masterful and subdued statement, richer and less obvious than that of his other caricatures.

Ironically it was this very technical proficiency that caused some to wonder whether Beerbohm had come to retreat from caricature, if not to abandon it altogether. Lynch cites the career of Leslie Ward (Spy) as an instance of the disastrous consequence of growing experience on a caricaturist who begins as a poor draftsman.[12] As his representational technique improves and as the crudeness of design falls away, as they are almost bound to do through constant practice, the satiric edge may become blunt. What began as caricature dissolves into portraiture. Lynch does not go so far as to say that this has actually happened to Beerbohm; yet the descent of Ward from mockery to harmlessness is clearly linked to greater attention to technique, and the tale is quite cautionary. What Lynch fails to observe, however, is that broad caricature is inappropriate in dealing with subjects who are dead since they cannot, properly speaking, be satirized at all. They can, however, be treated ironically, and for such treatment a touch of portraiture is far from amiss. The art critic Thomas Craven raised a more serious objection to *Rossetti and His Circle* when it appeared in book form.

Artistically the volume differs little from its predecessors. The drawing is more fluid and certain; the handling of line less ragged and amateurish; and the color harmonious and charming; but in many respects the work is more nearly allied with the modern pictorial cartoon than with caricature. The episodes unfold in a manner quite similar to the comic strip. To be sure the wit is highly refined, and the properties chosen with literary insight and exquisite taste — but there is the fat Rossetti, the protagonist of a comic sequence. This affinity not only explains the secret of Beerbohm's appeal, but also defines his position as an artist.[13]

The charge is one that must be answered, for Craven's criticism not only isolates Beerbohm's work from true caricature but also denies it a place even as minimal art. To create a comic strip, however witty or urbane, is no singular achievement. It is quite true that the individual pictures of *Rossetti and His Circle* do act as frames in a narrative sequence, much like the drawings in a comic strip. But it is also true that, although a series, the pictures make abundant sense as discrete entities. Moreover, the character of the protagonist of Beerbohm's "comic strip" is not static. Rossetti is not simply the fat man garbed in black who appears in each frame. Unlike Dick Tracy or Little Orphan Annie, who are unaffected by time or experience and who change neither their expressions nor their clothes, Rossetti evidences growth and alteration. One can discern, for example, a difference between his somnolent spiritual passion for Elizabeth Siddal (pl. 2; HD 1270; BLC 41) and his more physical infatuation for Fanny Cornforth (pl. 7; HD 1272; BLC 42). And there is a deepening of theme, not simply a march of chronological time, as one works through the sequence. Nevertheless, by the very establishment of a hero, of a figure whose character is somewhat predetermined and does not reside completely in his immediate pictorial presentment, Max exposes himself to the fundamental artistic sin to which the comic strip artist is prone, that of making the picture wholly subservient to the text. In at least one drawing, that of Leighton suggesting to Rossetti that he become a candidate for election to the Royal Academy (pl. 19; HD 919), the picture is almost intrusive. The effect does not depend on the graphic contrast between the worldly success of Leighton and the artistic purity of Rossetti. Indeed, only the feet

The sole remark likely to have been made by Benjamin Jowett about the mural paintings at the Oxford Union. 1916.
Rossetti and His Circle (1922). Courtesy of the Tate Gallery, London.

Design for Oxford Union: *Lancelot at the Shrine of the Sanc Greal*. Copy by H. Treffry Dunn. H. C. Marillier, *Dante Gabriel Rossetti: An Illustrated Memorial of his Art and Life*. London, 1904.

of Rossetti appear in the picture — at the end of a divan, literally slip shod, with a hole in the heel of one sock. This economy of pictorial expression is compensated for by the extraordinary length of the legend, over three hundred words, consisting of Leighton's self-exonerating harangue. This drawing works much like a Jules Feiffer cartoon, the humor owing next to nothing to its pictorial component. Another of the series, "The Touch of a Vanished Hand" (pl. 21; HD 369), appears to allude to the forgeries of Rossetti's paintings made and sold by Howell and his friend Rosa Corder, but neither picture nor text is clear enough to permit one to savor the irony of Max's invocation of the tag from Tennyson. But these are virtually the only lapses among the twenty-three drawings in which picture and text do not reinforce each other.

That Beerbohm moved away from pure caricature in *Rossetti and His Circle* is undeniable. But he did so for the same reason that he moved away from the realm of pure fantasy in *Zuleika Dobson* to the plausible world of *Seven Men,* with its mingling of actual and invented persons: to invest a real world with imaginative intensity. In the confrontation of Jowett and Rossetti at the Oxford Union (pl. 4; HD 837), an anecdote whose invention Max openly acknowledges by titling the picture "The sole remark likely to have been made by Benjamin Jowett about the mural paintings at the Oxford Union," that likelihood is confirmed by the careful attention paid to the background. Rossetti's mural of Sir Lancelot and his vision of the Grail had, of course, perished, but Beerbohm preserves it here as a work in progress, a faithful adaptation of the copy made by Rossetti's apprentice, Henry Treffry Dunn.[14] In the presence of such detail the apocryphal becomes authentic. Similarly, in the frontispiece to the volume, "Rossetti in Childhood" (HD 1269), Max depicts a young boy calmly and intently coloring a drawing while all around him Italian emigrés are gesticulating wildly, both singly and in groups. Beerbohm's drawing seems to anticipate and illustrate the following passage from a twentieth-century biography of the poet-painter:

> His parents had few English friends, but many Italian ones. Their house was a centre to which, night after night, it seemed as if

D. G. Rossetti, precociously manifesting, among the exited patriots who frequented his father's house in Charlotte Street, that queer indifference to politics which marked him in his prime and his decline. [c. 1916]. Rossetti and His Circle (1922). Courtesy of the Tate Gallery, London.

Gabriele Rossetti. 1853. Virginia Surtees, *The Paintings and Drawings of Dante Gabriel Rossetti: A Catalogue Raisonne.*
Courtesy of Oxford University Press.

all the Italian refugees in London must have come. The variety of the professor's acquaintance was indeed extraordinary, ranging from counts, barons, cavalieri, to organ-grinders, macaroni-sellers and plaster-cast vendors. Among the most distinguished of these political exiles were a count turned coal-dealer, and clay-modeller who was rumoured to have fought with brigands and also to have murdered somebody. Some of these visitors were merely eccentric; others were clearly insane. . . . the children, busy with their play, looking at pictures, colouring prints, would take in the scene, not as a strange, exotic sight, but as a normal incident of their daily life.[15]

The scene that Beerbohm drew was doubtless inspired by William Rossetti's recollections of his father's household, and Max uses it to establish the otherworldliness of Dante Rossetti and his apparent indifference to politics. The exiled patriots, therefore, are drawn in exaggerated postures and with crude facial delineation. One figure, however, that of Dante's father, is executed with more delicacy: the profile face is almost a portrait and the body is shown in a relaxed and natural pose, seated at a table. The contrast in the mode of representation between Gabriele Rossetti and his friends is enormous, and it is only when we realize that Max's presentment of the professor is a fairly faithful copy of a sketch that Dante drew of his father, even down to the very chair he is sitting on,[16] that we can ponder its implications. The reproduction of the original sketch endows Rossetti's father with permanence and memorability in Max's drawing while all the other elements fall into caricature and anecdote, just as in the drawing of the Oxford Union the mural appears to have more serious vitality than the almost grotesque figure of Jowett, whose head is far too oversized for its body. This appearance of realistic detail amid graphic hyperbole is the principal distinction between *Rossetti and His Circle* and Beerbohm's earlier caricatures. It is equivalent to the devices of verisimilitude in *Seven Men*, and its function is similar to theirs: to obliterate the line between probable and true history.

However much the drawings of *Rossetti and His Circle* may tend toward portraiture, Beerbohm does not let his viewer mistake their intent. No feelings of reverence toward the subject are allowed to well up, even though the initial graphic impression may be one of respect, if not of veneration. In the drawing entitled "Woolner at Farringford, 1857" (pl. 9; HD 1657; BLC 10), the Pre-Raphaelite sculptor is shown momentarily distracted from his work on a life-size bust. While Tennyson sits impassively, virtually the perfect model, having almost forgotten himself to marble, his wife impatiently asks: "You know, Mr. Woolner, I'm one of the most un-meddlesome of women; but — when (I'm only asking), *when* do you begin modelling his halo?" This drawing appears to be one of those in which the joke is wholly conveyed by the text until we look a little more closely. Max has lavished considerable care in painting the wall before which this little anecdote is played. Above the rich wainscoting the otherwise open expanse is severely crowded by the imposition of a latticework pattern both in the wallpaper and in the windowpanes. The only escape from this geometric prison lies in the four portraits hanging on the wall — all of them of Tennyson. The display place of the finished bust, one feels, will not be far from where it is being modeled — prominently framed in the curtained and valanced window. Far more subtly than in the Ibsen caricature of *The Poets' Corner,* Max has communicated wordlessly the egotism of eminence, a theme made all the more significant by the juxtaposition of this drawing of the poet laureate among those of the more self-effacing Pre-Raphaelite artists.[17] In the drawing that asserts his marginal identification with Rossetti's circle, "Spring Cottage, Hampstead, 1860" (pl. 5; HD 1279; BLC 43), Coventry Patmore, the celebrator of married love, is preaching his doctrine to Gabriel and Lizzie in their new and barely furnished home. As in the last-cited drawing, the caption delivers the initial thrust, but details of the drawing reinforce it. Although the teapot Rossetti holds in his hands is proclaimed the symbol of domesticity, emblems of incommodiousness abound. Patmore himself is far too big for the room. He is half-kneeling; were he to rise to his full height, he would be nearly twice the size of Rossetti, and his head would easily protrude through the garret ceiling. The obviously broken windowpane and the obviously broken chair leg are further testamentary evidence of the insufficiency of Patmore's creed to appeal to Rossetti's imagination. Instances such as these mitigate our sense of loss over Beerbohm's earlier outrageousness in his drawings and serve to assure us that exaggeration, which is the essence of caricature, need not be gross. So confident is Max of the fundamental purport of his work that he even allows himself the luxury of allusion. The likeness of Browning in the scene in which he introduces a "lady of rank and fashion" to Rossetti (pl. 15; HD 1273), who could obviously never paint such a woman, is derived from neither photograph nor portrait, but is instead a respectful adaptation of a full-length caricature of the poet executed over forty years earlier by Beerbohm's acknowledged master, Ape. Beerbohm thus implies that the extended range he has brought to caricature in *Rossetti and His Circle* justifies not only quotation but also reference to the very history of the art.

The change from physical distortion to situational incongruence as a basis for caricature is best exemplified by a comparison of the two drawings of Rossetti's back garden in Cheyne Walk. The impulse to portray a walled-in eccentricity is common to both, but in the earlier and better-known rendition in *The Poets' Corner* (HD 1268; BLC 49),[18] the intent is purely satirical: the picture is crowded with men and animals making very little contact with one another. For the later volume Max produced a more interesting composition in terms of both artistic design and mental stimulation (pl. 14; HD 1276). Instead of a perspectiveless jumble, there are two distinct focuses of attention: the unprepossessing and portly Rossetti in the left midground leaning against a tree, surrounded by a group of six admirers in various (and not always explicable) attitudes of obeisance, and the solid impassive figure of the painter William Bell Scott in the right foreground, arms crossed over his chest, wearing a respectable bowler on his head and a *nil admirari* expression on his face, "wondering what it is those fellows seem to see in Gabriel." There is, of course, no answer to his question, or at least none suggested by the drawing. Scott and Rossetti face each other diagonally across the picture, and there does not appear to be much physically to choose from between the two corpulent men. Yet Rossetti attracts both men of recognized talent, like Ford Madox Brown, Burne-Jones, Swinburne, Pater, and Morris, and beasts (Morris is attempting to introduce a kangaroo to Rossetti) whereas the technically more accomplished artist, Scott, can arouse nothing more than a terrified and suspi-

Mr. William Bell Scott wondering what it is those fellows see in Gabriel. 1916. Rossetti and His Circle (1922). Courtesy of the Tate Gallery, London.

cious glance from a wombat that slinks by him. By allowing us to observe the observer of the scene, Max creates a dramatic situation out of what would otherwise be a flat one. He is also able to ask whether the emperor is wearing any clothes without appearing to know the answer beforehand. In *Rossetti and His Circle,* then, we do not perceive any diminution or even mellowing of Beerbohm's powers of ironic observation, but we do see the resources of caricature heavily modified to elicit responses not merely immediate but also reflective. For Edmund Wilson the book was

> mainly a set of variations on the theme of Rossetti's relation, not to his romantic art, but to the influences of Victorian England that try to distract him from it. You see him — pre-occupied, obstinate, brooding, unkempt, ill-dressed — resisting importunity and pressure: the blighting smugness of the academic Jowett, the slick eloquence of the fashionable Leighton, Meredith's self-conscious nature cult, Mill's shy, pale and gentle rationalism, the bohemianism of Sala and Browning's society ladies.[19]

Visually these variations are established through strong physical contrasts (though, to be sure, not those of crude exaggeration) in accordance with the techniques of confrontation and introduction as bases for generating scenes, which techniques I discussed in chapter 3. In other words, although the legend is of far greater importance in *Rossetti and His Circle* than in Max's other albums and although one's appreciation of the drawings is certainly heightened by one's having a prior knowledge of the subjects, as in all caricature, the fundamental appeal to the eye in these drawings derives from a perception of disharmony, discrepancy, and paradox.

Rossetti, however, is not the only subject of these drawings. That otherworldliness, that commitment to the creation of imaginative realms transcending the commonplace, which qualities he so much exemplified, is manifested as well in his "circle," in those men of talent and genius who identified with his ideals or were otherwise inspired by him. Their presence in the volume multiplies the opportunities for pictorial contrast, for even though the representation of Gabriel himself is fairly restrained, Beerbohm's depiction of his friends is slightly more exaggerat-

Topsy and Ned Jones, settled on the settle in Red Lion Square. 1916. *Rossetti and His Circle* (1922). Courtesy of the Tate Gallery, London.

ed. The picture "Topsy and Ned Jones [William Morris and Edward Burne-Jones], settled on the settle in Red Lion Square" (pl. 6; HD 1072) is one of the few actionless scenes in the volume, but it is marked by pronounced visual contrasts. There is first the Laurel-and-Hardy aspect of the two men. What on earth can the two of them have in common — the chunky Morris, with a head of hair like the Medusa and legs so short that they do not touch the floor when he sits, and the wraithlike Burne-Jones, huddled into a corner of the settle alongside Morris's great girth, stroking his shapeless beard? The settle unites them, of course, that collaborative enterprise combining the craft of the cabinet-maker and the skill and vision of the artist. This massive piece of furniture, its panels portraying damozels and angels in blue and gold, takes up nearly half the picture and itself contrasts with the room's other stark furnishings: a besom leaning against the back wall and a plain table upon which lie a loaf of bread and a bottle of Bass's ale.[20] Comic in its external features, the drawing does not mock the pretensions or the earnestness of these two artists. It does wonder at them, however. And their obliviousness to any environment or atmosphere not of their own creation is made all the more striking by its placement immediately following the one of Patmore in the Spring Cottage garret.

So strong a personality as that of James McNeill Whistler could never submit to being part of a circle; yet in his flamboyant opposition to conventional Victorian verities he manifested an affinity to the Pre-Raphaelites, and in at least one of his extravagant passions, collecting Chinese porcelain, he set an example that was soon followed by Rossetti and Howell.[21] That passion is celebrated in the drawing "Blue China" (pl. 8; HD 241; BLC 53), in which a diminutive Whistler, scarcely as large as the Nankin vase he is displaying to Thomas Carlyle, stands as a representative of aestheticism against the moral earnestness of the old philosopher. Whistler is elegant and wasp-waisted, his delicate fingers extended in a gesture of connoisseurship. The figure of Carlyle, twice the size of that of the artist, looks coarse and ungainly; his face is heavily lined and shaded, revealing a disapproving incomprehension of what he beholds. In the background on a tall impractical table stands a tiny impractical vase containing an "arrangement" of branches, decorative perhaps to an Oriental taste, but very un-British. On the wall are three framed prints of drawings, each of a different size but all alike in the ampleness of their borders and the haziness of their subjects. It is obvious that Whistler is at home in these surroundings, where everything has been abstracted into colors and shapes, and that Carlyle is uncomfortable in them. This is no mere conflict of generations — it is a conflict of worlds.

As a final instance of the use of physical contrast to emphasize the strangeness and innocence of the mid-Victorian cult of aestheticism, one may adduce Beerbohm's "Riverside Scene" (pl. 17; HD 1643; BLC 47) of "Algernon Swinburne taking his great new friend Gosse to see Gabriel Rossetti." One of only three outdoor scenes in the album, its basic composition — two men promenading across the picture with the Thames, riverboats, and the Battersea shore in the background — is similar to that of Max's oil painting of Rossetti and Herringham.[22] Yet here the two men are hardly equal companions. It is not merely that Gosse is more than twice the size of Swinburne, even though they are wearing the same style of hat. Nor is it even the luxurious expanse of auburn hair, the principal source of color in the picture, that chiefly distinguishes Swinburne from the more conventionally shorn Gosse. Rather it is that Gosse appears earthbound while Swinburne is volant. Although he seems to be taking very long strides, Gosse cannot keep up with Swinburne, who seems to float ahead of him, dragging him by his left indexfinger, as a child might lead his nurse whose whole hand was too large for him to grasp. Elfin, eager, childlike, Swinburne, to a greater degree than all the others of the "circle," is depicted as a creature to be marveled at.

The juxtaposition of contrasting, though not necessarily conflicting, figures is thus a principal formula for the generation of scenes in *Rossetti and His Circle*. By removing Rossetti himself from the most dynamic of these contrasts, Beerbohm avoided obviousness and repetitiveness. He also experimented with confrontation across the dimension of time in his drawing, one of the later ones, "A Momentary Vision that once befell Young Millais" (pl. 3; HD 1039), in which the young artist, lithe and handsome, in the midst of painting *Ferdinand Lured by Ariel* (1849), drops palette and brushes in amazement as he beholds

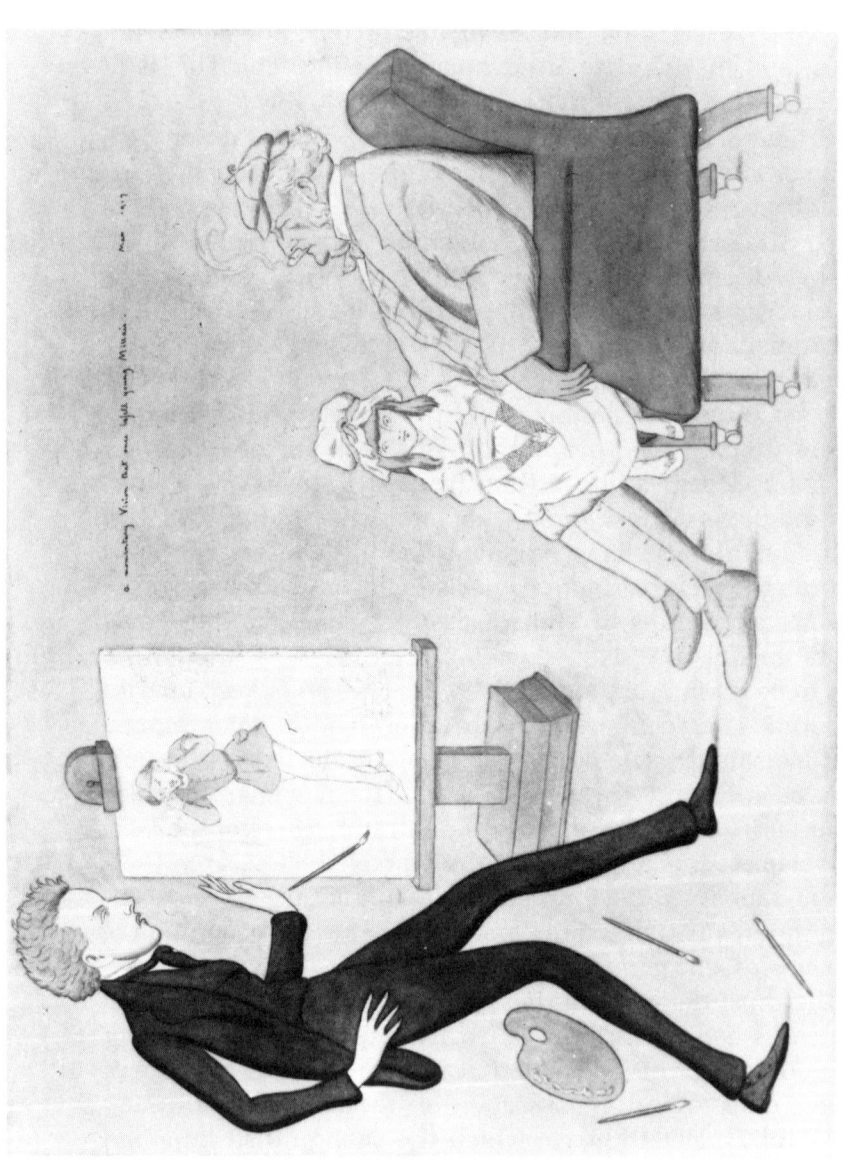

A momentary Vision that once befell young Millais. 1917. *Rossetti and His Circle.* (1922). Courtesy of the Tate Gallery, London.

John Everett Millais, *Ferdinand Lured by Ariel.* 1849.
Courtesy of Lord Sherfield.

himself in maturity: corpulent, complacent, commercially successful, with an insipid child model seated on his knee. Even Ferdinand in the painting, whose hands are at his ears, seems to be reacting in shock. Beerbohm's drawing perfectly relates physical contrasts to spiritual ones: the young Millais is bent on realizing in oils his interpretation of Shakespeare's vision; the old Millais is content to use his skill to cater to a vulgar and sentimental taste. Allowing the young artist to make the judgment himself preserves Beerbohm's ironic distance. Youth is, after all, intolerant, its determinations based on expectation rather than experience. But by placing the drawing third in the series, by informing us visually that Millais, one of the Pre-Raphaelite founders, will ultimately "sell out," Beerbohm prepares us to see the resistance of Rossetti and his other friends to Victorian commonplaceness as behavior heroic as well as eccentric.

In chapter 3 I pointed out that by means of a triangular arrangement of figures, most often conforming to the social convention of the introduction, Beerbohm is able to convey his "message" in an even more complex and subtle way. Such triangular arrangements characterize the introduction scenes in *Rossetti and His Circle*. In the drawing laconically entitled "An Introduction" (pl. 7; HD 1272; BLC 42), in which Gabriel brings together Ruskin and Fanny Cornforth, there is hardly any need for a legend at all. We do not require any words to proclaim Fanny's commonness. Her ridiculous hat, coarse features, bull neck, and scarlet dress would suffice to alarm the fastidious Ruskin. As she sails into the picture from the right, extending a meaty paw for the critic to shake, Ruskin's own right hand hangs limply, as though it would run away if it could to avoid an encounter with the other. Gabriel, standing in the middle, seems to be bringing the two of them closer together, though his eyes are fixed dreamily, obsessively, on Fanny. Ostensibly the picture dwells on the incongruity of the meeting between Rossetti's patron and Rossetti's latest model, but more deeply it probes the duality of Rossetti himself. Ruskin had been an early champion of Rossetti's soulful painting, providing considerable support and encouragement to him and Lizzie. But, as Max observes in his notes to "The Mirror of the Past," Ruskin "disliked Gabriel's *coarse* painting," for which Fanny was a frequent model ("Mirror," p. 44). Thus, quite apart from his probable difficulty in comprehending physical infatuation in the first place, Ruskin would have construed Rossetti's attachment to the vulgar Fanny as disloyalty not only to the dead Lizzie but also to the art she inspired. Significantly, a portrait of Lizzie hangs in the background, the apex of the composition, taking in the whole scene.

Another Rossetti portrait looks down upon the proceedings when John Morley introduces John Stuart Mill to Rossetti (pl. 18; HD 1280; BLC 60). This framed picture recalls the chalk drawing *Reverie*,[23] which Beerbohm must have sat under on the several occasions he visited Watts-Dunton and Swinburne at The Pines, where it hung prominently in the drawing room. One of the earliest works for which Jane Morris sat for Rossetti and but recently executed at the time Beerbohm alleges this meeting to have taken place (Spring 1869), the subject heralds Rossetti's last great passion and thus provides an ironic comment to Morley's proposal, which is nothing less than that Rossetti provide a set of illustrations for Mill's latest work now in the press, *The Subjection of Women*. Morley is grossly caricatured — an oversized head and elongated beak on a tiny body — tugging at Gabriel's coat to gain his attention. He is a practical politician, accustomed to mediating between parties, and sees no incompatibility between these two admirers of women. There is, of course, physical contrast between the ample Gabriel, who is pondering the suggestion in a suspicious but noncommittal way, and the lean, wizened Mill, who stands shyly to the side, radiating that deficiency "in warmth, in colour, in rich charm" that Morley hopes Gabriel's collaboration will reduce. Unlike Morley, Mill is not made to appear ridiculous — merely out of place. Beerbohm succeeds in making the thinker seem worldly, his sponsor crass.

The chief virtue of scenes involving triangular arrangements is that they demand study, for the relationships among the characters cannot be taken in all at once. And in some instances we cannot be altogether certain that we have mastered them. A case in point is what is probably the most familiar of the drawings in *Rossetti and His Circle*, "The Small Hours in the 'Sixties at 16, Cheyne Walk. — Algernon Reading 'Anactoria' to Gabriel

Mr. Morley of Blackburn, on an afternoon in the spring of '69, introduces Mr. John Stuart Mill. 1917. *Rossetti and His Circle.* (1922). Courtesy of the Tate Gallery, London.

and William" (pl. 11; HD 1275; BLC 44). It does not require any special knowledge of Rossetti's odd household in Chelsea, of which Swinburne was for a short time an inmate, to appreciate the strong contrasts: Gabriel dominates the picture, a behemoth reclining like an odalisque on a settee that can barely support him while the tiny Swinburne is perched on the smallest of stools, his legs not long enough to reach the floor. William sits gravely, almost in a trance, but seems to have one eye on each of the other two. We know that Rossetti's insomnia had begun soon after the death of his wife in 1862 and that before he became addicted to chloral, he would try to overcome it by being read to. Thus "the small hours" are readily explained. But while Swinburne pours forth profuse strains of premeditated art quite oblivious of his audience, Beerbohm makes it impossible for us to know for sure what effect the recitation is having on the Rossetti brothers. Even William's spirited defense of the poet in *Swinburne's Poems and Ballads: A Criticism* (1866) was qualified by reservations about the impurity of the theme of forbidden love found in "Anactoria." Edmund Gosse saw in the picture "a shocked William and a relaxed Gabriel"[24] whereas John Felstiner characterizes their attitudes in these words: "William is sitting dead somber; the widower Gabriel slumps on a chaise longue, scowling painfully."[25] My own guess is that the recitation has produced the desired therapeutic effect: that is, Gabriel has fallen asleep, perhaps unwillingly — hence the expression that Felstiner takes to be a scowl. I base this conjecture almost wholly on the representation of Gabriel's "spade" hand, hanging straight down. Elsewhere Beerbohm has used this feature in depicting ventriloquists' dummies, automatons, servants, and characters in trances, and I have interpreted it iconographically as a manifestation of diminished volition. William's expression may be read as one of mild anxiety as he checks back and forth between his brother and the rhapsodist. Having to be at the Inland Revenue office the next morning, he is unwilling to stay up any longer than is absolutely necessary; yet he does not quite know how to bring the reading to an end. Our enjoyment of the picture, however, does not depend on *our* knowing precisely what is going on but rather on the assurance that something memorable is taking place. It is, in the words of *The Times's* reviewer, "a great moment recaptured, even if it never happened."[26]

Although *Rossetti and His Circle* represents Beerbohm at the height of his technical skill as a graphic artist, the work is no less remarkable for its unity and comprehensiveness. Most obviously these characteristics manifest themselves in the chronological progression asserted in the arrangement of the twenty-three plates of the published volume. Despite the fact that only eight are assigned dates in their legends, five more imply as much by means of their reference to specific works or occasions (the painting of the Oxford Union, for example, or the composition of Swinburne's "Anactoria"), and the others are appropriately intercalated among these fixed points. Without the relentlessness of the methodical biographer, Beerbohm creates through his succession of scenes the illusion of a life passing before us, from the frontispiece depicting Rossetti as a child, drawing (it is significant to note, a portrait of a woman) amid the babble of the political exiles in his father's house, to the last plate where, although he is neither alive nor present in the picture, his gospel is being preached to the heathen Americans by his spiritual disciple, Oscar Wilde. The illusion is all the more striking because it is not enforced by the more obvious visual means. Thus, despite the fact that Rossetti is portrayed in the frontispiece as a child and in the first plate as an intense young man, the successive drawings do not depict the process of aging. Rossetti does not grow progressively more careworn or corpulent, though Beerbohm does note that by the midsixties he was wearing spectacles. Rather, Rossetti's twilight is treated quite subtly. In the last two pictures in which he actually appears he is shown reclining on a divan, and in both instances only a part of his body is seen, as though he were receding from view. He disappears altogether from the last two plates, where it is his influence rather than his physical presence that is depicted.

It is quite apparent that Beerbohm was less interested in charting a life than in illustrating a force. The invented scenes range over the real and likely events of Rossetti's life to produce, not chronicle, but response. Thus, in the drawing entitled "Rossetti's Courtship" (pl. 2; HD 1270; BLC 41), the fact of the artist's long and peculiar engagement to Elizabeth Siddal is subservient to his conception of her. Rossetti himself is depicted as dreamy and listless; slip shod, he leans against the mantlepiece in a room whose furnishings consist of nothing more than an easel and whose bare floor is littered with abandoned sketches and traversed by a tiny mouse in the foreground. In the midst of this drab squalor stands Lizzie, impassive and marmoreal, her bright red hair set off by the deep blue of her gown. Because there is no physical contact between the two lovers, because she provides the only intense color in the picture, and because her remote, heavy-lidded expression so much resembles that of the idealized damozels of Rossetti's early portraits of her, it is virtually impossible for us not to see her as the embodiment of Rossetti's artistic inventions rather than as an actual person. Beerbohm labels his composition, giving it both a geographical and a temporal locus, but for all that it is an imaginary reminiscence of an imaginative experience. Similarly, the fact of Rossetti's painting the walls of the Oxford Union in 1857 is recorded two plates later, but as has been observed, that fact is subordinated to the repudiation of Victorian complacency in the person of Benjamin Jowett. Juxtaposed between these two plates is the "Momentary Vision of Millais," the Pre-Raphaelite who abandoned the lofty artistic ideals that the Brotherhood had sought to articulate in its youthful manifesto. A consideration of the first five plates of the volume alone (frontispiece, "British Stock and Alien Inspiration," and the three just mentioned) is sufficient to persuade us that the course of the artist's life may have provided the outline, but hardly the final form, of *Rossetti and His Circle*.

That outline, however, is remarkably suggestive of fullness. Without creating a gallery of crowded tableaux, Beerbohm introduces a surprising number of people — well over thirty — into the series. The principal women in Rossetti's life, Elizabeth Siddal, Fanny Cornforth, and Jane Morris, appear either in their own persons or in Rossetti's allegorical presentments of them. His father, brother, and sister also appear, but in ways that do not suggest a family portrait. The Pre-Raphaelite Brotherhood does not pose as a group; its chief members — Millais, Hunt, and Woolner, as well as Brown — are captured in the same candid way as the others. This is no less true of Rossetti's more intimate friends, those who looked after his personal and business affairs, Hall Caine, Theodore Watts-Dunton, Frederick Shields, and Charles Augustus Howell, than it is of those whose companionship may have been more intense but of shorter duration, men like Meredith, Swinburne, Patmore, Morris, Burne-Jones, and Whistler. What is implied by such a casual mode of associative biography (Rossetti is often not even present in the pictures in which they appear) is the pervasive influence of Rossetti on all the sensitive natures that came anywhere near him. Even those who do not actually step into the magic circle to experience the aureole are nevertheless judged by it. Beerbohm engineers confrontations between the Rossettian visionary ideal and the established representatives of mid-Victorian thought and art, such as Browning, Tennyson, Ruskin, Mill, Carlyle, Disraeli, Jowett, Sala, and Leighton. Although Max's selection of these worthies is personal, it is by no means eccentric. In each instance we perceive the uniqueness of Rossetti's purpose, his isolation even from the recognized apostles of high culture. Finally, Beerbohm suggests the continuity of the Rossettian ideal beyond Rossetti's actual lifetime by his depiction of another Oxford don besides Jowett, Walter Pater, as a devoted admirer and by his conferring the mantle of aestheticism on Oscar Wilde. The presence in the volume of Edmund Gosse, who was apart from Caine the only man still living when the picture was drawn, carries the myth forcefully into the twentieth century, endowing it with continued vitality as well as venerability. In *Rossetti and His Circle* we are well beyond the literary jokes of *The Poets' Corner*. We are also well beyond a chronological string of invented anecdotes. By imagining and arranging these scenes, Beerbohm engages us to consider Rossetti less as a man or as a creator of beautiful things than as an inspirational force.

The precise nature of that inspiration is somewhat elusive, for Beerbohm himself is still the detached and ironic observer. However much he is drawn to contemplate the phenomenon of Rossetti, it is as subjective historian rather than as worshiper that he does so. He sees the comedy and the absurdity in the postures of Rossetti and his friends; neither can he regard himself either literally or spiritually an adherent. But for all of his self-exclusion, Beerbohm's attitude is never condescending. He is constantly full of wonder, of admiration in the Latin sense of the word, both at Rossetti's attempts and at those he encourages in others, to transcend the quotidian, to inhabit worlds of the imagination richer than those of common reality. I do not mean to suggest that Beerbohm has created a hero as strangely complex as Don Quixote, but he has quite clearly interpreted the Rossetti myth as something at once comic and noble. The accomplishment is all the more remarkable because it is achieved almost wordlessly (the legends label rather than establish situations) and, for all the technical improvements displayed in the work, it is achieved more through the cruder devices of the caricaturist than through the subtle refinements of expression of the trained artist. Not only does the artist-hero of *Rossetti and His Circle* command our respect, even though rendered in a reductive mode of portraiture, his own artistic compositions are also subjected to reduction; in one plate the process is carried a step further when the viewer is confronted with childish daubs representing forgeries of those compositions (pl. 21; HD 369) — in effect, caricatures of caricatures. Unable to indulge in verbal parody, Beerbohm simplifies Rossetti's career, presenting him solely as a painter, there being but few visually attractive possible means by which a writer at work can be portrayed. Yet Beerbohm makes the most of these few in his imaginary reminiscences of Swinburne's rhapsodic recitation, Meredith's hortation, and Wilde's lecture. Despite the constraints imposed by caricature, however, Beerbohm reveals an attitude toward his subject comparable in its sophistication to that expressed in *Seven Men*.

But caricature is virtually by definition bold and not delicate. Even in the less harsh mode of caricature Beerbohm adopted in *Rossetti and His Circle* there is little opportunity for effects of much subtlety. Most of the pains he took were directed toward establishing immediate recognition of the figures in the drawings as likenesses of real, though no longer living, people. Their postures and gestures, therefore, rather than their facial expressions, must convey the basic meaning, a treatment further necessitated by the miniaturizing effects of reproduction. Consequently, to refine the drawings beyond scenes of raw encounter, Beerbohm, like many a satiric artist before him, had recourse to the emblematic use of backgrounds. But unlike such a satirist as

Sir Max Beerbohm

Hogarth, for example, whose drawings have literally to be deciphered, Beerbohm's use of background is essentially unobtrusive, however supplemental it is to the main design. This restraint is as much a matter of limitation as of choice: Beerbohm was no draftsman; nor for that matter was he a very keen observer of "the human form divine." Even had he wanted to, he could never have produced anything approaching the rich detail and crowded interiors of the nineteenth-century paintings whose artists he celebrated. However modestly he does so from an artistic standpoint, Beerbohm nevertheless utilizes background to reinforce the basic theme of the work — the conflict of the artistic imagination with the real world — and to suggest a few variations on that theme. In particular his effects are produced through fenestration and decoration.

By fenestration I mean more than the mere presence or placement of windows, though that, of course, is its basic meaning. Max himself had given sufficient thought to the implications of things seen through windows to devote a radio broadcast to the subject, in which he spoke of their rich artistic potentiality: "People seen or things said indoors or out-of-doors have not the same arresting quality as things said or people seen half-indoors, half-out. There is much virtue in a window. It is to a human being as a frame is to a painting, as a proscenium to a play, as "form" to literature. It strongly defines its content. It excludes all but what it encloses. It firmly rivets us. In fact, it's a magic casement."[27] Because windows admit not only light and air but glimpses of an exterior as well, they may be used to suggest a larger and different environment, one removed from the controlled interior atmosphere. Similar implications, Beerbohm seems to suggest, may be created by framed pictures. In a larger signification, therefore, we may employ the term *fenestration* to refer to the framed "holes" in interior scenes through which other scenes, whether complementary or opposing, may intrude. Of the twenty-three scenes of *Rossetti and His Circle* only three take place in the open air, but in only five of the remaining twenty is there no window or picture to hint at an alternate scene. To be sure, none of them open "on the foam of perilous seas"; yet in most of them what is seen in the smaller frame provides a commentary on what is seen in the larger one. In "Rossetti's Courtship," for example, the fenestration anthenticates the setting: "...the fine view of the Thames below his windows, the hurry and bustle of the quays, the constant passing of boats and barges.... The studio had windows looking southwards, and on fine days was bright with sunshine."[28] Only, as Beerbohm draws the picture, it is not a fine day. All is gray through the window, and rain falls in diagonal sheets. Lizzie stands in the middle of the room, but the perspective is such that her head with its radiant hair appears framed by the window. In the absence of light from outside or from a fire in the grate, Lizzie's illumination, we come to understand, can have its source only in Gabriel's imagination. In this instance the world of reality, both in its interior and exterior settings, is shown to have less color and less intensity than the world of the artist's conception. Quite frequently in Beerbohm's drawings windows will look out onto blank space, and this is particularly the case when the interior is dominated by an artistic work. Mention has already been made of Beerbohm's fidelity to the sketch of the Grail scene that Rossetti painted on the walls of the Oxford Union. The effect of the two round windows piercing the composition to gaze out on nothing while around them a host of figures and trees are being summoned to life by the artist's brush is deeply ironic and serves to heighten the confrontation between Rossetti and Jowett, who, as he is here portrayed, can see nothing. Similarly, in the depiction of Morris and Burne-Jones, the actual window has been pushed to the side of the composition and truncated, its functions taken over by the settle: the panes have become panels, richly illuminated, and Morris, as though he were sitting in a window seat, seems to be composing in its light.

The effects achieved by decoration do not differ qualitatively from those of fenestration, but, because the secondary vistas are unframed and exist wholly in an interior setting, their impact tends to be more striking. The distinction may be more artificial than real, however, for in some instances it is difficult to separate fenestration from decoration. In the plate just mentioned, for example, a real window has been displaced by an artificial one. But the settle so dominates the scene and is so overwhelmingly the product of human artifice and ingenuity that it becomes far more than an emblem of an alternate world since it is worthy of study in itself. This use of decoration to assert the superiority of art is even more apparent in the drawing entitled "*Quis Custodiet Ipsum Custodem?*" (pl. 20; HD 1277; BLC 48), which represents Theodore Watts-Dunton and Frederick Shields, as the elder of Rossetti's "guardians," expostulating with the younger Hall Caine, urging him not to read his compositions to Rossetti, who is reclining in the background in a posture reminiscent of the earlier scene in which Swinburne read to him. (As in "The Mirror of the Past," so in *Rossetti and His Circle* Beerbohm indicates the passage from the artist's prime to his decline by substituting Caine for Swinburne as a companion. In Beerbohm's presentments of them the two men bear some physical resemblance.) The principal drama is apocryphally anecdotal: the daily activities of the languid and indifferent Rossetti are carefully regulated by nurses who quarrel among themselves. But the scene is enacted in a gorgeous setting. In the words of one commentator, the drawing is "quite apart from its merits as caricature, the most decorative piece of work that Max has ever done. The walls, with Rossetti's pictures, the wallpaper, the carpet, and above all the screen are most exquisitely drawn, and the old golds, browns, and yellows with which they are tinted definitely appeal with great force to a side of our taste which had never yet been excited by Max before."[29] The effect of the richness of scene is to assert that, however incapable Rossetti may have become of looking after himself, he nevertheless succeeded in immersing himself in an atmosphere of delicacy and beauty. A similar contrast is evoked in the volume's last plate (pl. 22; HD 1784; BLC 55), in which Oscar Wilde is lecturing in America. Here there is both fenestration and decoration of sorts. The audience is somberly clad and dull of expression, sitting in uniform rows, all posed with hands on knees and shod in footgear so shapeless that it is impossible to distinguish left from right feet. On the wall hangs a framed portrait of Lincoln, scowling dourly on the proceedings, which likeness is surmounted by a pair of crossed American flags. This treatment, of course, contrasts sharply with the Rossettian interiors of the earlier plates. The lecturer, though of ample girth, is dressed in a well-fitting, textured velvet suit with knee breeches, his stockings revealing finely turned calves that culminate in delicately slippered feet. In his left hand he holds a single lily, whose very leaves seem to droop artistically. Wilde and his flower are all curves; his auditors and their surroundings are all angles or amorphousness. The whole picture in its pronounced contrast might well illustrate the superiority of sinuous to straight lines, as do the figures in the plates to Hogarth's *Analysis of Beauty*. Here the decoration is minimal but the effect is marked. Both Wilde and the Americans are presented as preposterous; but the exaggerations of the aesthetic posture are seen ultimately as more pleasing than the dullness of common sense. Enforcing his contrasts by these means, Beerbohm renders his caricature more discriminating and ironic.

Rossetti and His Circle constitutes Beerbohm's most elaborate and contrived use of caricature for the purpose of ironic statement. But however informed with narrative implications, transcending by far the crude series drawings of an earlier decade, and however invested with factual and imaginative detail, the work displays a maturity of expression rather than any fundamental alteration of perspective from *The Poets' Corner* of 1904. There is greater assurance, both conceptually and technically, in the later work. The sophomoric irreverence, carried over from the many sketches of masters and dons he had doodled at Charterhouse and Oxford, is displaced by a measure of sympathy and understanding. Yet in no sense can the work be viewed as a venture either into personal biography or even into cultural history. It is far too idiosyncratic for that. As in all of Beerbohm's creations, it is the observer rather than the observed who is illuminated[30] because Max is concerned less with actual men than with the myths that surround them, less with celebrating their actual achievements and struggles than with testing their projections and emanations. The myth of Rossetti, largely swept away by modernism in art and literature, still persists as a manifestation of taste and genius equally eccentric and recherché. Although the respectable Victorians, such as Tennyson and Arnold, seem to be recovering some of their luster tarnished in the first half of our century, it is doubtful whether their more romantic contemporaries either in art or poetry can ever again be seen as inspirational figures. Yet to the retrospective Beerbohm, who remained an alien in the century into which he survived, the Rossetti myth continued as potent as it had been in his childhood. Less than a year after the artist's death, even though his paintings had still not achieved total acceptance, Rossetti was being hailed as a force instrumental in the transformation of the aesthetic consciousness of the nation:

> In an age when painters have few beliefs, and hold those very lightly, this man scarcely stirred a step in art except in obedience to his own inspiration, and was strong enough, despite all his failings, to modify the practices, if he did not actually change the creeds, of half the artists of his time. To him . . . Millais owed his poetical inspiration, and his most beautiful pictures were painted under that influence; to him Holman Hunt was even more indebted; from him, though soon able to strike out a line for himself, sprang Mr. Burne Jones, fully equipped for the fight, like a second Minerva, from the brain of a second Jove; to his early friendship with William Morris at Oxford, when he went there to paint the frescoes in the Union, we probably owe the determining impulse which set the author of the "Earthly Paradise" on the road to that decoration which has changed the look of half the houses in London; and to him probably, if we could trace it back, we owe, almost equally with Ruskin who defended him, the growth of the feeling that art was more than a mere trade, and that an artist has duties to himself and his art as well as to his pocket and his public.[31]

It was to this myth, born a generation earlier than the Edwardian world in ruins of his time, that Beerbohm responded in *Rossetti and His Circle,* and his object was no less to comment upon it than to celebrate the age that sustained it.

The influence of Rossetti on other artists is certainly chronicled in Beerbohm's depiction. That influence, however, lay less in Rossetti's actual accomplishments than in his commitment to the realization of his imaginative dream in art, and it is this aspect of the Rossetti myth that most engages Beerbohm's scrutiny. We see this commitment clashing not only with the cruder sensibilities of a Jowett or a Sala but also against the equally idealistic but more philosophical and political commitments of men like Morley and Mill and those of the less mystical, more socially conscious, poets like Tennyson, Browning, and Patmore. The investigation is carried on in imagined scenes both private and domestic, though hardly intimate. Beerbohm is not particularly interested in piercing Rossetti's mask, in penetrating to the inner man. What the man stood for rather than what actually happened to him is the subject of Beerbohm's album. That is why, for all the richness of Max's invention, the work is biographically antiseptic. There is no allusion whatever to the more sensational aspects of Rossetti's life, which even Victorian reticence had difficulty in suppressing: the exhumation of his dead wife, the estrangement from William Morris resulting from his growing attachment to Jane Morris, and the physical degeneration and suicidal despondence induced in part by his addiction to chloral. The women in Rossetti's life are treated almost exclusively as adjuncts to his art. Elizabeth Siddal is portrayed soulfully and mournfully, Fanny Cornforth grossly and sensually, in Max's parody of Rossetti's employment of them as sitters. Jane Morris does not appear in person at all, but her portraits look down from elaborate gilt frames in the last scenes of the series. Beerbohm's inclination and talents would hardly have led him to the presentation of lurid and arresting incidents; yet that fact alone is insufficient to account for the chronological imbalance of *Rossetti and His Circle*. The last decade of Rossetti's life, which witnessed not only his physical decline but also his growing reputation as both artist and poet, figures scarcely at all in the album; and as I pointed out earlier, the actual presence of the man appears to recede in the last drawings. This, I think, is Beerbohm's way of suggesting that Rossetti, as the source of inspiration to others that Quilter speaks of, had become essentially a spent force. For Max, the high points of Rossetti's life (like his own?) had all been reached before his thirty-fifth year, particularly in the heady fifties: the days of the Pre-Raphaelite Brotherhood, of the patronage of Ruskin, of his courtship and marriage to Lizzie, and of the Jovial Campaign at Oxford with Morris and Burne-Jones. After Lizzie's death Rossetti's youth and exuberance came to an end and with them the exclusiveness of his commitment to the life of the imagination. "I think he began to sell his soul, or rather to sell what was left of it," Max wrote to Robert Ross, "soon after he went to Tudor House [October 1862]."[32]

Beerbohm's fascination with Rossetti, then, rests ultimately on that artist's dedication to his artistic purpose and on his capacity to inspire others to a like purpose. Presented as physically drab and unprepossessing himself, Rossetti seems to endow everything he touches with form and color. Under his influence the commonplace is overwhelmed: bare walls glow, however transiently, with medieval visions; bare rooms are furnished with objects that feed the soul. But Max is far from the uncritical hero-worshiper. He is fully aware of the comedy inherent in the aesthetic posture, as the confrontation scenes amply attest. He knows too that, though nobler than many another passion, the quest for beauty, like all single-mindedness, leads to tunnel vision. The young Rossetti of the frontispiece is as oblivious to the fervor for political liberty of the Italian émigrés surrounding him as Oscar Wilde, depicted in the last drawing as his apostle in the wilderness of North America, is to the portrait of Lincoln in the lecture hall and to the ideals that it represents. At issue is not whether Rossetti or Wilde should have been more politically conscious, for elsewhere Beerbohm has suggested that Swinburne's devotion to political causes was not particularly salutary to his poetry. The point is rather that single-minded men, whatever their devotion, must appear to the candid observer, however he may admire them, a trifle absurd.

But if Beerbohm offers us little in the way of insight or penetration into the Rossetti phenomenon, in his articulation of wonder he provides a form of annotation to it. As is the case with almost all of Beerbohm's caricatures, those unfamiliar with the legend may readily extrapolate its configuration from the drawings while the more knowing may take delight in beholding the familiar in its genial distortion. There is a particular pleasure in seeing how this or that eminence will be "taken off." What chiefly distinguishes the collection in *Rossetti and His Circle* from Max's other drawings, however, is its seriousness both in intent and execution; its closest verbal counterpart is the treatment of Swinburne and Watts-Dunton in "No. 2. The Pines," which also strikes a balance between reverence and irreverence, pathos and ludicrousness. Both, moreover, fix impressions firmly in the mind: however limited in depth it may be as objective analysis, Beerbohm's testimony is memorable, ineffaceable, an unignorable part of the criticism that surrounds these men. The remarkable thing is that there is virtually no change in perspective here from the earliest of Beerbohm's work. The critic of performances is still performing. There is no more inconsistency in outlook from *Caricatures of Twenty-Five Gentlemen* to *Rossetti and His Circle* than there is from the weekly drama notices in the *Saturday Review* to the sketches in *Seven Men*. But there is greater mastery in managing it. That management, however, cannot be accounted for by technical proficiency alone. Beerbohm's triumph is one of form, of finding the perfect vehicle for his gifts; through the imaginary reminiscence, that mingling of fact, legend, and fiction as personal recollection, he succeeded in investing those gifts with poignancy and intensity. In *Seven Men* he teases us into accepting the remembrancer as the only true historian. In *Rossetti and His Circle* he accomplishes a far more difficult task, that of composing a graphic history reconciling the distortion inherent in caricature with the subtle ambiguity of sensitive reflection.

CHAPTER VII

The Fading of Memory

To define, as I have done, the career of Sir Max Beerbohm in terms of a quest for significant form, to identify the sources of that form in the imaginary reminiscence, and to isolate, moreover, the perfect attainment of that quest in the works of his pen and brush composed essentially in the war years of 1917–1918 (namely, *Seven Men* and *Rossetti and His Circle*) do obvious violence to the configuration suggested by a casual observation of Beerbohm's record of production. For one thing, such an interpretation relegates to the status of an interesting dead end the most substantial of Beerbohm's achievements in prose, his only finished novel, *Zuleika Dobson,* while elevating the inchoate "Mirror of the Past," a curiosity known intimately perhaps to no more than a handful of scholars and bibliophiles, to the eminence of a seminal work. For another, it would seem to ignore the fact that the succeeding decade saw publication of two more volumes of essays, *And Even Now* (1920) and *A Variety of Things* (1928) — to say nothing of the republication of a selection of his drama criticism in *Around Theatres* (1924), as well as three considerable volumes of caricatures, *A Survey* (1921), *Things New and Old* (1923), and *Observations* (1925), all of which followed successful London exhibitions. If a twilight must be indicated, surely it would seem more appropriately located in the thirties and forties, when the writings and caricatures are indeed more sporadic and occasional, manifesting a weakening of concentration, if not of charm. In a survey purely biographical or chronological the slighting of *Zuleika Dobson* would be un-

The Fading of Memory

pardonable, nor is it much of a defense to claim that it is in no danger of being neglected by critics and literary historians. My contention, however, is that brilliant though the novel may be, it is not central but peripheral to that successful fusion of talents and uniformity of vision achieved in *Seven Men* and *Rossetti and His Circle*. The concern of this chapter, therefore, will be to trace Beerbohm's attempts — by no means unsuccessful but always more limited in scope — to extend or to build upon the masterful accomplishments of the war years.

Essential to our understanding of those accomplishments is the acknowledgment that Beerbohm's best work, whether as a writer or caricaturist, is always retrospective, so that to speak of publication dates rather than dates of composition is more than usually misleading. Among all artists there is of course a lag between conception and execution and between execution and exhibition. This is particularly so with miniaturists like Beerbohm, whose volumes for the most part are accumulations of pieces wrought at different times. His essays generally appeared first in magazines, their collective force dispersed for years until they were united in book form. Thus the constituents of *Seven Men*, though largely the product of a concentrated period of creative activity, did not appear together until 1919, and the augmented volume that joined "Argallo and Ledgett" (1928) to the earlier sketches did not appear until 1950. The drawings of *Rossetti and His Circle*, dating from the same years, had first to be exhibited before being reproduced, and their publication in book form had to await the more favorable postwar climate of 1922. Between 1919 and 1922 Beerbohm published *And Even Now* and *A Survey;* six of the twenty essays of the former and fifteen of the fifty-one caricatures of the latter actually predate the war.

But Beerbohm's compositions are retrospective as well in a profounder sense. Whether or not they are reminiscences real or imaginary, they commonly extol the past. *Zuleika Dobson* looks back to an Oxford twenty years earlier; the "remembering" essays and character sketches celebrate the *fin de siècle* and Edwardian heyday; *Rossetti and His Circle* plunges even further into a past not personally experienced. Successively Beerbohm had mined his own experiences and those of his elders, suffusing all with a rich imaginative irony. What had happened by 1922 was that the ore gave out. The years of seclusion in Rapallo had given him time to reflect upon what he had seen but had furnished him with no new stock upon which to reflect in future years. Paradoxically the culmination of his productive retirement came not in the land of his adoption but in his native land — though far from his native scene — to which he was driven by war. (To a far slighter degree he experienced another creative resurgence in his sojourn in England during the Second World War.) Theoretically, of course, there was nothing to prevent him from turning to history as a substitute for experience, and indeed there are some experiments in which he attempts to flesh out the bare bones of fact with the intimacy of recollection. Certainly his almost unqualified admiration of Strachey suggests that this was a thing he thought worth doing. Strachey's purpose, however, was rather different and his irony more relentlessly mocking. "He had," observes Max with considerable understatement, "like the rest of us, imperfect sympathies."[1] Max, on the other hand, for all of his irreverence, had ever been "a small boy seeing giants."[2] His own course, therefore, took a different turn. Upon his return to Italy late in 1919 there was no diminution of energy, as his continued publication attests. But the prewar world he had so celebrated even while laughing at its artifice and pretense was quite obviously no longer vital in his artistic imagination, just as its contours were no longer visible in the war-scarred terrain of modern life. He would continue his role as a *laudator temporis acti* but as a censorious and occasionally shrill critic of the present, not as the sly and genial conjuror of memory.

It was not merely, however, that Beerbohm had exhausted his stock of materials and had rather lost touch with the contemporary scene and contemporary artists. He had perhaps lost as well the impulse to create a unified major work. That impulse, so frustrated in "The Mirror of the Past," had been realized, however obliquely, in the welded fragments that constitute *Seven Men* and *Rossetti and His Circle*. Never at ease in the century he had survived into and nearly fifty at his return to exile after the war, Beerbohm may have had some sense that the greater part of his career, at least as a writer, was over. I believe such awareness is implied by his authorization of the collected edition of his prose, whose first volumes appeared in 1922.[3] His very first book, we recall, had also been a "collected" edition — seven essays, with a bibliography assembled by John Lane — impishly entitled *Works*. Over twenty-five years separate the two compilations. The archness of the dandified *enfant terrible* is still discernible in the middle-aged recluse; yet there is a kind of drawing in, an awareness that this time the garnering is to be very nearly total. The tenth and last volume of the collected edition, *A Variety of Things* (1928), contains ten pieces, all but two of which were written before 1922. Although the uniform edition was limited to 780 sets,[4] its leaves thereby destined to remain unopened on the shelves of bibliophiles, it is nevertheless reasonable to believe that Beerbohm felt its contents represented fairly definitively what he thought worthy of preservation.

The curious fact of the matter is that even though the *scope* of Beerbohm's invention visibly contracted after the war, his powers as an artist suffered no comparable diminution. The essays of *And Even Now*, for example, are among the best and purest he has written. Manner and matter are perfectly integrated in them. But even though excellent of their kind, they mark on the whole a retreat to the more traditional essay that antedates *Seven Men*. At no time in his life was Beerbohm consumed with soaring ambition, a characteristic of himself he readily acknowledged as an old man: "I had merely some modest wishes — to make good use of such little talents as I had, to lead a pleasant life, to do no harm, to pass muster."[5] Yet in the ten years following the publication of *Zuleika Dobson* he had been caught up in a desire to "do something big," in the words of his fictional character James Pethel. And if he had now abandoned that quest, the reversion to earlier form was not total. Too much had been learned and accomplished in those years. The imaginary reminiscence, though it no longer manifested itself in major works, had yet a profound impact in modifying the essays and caricatures Beerbohm produced in the twenties. And we may best appreciate that impact not by methodically describing the contents of one volume after another but by classifying the experiments and innovations in form that develop in the essays from *Seven Men* and in the caricatures from *Rossetti and His Circle*.

Sir Max Beerbohm

As has already been noted, many of the essays in *And Even Now* were originally composed well before the outbreak of the war; some of them, like "'How Shall I Word It?'" "Kolniyatsch," and "No. 2. The Pines," have already been discussed in an earlier chapter. A considerable number of the remainder are classic examples of the personal essay, timeless in their treatment of the subjects they discuss, remote from the merest suggestion of narrative or fiction, whose very titles — "Hosts and Guests," "Servants," "Going Out for a Walk," "On Speaking French" — recall to us the genial whimsy of the nineteenth century, if not of the eighteenth. These are understandably among the most frequently anthologized of Beerbohm's pieces, little gems of the art of discursiveness. Some indeed are more intimate in their expression of personal feeling, like "The Golden Drugget," which describes almost lyrically the fascination for the author of a roadside inn near his home in Rapallo. "The Crime" is a minor masterpiece of reflection, action, and retribution, all solitary and confessional. Any of these essays might well have been composed ten years before; yet the volume is tinged with a note of sadness for the loss of earlier and simpler times. In "Something Defeasible" that note becomes almost strident as Max sees in a child's delight at the destruction of his sand cottage an emblem of civilization falling into chaos. Dated July 1919, this essay is Max's equivalent of Yeats's "Second Coming." None of these essays, however, appear to be significantly influenced by Max's experiments in form that preceded them.

The "remembering" essays themselves are represented in *And Even Now* only by "No. 2. The Pines," whose appearance as a composition under Beerbohm's name was now made possible by the intervening publication of Gosse's biography of Swinburne in 1917, to which he had originally submitted the piece for excerption. But the subjects of the other finished essays of this group — Moore, Caine, Yeats, and others — were still very much alive. Thus the fastidiousness that had kept Beerbohm from elaborating the contents of the holograph notebook and had shifted him from real to fictional reminiscence in the teen years of the century was no less present in the twenties. The appropriate time arrived too late for their inclusion in the collected edition; indeed, although Max broadcast them over the BBC, they were not gathered together in print until the posthumous edition of *Mainly on the Air* appeared in 1958. One exception is worth noting, however. For the first number of *Life and Letters,* a journal edited by his friend Desmond MacCarthy, Max contributed "Two Glimpses of Andrew Lang."[6] Compounded of personal reflection on details of Lang's appearance, gesture, and language on the two social occasions from Max's worldlier days when he encountered him, the essay is clearly a product of the "remembering" essay phase. It may also have cost Beerbohm many pains to compose, for the sole entry under Lang's name in the holograph notebook reads, "Written — unberufen!"[7] Those pains are well concealed, however, in the seeming artlessness of recollection. Max's "glimpses" reveal more quintessential character than many a full-length biography; and although Lang had been dead sixteen years when it was published, the sketch does not present him at all as a figure of the past. As with his caricatures, by dealing with an established public figure, albeit one known essentially through print, Max can bypass facts readily available to the reader through other sources and concentrate on impressions. Without the slightest alloy of sentiment Beerbohm portrays Lang as supercilious and aloof, a literary celebrity unredeemed by any spark of humanity. That the appraisal is implied rather than pronounced, that it is based on casual incidents meticulously observed and analyzed by one who does not profess to judge but merely to remember, makes the estimate that much more devastating. No aspect of the man is without moral implication:

> Now and again, as he stood propped against the angle of the wall, he inserted with long brown fingers a monocle through which the rays of the eye were refracted with surpassing brilliance. And his manner of doing this seemed to indicate, not that there was any one whom he particularly cared to inspect, but that he took a languid pleasure in the gesture. If to superficial observers the fixing of that monocle might have convicted him of curiosity, the marked way he had of letting it drop promptly down again to his waistcoat must have acquitted him of having found the slightest profit in the investigation.[8]

213

Sir Max Beerbohm

It is apparent that Beerbohm's restraint in publishing his "remembering" essays was not misplaced; such analysis, he had learned, could be applied uncensurably only as ambiguous tributes to the illustrious dead or as ironic ones to the less than illustrious characters of his fiction.

With his literary canon more or less established by the mid-twenties, Beerbohm perhaps felt no longer constrained to confine his reminiscences of contemporaries to "remembering" essays. Some of the materials from the notebook leak out into other, more fugitive forms. In 1925 he supplemented the obituary notice in *The Times* with a few recollections of William Archer drawn from that source.[9] From the same place a few months later came recollections useful in composing an introduction to John Rothenstein's work about his father, *The Portrait Drawings of William Rothenstein 1889–1925, An Iconography*.[10] Clearly he could not simply await the death of friends and acquaintances, with the attendant added risk that they might no longer be noteworthy personages, before committing his memories to the press. Whether the dream of a whole volume of "remembering" essays had faded or not, the fact of the matter is that Max's post-World War I recollections are essentially not of particular persons and incidents but of general and large occurrences. They chronicle, not the awe and trepidation of a sly initiate into the dazzling world of the great, but the wistful passing of a colorful and less frenzied era. The point of view remains technically the same as that in the earlier pieces — we still have the personal responses of Max — but the immediacy of the scene, the clarity of its detail, and the evocation of its emotional affect are all displaced by summation. In short, they are no longer the reminiscences of youth but of age.[11]

Beerbohm's real reminiscences were thus inhibited on the one hand by the depletion of his stock and his inability to publish those essays already composed and on the other by the perspective of middle age, which dimmed the acuity of vision and poignancy of recalled experience. In *Seven Men* he had overcome these disabilities by transferring reminiscence from fact to fiction. The formula he employed, however, could not be indefinitely repeated. Not only were there a limited number of literary or quasi-literary types to be caricatured, there were as well only a limited number of ironic postures for the narrator to assume. And sooner or later the reader would tire of the ingenuity of the hoaxes. The artistic problem for Beerbohm as a writer after the war was how to move beyond the success of *Seven Men*. "Argallo and Ledgett," as we have seen, finished off the series, but it also finished off Max as *eiron*, to say nothing of the literary establishment of writers and critics. If he wished to continue composing imaginary reminiscences, even on a limited scale, he would have to experiment with different subjects and different postures. As the experiments he made were desultory and no longer motivated by a desire to achieve a *chef d'oeuvre*, we may speak of them, as we have of his more traditional postwar essays, without any strict regard to chronological order but rather in terms of distance from the norm of *Seven Men*.

Closest to those sketches in conception is the portrait of T. Fenning Dodworth (1922), not a *soi-disant* poet but a *soi-disant* statesman, a Tory hanger-on continually defeated in his bids for a seat in Parliament and reduced to hack political journalism. He is yet one more of the failures rescued from oblivion by Max's attempt to set the record straight, to flesh out the bare biographical bones of *Who's Who* and the casual allusions of political diarists. Max ironically extols this imagined leader without a following as he had extolled writers without talent, seeing him as "one of the most remarkable, the strongest and, in a way, most successful men of our time."[12] Like "Savonarola" Brown and Enoch Soames, Dodworth is insulated against failure by self-image. In Behrman's words, "he had fought all the battles and won them in the trophied caverns of his own self-esteem."[13] Unlike Brown and Soames, however, Dodworth is merely a fiction of the author; he does not turn out to be a figment of the narrator's imagination. Indeed, the narrator's function in this sketch is reduced virtually to that of commentator. There are no real incidents to speak of, no opportunities for the narrator to react immediately to Dodworth's situation, no occasions for any sympathetic commerce between them. We realize that just as Beerbohm has deliberately moved outside the cozily familiar literary world, he has no less deliberately fashioned another persona for himself, that of the uninvolved spectator whose affection for his hero amounts to no more than a sentimental admiration of his indefatigability: "*Dear* old Dodworth? Well, no — and yet, *yes,* too. I don't like him, perhaps; but there is no man whom I so delight to see, to watch, and to think of" ("Dodworth," p. 150). The return from the fictions of *Seven Men* to the purer essay form of "T. Fenning Dodworth" need not be regarded necessarily as a retreat. The portrait that emerges is of a character far more likely to exist in real life than any of the improbable caricatures of earlier sketches. But a character without a story is like a photograph of an unidentified person — full of unrealizable potential. For conflict and tension we then turn to a consideration of the narrator. We already know that he is not Beerbohm himself but a persona; nevertheless, the persona is one who shares a number of characteristics with the Max we have encountered in *Seven Men.* He is naive but not fatuous, and by his control of the pace and manner of his exposition he shows himself well aware of the nature of Dodworth's "success." However fascinated he may be by the phenomenon of Dodworth, the adulation is ironic. We know that the praise of his wit is hyperbolic for we are given specimens of it. We know too that the narrator cannot accept Dodworth's continued setbacks as triumphs because they are recorded so ludicrously. The laughs are all on Dodworth. Yet there appears to be an inconsistency. Beerbohm seems not to have decided whether he was creating a persona who was a conscious master of facetious understatement or a dolt whose language duplicates that of inept memorialists. In the following passage, for example, it is hard to know whether the person described or the person describing him is the more preposterous.

> One of his eyebrows is slightly raised; the other is slightly lowered, to hold in position a black-rimmed single eyeglass. His nose is magnificently Roman. His lips are small, firm, admirably chiselled, and every word that falls from them is very precisely articulated. His chin is very strong, and his chest (in proportion to his height) deep. He has the neatest of hands and feet. Draped in a toga, and without his monocle, he might pass for a statuette of Seneca. But he prefers and affects a more recent style of costume — the style, somewhat, of the Victorian statesmen who flourished in his youth: a frock-coat and a rather large top-hat, a col-

lar well open at the throat, and round it a riband of black silk tied in a loose bow. ("Dodworth," pp. 135–136)

I suspect that in "T. Fenning Dodworth" Beerbohm was trying to extend reminiscence to a consciousness outside his own — as he had tried, unsuccessfully, to do in "The Mirror of the Past" with the invention of Sylvester Herringham. But his "dreadful little talent for 'parody'" once again intervened. What confirms this suspicion is the fact that Beerbohm left other attempts at invented reminiscence in which he either altered his own perspective slightly (from that of *Seven Men*) or openly ridiculed the pomposity and imperceptiveness of the casual writers of memoirs by stylistic imitation. The consequence here is that the narrative voice alternates uncomfortably between that of "Enoch Soames" and "Kolniyatsch."

The most accomplished of the variations on the *Seven Men* formula of imaginary reminiscence, "T. Fenning Dodworth" is not the most innovative. Two slighter pieces, but recently collected, evidence Beerbohm's ongoing concern with the ways of presenting character with a minimum of story and of recalling with vividness a past far different from the present. The first of these, "Miss Dustworth and Miss Libman," is an undated, unparagraphed sketch of about fifteen hundred words found among Max's papers after his death.[14] It is an investigation of the eccentric lives of two spinsters of uncertain means who are devoted to the theater; as guests of the management they help to fill up unpacked houses. What is most remarkable about the piece, apart from its being written about women, is the nearly objective reportorial stance that Max assumes without relinquishing his own person. He composes his double portrait out of short factual statements descriptive of the shabbiness of the women's outer existence: "A charwoman comes in and 'does for' them at noon. They are not early risers. They are fond of Guinness's stout. They don't read books very much. They never leave the four-mile radius. They used to go for a fortnight to Southsea every August, but sea air no longer agrees with them" ("Dustworth," p. 106). These statements are complemented by somewhat longer ones descriptive of the shabbiness of their inner existence:

Sir Max Beerbohm

> They knew the Marquis de Leuville slightly. He once came to tea and borrowed fifteen shillings from one of them — from Miss Libman, as a matter of fact. Miss Dustworth happened to have nothing in her purse. The Marquis did not come back next day to repay the loan, though he had said he would. After the lapse of a week Miss Dustworth insisted that, as the Marquis had come to see *her*, she must make good the loss to Miss Libman. Miss Libman's pride was wounded. She said that some people never supposed any people would come for the purpose of seeing anyone but themselves. She refused the fifteen shillings. For three days neither lady spoke to the other. ("Dustworth," p. 108)

Since there appears to be no real contact between the women and Max, he can view them only from afar, but, as in "T. Fenning Dodworth," he admits that he doesn't particularly like his subjects, finding their pretensions to gentility, their opinions, and their petty disagreements "rather dreary." Yet he confesses a fascination in contemplating them, much to his wife's displeasure. He addresses the reader personally, almost as in a letter, challenging him to deny, if he can, the appropriateness of such subjects for memorialization: "Perhaps I have written to you at too great length about them. I admit they are not remarkable women; not ladies, exactly; narrow, uncultivated, without any fairness of vision. But am I mistaken in thinking there is a sort of awful cosiness about them? Florence thinks I am utterly mistaken in this opinion. Which of us is right? I will abide by your decision" ("Dustworth," p. 108). This is a strange way to end the piece, if indeed it is ended; such an end leaves us baffled at Beerbohm's intentions in writing it. There is unquestionably a movement away from the involved narrator of *Seven Men;* yet the indecisive recorder, who does not know quite what to make of his data, is neither parodied nor mocked. And the two women, though not particularly differentiated from each other, are a marvelous pair, worthy of having a fiction created around them.

No such ambiguity attends "Then and Now" (1940), which purports to be the recollection of a centenarian, Vera Lady Elderton, whose name alerts us at the outset that we are to be spoofed. The joke is that the reminiscences, all haphazard and without any particular point to them, are either wildly improbable or hopelessly garbled. She distinctly recalls, for example, the

The Fading of Memory

raids by hungry bears that descended in Grosvenor Square from Hampstead in the 1840s and her parents' entertaining Charles Lamb, even though he had died six years before she was born. According to her, the Duke of Wellington acquired his sobriquet "because of the iron shutters that he had put up at Apsley House when the mob broke his windows at the time of his opposition to the first Franchise Bill."[15] She also mutilates Disraeli's peace-with-honor pronouncement upon his return from the Congress of Berlin and renders Whistler's famous repartee to Wilde as follows: "Well, Oscar, I have noticed in the course of years that you do not always avoid the vice of plagiarism, and I will think it not unlikely that sooner or later you will repeat what I have just said, leaving your hearers to suppose that you, not I, originated it!" ("Then and Now," pp. 97–98). An amusing trifle, "Then and Now" perhaps suggests no more than that neither accurate memory nor reasonable understanding are necessarily bestowed upon the mere survivor of events. This theme is a familiar enough one in Beerbohm. Yet a deeper criticism appears to be implied. Lady Elderton's ineptness is in no way the consequence of senility or impaired faculties. She is as spry as ever, busy in her war work, thoroughly at home in the century in which she now lives. Indeed, she finds the tall buildings of modern London preferable to the dismal Mayfair of her childhood and regards science "an immense blessing and improvement in every way" ("Then and Now," p. 98). Max has created her as a polar antithesis to himself. Energetic and muddled, Lady Elderton, we come to realize, has joyously accommodated herself to change only because of her insensitivity to the destruction of traditional values worthy of preservation.

The slight essays just described illustrate Beerbohm's attempts to continue the imaginary reminiscence essentially according to the formulas of the "remembering" essays and *Seven Men*. The range is extended slightly beyond the circumscribed literary world of late Victorian and Edwardian days. Dodworth is a would-be statesman, not a poet; Dustworth and Libman haunt the theater, but not with quite the same motives of a "Savonarola" Brown; and Lady Elderton's renown, had she died earlier, might have been as a lionizing hostess, but as a survivor into the Age of the Common Man she is made to suffer reminiscential unreliability and dullness. More interesting than these slight variations in subject, however, are Beerbohm's efforts in these essays to modify the point of view. They demonstrate once again that he could never wholly remove himself from the central narrator, nor could he alter the character or perspective of that narrator from his own without slipping into parody. Without the capacity to *invent* characters and without the opportunity to *find* new ones, Beerbohm seemed destined to tread again the same round of memory unless, as in *Rossetti and His Circle,* he could find other formulas to generate probable scenes for him to respond to. *And Even Now* contains a number of such experiments.

The foundation of the imaginary reminiscence in its purest form lay in the recollection of a personal witness. This essential characteristic had governed the invention of Sylvester in "The Mirror of the Past," for the mirror itself was a thing of no value without an interpreting observer. There is an alternative, however, to actually being there. If the originals are vivid enough to initiate the evocation, one can interpret scenes witnessed obliquely through one's reading, which is, after all, an extension of experience and observation. The originals, of course, must not be fictional — biography or autobiography is best — or the fancies conjured from them will be no more probable than they. Also, if the secondary reminiscence or conjecture is to have any validity, it must be seen, not as complementing the design of the original writer, but as a reasonable response private and apart from it. When Beerbohm cites episodes from his reading of Goethe and Boswell, he does so in the same way that he cites the mannerisms of Andrew Lang, as the basis for an imaginative composition of his own. In "Quia Imperfectum" Beerbohm creates out of passages from the German poet's *Travels in Italy* an intricate and plausible conjecture of estrangement between Goethe and the artist Wilhelm Tischbein, an estrangement brought about as much by Goethe's Olympian detachment as it is by Tischbein's presumed infatuation with the future Lady Hamilton, both of which justifications are interpolated from the lines of the journal.[16] What has launched Beerbohm on his imaginative quest is a need to explain why Goethe, who speaks at the outset so enthusiastically of a portrait Tischbein is painting

The Fading of Memory

of him, never mentions its completion or disposition. Assuming that the portrait was never finished, Beerbohm determines to give it a place of honor in his museum of incomplete works, along with "Penelope's web and the original designs for the Tower of Babel, the draft made by Mr. Asquith for a reformed House of Lords and the notes jotted down by the sometime German Emperor for a proclamation from Versailles to the citizens of Paris."[17] Facetiousness gives way to fascination, however, as Beerbohm begins to extract from the classically austere prose of Goethe's reminiscence the less than noble feelings of real human beings. However conjectural, Beerbohm's analysis begins to impose itself on our imaginations as quite likely. Because we know, moreover, that the characters are "true," we feel reasonably assured that we cannot be tricked as we are in "Enoch Soames" or "A. V. Laider." So confident, for example, was the BBC that it broadcast "Quia Imperfectum" in connection with the Goethe Bicentennial in 1949.[18] The plausibility of Max's conjecture, however, rests on a false premise — namely, that there is a mystery to unravel in the first place. Not only was Tischbein's portrait, *Goethe in the Campagna,* finished, it is one of the most frequently reproduced presentments of the poet. Yet Beerbohm asserts quite vigorously that he has sought vainly for the painting:

> If you know where that portrait is, tell me. I want it. I have tried to trace it — vainly. What became of it? I thought I might find this out in George Henry Lewes' "Life of Goethe." But Lewes had a hero-worship for Goethe: he thought him greater than George Eliot, and in the whole book there is but one cold mention of Tischbein's name. Mr. Oscar Browning, in the "Encyclopedia Britannica," names Tischbein as Goethe's "constant companion" in the early days at Rome — and says nothing else about him!... What became of the expropriated canvas?... Somewhere, I am sure, in some dark vault or cellar, it languishes. ("Quia Imperfectum," pp. 215–216)

But Beerbohm's research cannot have been that assiduous. Although in private hands for a century, the portrait (which was completed in Naples, not abandoned in Rome, as Max asserts) passed into the collection of the Städelsches Kunstinstitut in

Sir Max Beerbohm

Frankfurt am Main in 1877, since which time it has been prominently displayed as one of the museum's chief treasures.[19] We shall probably never know if Beerbohm actually believed the portrait to be incomplete and lost. But it suits his purpose to say he does. For in so doing he is able to give primacy to an imaginary portrait, just as Walter Ledgett comes to prefer to his actual life the adventures imputed to him by fictitious letters. Although he enjoins his readers to find the missing painting for him, Max is more than content with the portrait in his mind, whose outline was drawn by Goethe's words and whose colors have been supplied by his own imagination.

> I have formed so clear and sharp a preconception of the portrait that I am likely to be disappointed at sight of what you bring me. I see in my mind's eye every falling fold of the white mantle; the nobly-rounded calf of the leg on which rests the forearm; the high-light on the black silk stocking. The shoes, the hands, are rather sketchy, the sky is a mere slab; the ruined temples are no more than adumbrated. But the expression of the face is perfectly, epitomically, that of a great man surveying a great alien scene and gauging its import not without a keen sense of its dramatic conjunction with himself. ("Quia Imperfectum," p. 217)

It looks remarkably like the real thing; if anything, it is almost better.

Beerbohm conjures up another imaginative amplification from biography in "'A Clergyman'" (1918), where he dilates upon a casual incident in Boswell's *Life of Johnson,* investing it with dramatic intensity. He re-creates the plight of a shy young man whose timid conversational gambit meets with immediate and total defeat by the Great Cham. Unlike the conjecture of "Quia Imperfectum," however, the scene here expanded is not introduced with elaborate justification but as a frank indulgence in imaginative annotation: "Fragmentary, pale, momentary; almost nothing; glimpsed and gone; as it were, a faint human hand thrust up, never to reappear, from beneath the rolling waters of Time, he forever haunts my memory and solicits my weak imagination. Nothing is told of him but that once, abruptly, he asked a question, and received an answer."[20] Max sees the clergyman, whose name Boswell cannot recall, anxiously

The Fading of Memory

squirming for an opportunity to participate in the table talk on the one subject that he may presumably speak of with some authority — contemporary sermons. But his innocent question, "Were not Dodd's sermons addressed to the passions?" meets with a crushing rebuff from Dr. Johnson: "They were nothing, Sir, be they addressed to what they may." Beerbohm's imagination renders the clergyman's annihilation complete. But he goes even further. To make the scene still more immediate for us, he proposes to abstract from it the fact perhaps most difficult for moderns to accept, namely, that all the animated discussion had as its subject the style and effectiveness of sermons. He then creates an archetypal scene in which contemporary novelists are made to substitute for the eighteenth-century divines; for Atterbury, Tillotson, Jortin, and Sherlock, read Wells, Galsworthy, Corelli, and Caine. Seeing his neo-Georgian contemporaries as types of paleo-Georgian worthies suggests, of course, that our tastes and preferences in art, which seem to us matters of such great moment, will pass, as did those of Johnson's age, into curious and inexplicable crotchets. But this perspective gets as well at the essence of the scene, inviting us to see the fundamental timelessness of reminiscence and the interpenetration of our personal experiences of life with those of our personal experiences of literature. Once again Beerbohm celebrates a personal, idiosyncratic response to public performance.

Like most of the essays in *And Even Now*, the two just discussed take literature itself as their basic point of departure. As imaginative extensions of literary texts, however, they are subject to a particular scrutiny from which the other essays in the volume are exempt, namely that of the scholar. It is all very well to parody trendy literary journalism in "Kolniyatsch" and letter-writing manuals in "'How Shall I Word It?'" but "Quia Imperfectum" and "'A Clergyman'" are more serious efforts and purport, however subjectively, to illuminate the books they discuss. It is true that we do not run to Beerbohm for explication; yet our enjoyment of his embroidery on the fabric of the text is to a high degree dependent on its appropriateness. The inventions of *Rossetti and His Circle* have a likelihood for us because they seem the product of a total immersion in Rossettiana, albeit at the shallow end of the Pre-Raphaelite pool. But no such assurance attends Max's other readings. Much of the power of "'A Clergyman,'" for example, derives from Beerbohm's rescue of the cleric from oblivion by caring about him and giving him a story, much as he earlier rescued Enoch Soames. The significance of the act is heavily dependent on the clergyman's otherwise remaining obscure, anonymous. To have him identified in the definitive edition of the *Life* as Mr. Embry,[21] even without further elaboration, though it cannot reduce the intensity of Beerbohm's scene, nevertheless diminishes the passionate need for imagining it. It is as if Soames had been named in Holbrook Jackson's book. Similarly, although Max's ingenuity in extracting the probable but not openly expressible feelings of Goethe and Tischbein from letters and journals continues to delight us, the "truth" of the essay is never quite the same after we have realized that it is based on a false assumption. There is a difference, then, in writing imaginative responses between those stimulated by people and those by books. Beerbohm's reaction to Yeats, despite the fact that it may not have been particularly sympathetic or understanding, was nevertheless real, occasioned by things Yeats actually said and did, the product of authentic, if not total, encounter. But that authenticity becomes tarnished when, invited to participate in imaginary reminicence from a textual source, we have reason to suspect misreading.

"Quia Imperfectum" and "'A Clergyman'" build imaginative scenes out of hints from literature. Externally supplied with characters and situations, Max had only to elaborate upon them to produce an illustrative "reminiscence." But he could on occasion generate a plausible remembrance from even slighter materials, as attested by "William and Mary" (1920), which "stands unique among Beerbohm's works."[22] Like all of Beerbohm's tales, this one is heavily ironic, only here the effect is one of pathos rather than of satire. Lord David Cecil describes the genesis of this most fictional of Max's fictions as follows:

> The story was inspired by the memory of an empty house in the country he visited some years ago when staying with Herbert [Beerbohm Tree]. He had rung the bell and listened to it echoing forlornly through the desolated rooms. "I invented a story round the strange emotion caused by the weird ringing of the bell," he

said. What sort of people had lived there? he wondered, and gradually the figures of an imaginary couple had formed themselves in his imagination. The story relates how Max had made friends with a happy young married pair called William and Mary, how the friendship was ended by their death and of his solitary pilgrimage years later to the house, now desolate, where he had witnessed and shared their happiness.[23]

Apart perhaps from the fairy tales, no other work of Beerbohm's strikes so sentimental a chord. Yet one cannot help feeling that "William and Mary" is but another experiment in the generation of imaginary reminiscences, a quest that goes somewhat awry in "A Relic" (1918). The title of this piece refers to the broken remains of a fan picked up by Max years ago on the terrace of a French casino. The fragments of white bone now before him recall to him that he had been witness to the conclusion of an angry scene between a young woman and a middle-aged man even though he was ignorant of the origin and substance of their quarrel. As a very young man himself and a candidate for literary fame, Max had tried (vainly) to construct a fiction appropriate to their public display of passion: "I was determined to make a story of what I had seen — a *conte* in the manner of Guy de Maupassant."[24] Having settled on the first sentence of his tale, which was to be repeated as the last one as well, Max proceeds, rather like "Savonarola" Brown, to allow the characters to determine their own destiny with a minimum of editorial supervision. Needless to say, none of the strained false starts ever comes to anything. The tale refuses to adhere to Mlle. Angélique and M. Joumand, sticking instead to Max himself, becoming a reminiscence of his callow attempts to become a writer. "A Relic" and "William and Mary" are thus in a measure complementary: the one proclaims his limitations as an artist, his incapacity to write convincingly of anything he has not personally experienced or to assume a manner not his own; the other is a *tour de force,* demonstrating exactly the opposite, that he could, in fact, invent wholly fictional characters and circumstances and could treat them, moreover, in a thoroughly tender and unsardonic way. What was essential, however, was that in all instances the narrative remain a reminiscence.

Sir Max Beerbohm

Although the great prose work was to elude him, although he would never again create characters of such monumental eccentricity as those in *Seven Men*, Max continued to experiment in these ways with generating fictional reminiscences. That the concern was fundamentally a formal one may be inferred from the existence of essays whose purpose can only be regarded as offering instruction in the composition of memorable scenes. In "A Point to be Remembered by Very Eminent Men" (1918), the men are literary and the point is that they ought never to introduce themselves to their worshipers except in their own homes, making their respective grand entrances only after deliberate delays of no less than ten and no more than twenty minutes. Beerbohm discusses the psychological rationale for his prescription, to be sure, but he pretends to derive its authority from the actual practice of autobiographers in the way they have recorded their first meetings with the great. Beerbohm thus implies that there are conventions in the construction of scenes in autobiography (or memoir) just as surely as there are in drama. "Fenestralia" (1944) is a rather late essay devoted completely to the recollection of people or events seen through or in open windows. Max throws together personal and historic incidents with biblical, literary, dramatic, and artistic scenes to demonstrate that the most memorable have been consciously composed, framed spatially. A much slighter affair, "A Note on the Einstein Theory" (1923), attempts, rather feebly, to provide some homely anecdotal adjunct, the equivalent of Newton's apple or Watt's tea kettle, to the theory of relativity. His purpose is rather like that of the modern image maker: however kindly and genial Einstein may appear in photographs, his work can never impress the lay consciousness until invested with some personal characteristics. In these three essays Beerbohm shows himself at least as interested in the engineering required to make events memorable as in the events themselves. The attention to form is certainly not new; only after *Seven Men*, however, does Beerbohm devote whole essays to the abstract discussion of it. It would not be amiss therefore to regard *And Even Now*, the most varied and stylistically accomplished of all of Max's collections of prose, as a book of essays in the most fundamental sense of the term, for almost all of its pieces are attempts to construct

The Fading of Memory

reminiscences in strikingly new and original ways. That quest to make vivid the memorable moment may be said to inform the book with its unity. But Beerbohm's concern, as we have seen, did not end with the publication of this volume; indeed, it continued, however sporadically, well into his declining years.

In treating of Beerbohm's caricatures drawn after the monumental series *Rossetti and His Circle,* one faces the same problem of selection and multifariousness encountered earlier in this study. Once again I have chosen to confine the discussion essentially to those drawings that have been reproduced in books, either in his own albums or as illustrations in other works, on the principle that these are the likeliest to be known and were presumably thought worthiest of preservation. There are, indeed, some notorious exceptions. In his exhibition at the Leicester Galleries in May 1923 Max seemed to tread very closely to *lèse majesté.* A series of drawings, "Proposed Illustrations for Sir Sidney Lee's Forthcoming Biography [of Edward VII]" (HD 505 –512), now in the queen's collection, has never been reproduced, nor has its existence been widely publicized. Another drawing, one of Max's uncanny previsions, chronicles the wedding in 1972 of the then Prince of Wales (later Edward VIII and duke of Windsor) to a commoner (HD 528); creating a furor in the press, it was withdrawn from the exhibition and passed into private hands. These controversial instances apart, however, we may confidently assert that the best of Beerbohm's post-World War I caricatures have been reproduced in some form. And their number is by no means small. Of the more than fifteen hundred dated caricatures listed in Hart-Davis's *Catalogue,* almost a third were drawn after *Rossetti and His Circle;* of all the caricatures reproduced in album form very nearly half were published subsequent to the completion of the Rossetti series.[25] Whatever falling off in industry he may have experienced as a writer, Beerbohm certainly returned to his drawing table in Rapallo with assiduity.

Although the exceptions are significant, and will be discussed at length below, for the most part — at least in terms of numbers of drawings — Beerbohm's return to Italy constituted for him a return to artistic normality, a picking up where he had left off after the adventurous interlude of *Rossetti and His Circle*. Certain stylistic attributes of that work could not, of course, be unlearned. For example, although the backgrounds in the drawings of the twenties never assume the importance that they do in *Rossetti and His Circle*, on the whole these compositions are far more elaborate than those of the earlier teens. There is also a softening of visual hyperbole in favor of implied situational paradox, less distortion of physical features and less exaggeration of postures. But even though their general tendency is more intellectual than that of the prewar drawings, they revert nevertheless to earlier conceptual formulas for their generation — portrait, group, confrontation, and introduction — essentially without the intensity of a fully imagined scene.

Beerbohm, it must be allowed, does not quite return to the beginning of his career, to the simplicity of the single portraits of *Caricatures of Twenty-Five Gentlemen*. Portrait caricatures, in fact, do not figure very prominently in the postwar collections, no doubt because of Beerbohm's isolation from fresh visual impressions of current celebrities. Of the eleven single portraits in *A Survey*, the six drawn before the war appear to have greater "bite" though less timeliness; that of Alfonso XIII of Spain (HD 12) is a true caricature, but those of Lloyd George (HD 951) and the deposed Kaiser Wilhelm (HD 1798), eked out with provocative captions, seem wrought less out of fascination with their subjects than a desire to appear *au courant*. There are, to be sure, some memorable portrait caricatures in the later volumes, but they are not numerous. That of Aldous Huxley (HD 780) in *Things New and Old* seems rather more superficial than it might be; that of Lytton Strachey (HD 1604) in *Observations* is more masterful and sympathetic, though Max draws his subject frozen in so pronounced a scholar's slouch that he is virtually reduced to a caryatid upholding an invisible entablature. But then Max regarded Strachey as a kindred spirit, drew several other caricatures of him, and had, moreover, when in London to arrange an exhibition, asked Strachey whether he "might professionally stare at him."[26] Generally, however, the portrait caricatures of the postwar years manifest an unimaginative blandness. By 1931, when he drew eight portraits each as a weekly supplement to the *Spectator*, they had dwindled to spirit-

The Fading of Memory

less illustrations. Even H. G. Wells (HD 1759) could no longer excite Max's languid pencil: only an overhead light worked by pulleys gives testimony to what Max had found so oppressive in Wells, a tendency to prefer mechanical solutions for human problems.

The published group portraits of the period are also neither numerous nor particularly distinguished. The chief problem attending such compositions is that the pretext for assembling the group is so thin that there is really no opportunity for the personages caricatured to strike interesting poses or to react to one another. A notable exception is the caricature in *A Survey* entitled *"Tout peut se rétablir"* (HD 1749), depicting a greatly agitated Sidney Webb convoking an "Urgent Conclave of Doctrinaire Socialists, to decide on some means of inducing the Lower Orders to regard them once more as Visionaries merely." Born of a horror of Bolshevism, the drawing is an assemblage of honorable, well-meaning, but impractical idealists. By mingling the readily recognizable figures of Webb, Shaw, Wells, and Cunninghame Graham with more shadowy and indistinct grotesques, Beerbohm succeeds in conveying a feeling of their collective perplexity. One senses that these men, stroking their beards or looking dreamily vacant, cannot comprehend that their reverie has become the world's nightmare; they seem incapable of dealing with any but theoretical issues. Tied more closely both to the technique and to the spirit of *Rossetti and His Circle* are two group caricatures not reproduced in Max's albums that, though wholly imagined in their details, commemorate actual events. Both have been used to illustrate books, where they are accompanied with keys to identify the personages caricatured. The first is Max's rendering of "The Red Cross Sale at Christie's, April 1918" (HD 679), to which, it might be recalled, he had contributed his "Further Recollections by Viscount M., O.M."[27] With the clock and the auctioneer's rostrum in the center background of the composition, forty-three celebrities of the artistic, literary, theatrical, and financial worlds are arrayed, seeing and being seen, in various attitudes of connoisseurship. Paintings of various styles and periods fill the walls, but they seem far less interesting than the parade of self-important figures shuffling by them. The drawing is executed, moreover, with the same loving physiognomical precision of the Rossetti series. On the occasion of his seventieth birthday Edmund Gosse was presented with a bronze bust of himself, to which more than two hundred friends had subscribed. Max himself was not present at the ceremony, which he nevertheless recorded in "The Birthday Surprise" (HD 612), his own personal tribute to Gosse.[28] A startled Gosse steps back from the simulacrum of himself, surrounded by twenty-seven well-wishers, all standing about in characteristic postures familiar to us from other caricatures by Max. Although drawn with a freer hand than the auction-sale group of the year before, this caricature delights us no less for its crowding together of so many diverse types, persuading us that they did indeed appear simultaneously on a single stage. Perhaps the best known of Beerbohm's group portraits is "Some Persons of 'the Nineties' little imagining, despite their Proper Pride and Ornamental Aspect, how much they will interest Mr Holbrook Jackson and Mr Osbert Burdett" (HD 1650; BLC 51), which assembles a dozen real literary and artistic worthies, including Max himself, as well as a hint of the dim Enoch Soames being harangued by Yeats. Remarkable more for its evocation of a thirty-year-old past than for any authenticity or analysis, the drawing appears to have been occasioned by the publication of Osbert Burdett's book *The Beardsley Period*. Although the renewed and critical interest in the era in which he came of age may have stimulated Beerbohm to bring together his visual memories of these men, the drawing is in no sense an illustration of that interest. One might note, by the way, that the diminutive Rothenstein, who so animatedly engages Beardsley in conversation while a languid Max looks on in the right foreground, is not even mentioned in Burdett's book. Beerbohm is less concerned with what posterity may make of the men of the nineties than in conveying what they thought of themselves. They are all in evening dress, many with walking sticks, and each in his own way appears to be performing for his neighbor. The drawing's legend, which does not condescend to identify the persons portrayed, declares them unconcerned about what posterity may think of them. Beerbohm's point, one that he asserts frequently in the postwar years, is that whether or not his generation possessed men of genius or of talent merely, it pre-eminently had style, an element deplorably absent in the twentieth century.

Group caricatures, as I pointed out in an earlier chapter, however meticulously executed, rarely display the well-defined contrasts of which caricatures of confrontation are capable. And it is to this latter general class that most of Beerbohm's postwar album drawings belong. Confrontations, such as that between Ibsen and Archer, had been the basis for some of Beerbohm's most memorable prewar caricatures, as well as for many of the most effective scenes in *Rossetti and His Circle*. Moreover, confrontation is the fundamental organizing principle behind the highly successful series of drawings in *Observations*, "The Old and the Young Self," described below. Beerbohm's nonseries confrontations, however, generally seem feebler than his earlier work in this category. Partially — but only partially — this is due to a considerable shift in Max's subject matter from literature and art to politics and musings on the state of the world generally, a shift frequently explained as a consequence of his greater reliance on newspapers rather than personal encounters as a source of inspiration and information. Yet from the very outset of his career Beerbohm was fascinated by political figures. That interest, however, had always resided more in their personalities than in their programs. One could be fascinated by a Lord Rosebery; it was difficult to be so about Stanley Baldwin — or, in 1920, about Winston Churchill compared to his father, Lord Randolph.[29] Thus the change in the atmosphere in which political activity took place (and this is true to a lesser extent of literary and artistic activity as well), quite as much as a loss of firsthand observation, led Max to move away from caricatures of personal confrontation to editorial cartoons. For example, Sir Edward Carson engages not with a real adversary but with John Bull (HD 248), and the caption must tell us what it is all about; Independent Liberalism, depicted as a great-domed, spindly intellectual, stands in the palm of a gross, microcephalic figure called Labour (HD 1995); and a similarly corpulent bully, though somewhat better dressed, identified as a Captain of Industry, berates a meek clergyman for failing to keep the masses in check, actually piercing his breast with massive index finger (HD 1998). These instances are all drawn from *A Survey,* which features as well, it should be added, a delightful imaginative rendition of Hilaire Belloc's audience with Pope Benedict XV (HD 122; BLC 38).

The tendency toward generalization and allegorization extends to the later albums as well, even if it cannot be said to pervade them thoroughly. Nor are the results necessarily unpleasing. "The Insurgence of Youth" (HD 2027), for example, is conceived in the tradition of the he-she dialogues of social satire of George Du Maurier. But here Max so totally effaces his usual style in delineating a bored and cynical flapper and her effete male companion that the drawing itself hardly requires the addition of their foul-mouthed political observations. Their graceless postures alone indict them for shallowness and insensitivity. Even though no particular persons are satirized, a generation has been characterized, without recourse to the more usual personified abstractions Beerbohm employs in this period. For the most part, however, the confrontations of nonspecific persons are not very effective. Even those of flamboyant real people do not always work. Max had successfully caricatured both Paderewski and D'Annunzio in the heyday of their artistic careers. He brings the two together in *"Post Taedia Longa Laborum"* (HD 401; BLC 15) to make an observation on their postwar political careers. But neither the drawing nor the legend conveys much more than the fact that they have been active in both art and politics. Indeed, in treating only one kind of subject — royalty — do Max's confrontation caricatures of this period seem to have any cutting edge. Understandably, these do not constitute a very large proportion of the whole, and the two Edwards are his principal targets. The retrospective drawing entitled "The rare, the rather awful visits of Albert Edward, Prince of Wales, to Windsor Castle" (HD 503), executed in 1921 but suggesting the earlier manner of *The Poets' Corner,* possesses the "truth" of the imaginary reminiscence. The fully grown Prince of Wales, hands clasped behind his back, stands in a corner, while Queen Victoria, her hands clasped in her lap, sits in the foreground, awaiting her son's reformation of character. The point is hardly subtle; yet it says much about the personalities of both sovereigns. Three years later Max depicted Edward VII's grandson in "The Prince of Wales in New York" (HD 530), besieged by a chorus of shrill and muscular viragos, each intent upon claim-

The Fading of Memory

ing him as a social prize. It is difficult, of course, to divest ourselves of our knowledge of subsequent history in savoring this caricature, yet the prince seems not altogether as distressed by the attentions of these harpies as he might be. Perhaps because the postwar world offered so few truly public personages of any elegance or panache, Beerbohm's caricatures of confrontation became correspondingly more subdued.

This weakness is even more pronounced in the very few drawings of this period that attempt to establish triangular relationships among the figures caricatured. Beerbohm had brought the introduction scene to perfection in *Rossetti and His Circle* in such drawings as "John Ruskin meets Miss Cornforth" (HD 1272; BLC 44) and "Mr. Morley brings Mr. Mill" (HD 1280; BLC 60). But the greater depersonalization of Max's subject matter in the postwar era rendered subtlety of response irrelevant. There is, moreover, something inherently absurd in representing personified abstractions conforming to the social conventions of a bygone age. In a drawing such as "Logic and Mathematics reconciled through the bitterness of beholding the passionate advances now made by Mr. Bertrand Russell to Physics" (HD 1346; BLC 73), even though one appreciates the delicacy of the allusion to the philosopher's amorous proclivities, the wit lies all in the title; it is not a scene that can be truly envisioned. Parody offers some relief to the problem: "Literature, Mr. Guedalla, and the Law" (HD 655) depicts the central figure tugged in opposite directions by the two muses, and the effectiveness of the drawing, both in terms of composition and in terms of intellectual delight, derives from the imitation of Sir Joshua Reynolds's *Garrick between Tragedy and Comedy*.[30] But even where the persons are wholly real, the introduction scene no longer seems an appropriate vehicle for comic observation. Certainly the idea of Victor Emmanuel's introducing Mussolini to George V as one constitutional monarch to another (HD 1079) is no more farfetched than Henry James's making a match between the Mona Lisa and the Man in the Iron Mask (HD 809). But the earlier drawing afforded some insight into the workings of James's genius whereas the later one leaves us unsure of what mark has been aimed at. It is impossible to read much into the expression of the two kings, though they obviously contrast with the coarse-featured Mussolini who towers above them. The point of the drawing may be the anachronism of the bemedaled and beribboned monarchs in the age of the proletarian strong man, but the pictorial means seem inadequate to represent it forcefully. In short, Beerbohm's reversion to earlier formulas to generate the scenes of his caricatures was inadequate to accommodate either the alteration of his subject matter from the confined area of upper-class culture to the broader one of global affairs or the shift in perspective from one of personal impression to that of a citizen of the world.

However comfortable Max may have felt with these old formulas, however, he was not averse to experimenting with new ones. In 1917, whether before or after the completion of the Rossetti series we do not know, he executed a series of what he called "doubles," caricature improvisations based on the symmetrical patterns produced by folding in two a sheet of paper to which random blotches of color had been applied (HD 1879–1903). Exhibited in the spring show of 1921, none appeared in book form until Hart-Davis reproduced four in the *Catalogue*. Rather like Rorschach inkblots that have been doodled over, Max's "doubles" are interesting more as extemporaneous curiosities than as ingenious compositions. Work on the Rossetti series, however, did influence two more significant and rather disparate groups of drawings. The first, a set of sixteen "Studies in the Eighteen-Seventies" (HD 1904–1919), capitalizes on Beerbohm's talent for imposing fictions as realities upon his viewers. Conceived as *Vanity Fair* portraits, antedated to disarm suspicion, these caricatures seem authentic. Their authenticity is belied only by the ironic letterpress that accompanies them. A self-consciously ascetic Father Vernon (HD 1915), for example, attired in biretta and well-tailored cassock, is described thus: "Amidst all that he has suffered for the Faith of his adoption, he has the comfort of knowing that ladies of even the highest fashion have professed to find no flaw in his dialectics." And Father Vernon is but one of the pillars of the community who are being toppled even as they are being extolled. The illusion of personal witness is compelling, and so pointed are the barbs of the text, which amplify hints in the drawings, that we find it hard to believe that the studies are inventions. For Desmond MacCarthy

The Fading of Memory

they possessed the truth of historical fiction: "These portraits of by-gone types . . . are as convincing as figures in a novel of genius. It is hard to believe that if their shades returned they would not feel the same mixture of resentment and gratification as visitors to the Leicester Galleries who today find themselves ridiculed and immortalized by 'Max.' The longer we look at them the more they seem to belong to their period."[31] Wholly unsatirical in character, on the other hand, are the five "sentimental" drawings — illustrations really — that make up *Heroes and Heroines of Bitter Sweet* (1931), a portfolio celebrating the Noel Coward play. Deriving from the painstaking draftsmanship and artistic maturity of *Rossetti and His Circle*, these drawings, though highly stylized, are utterly free of any comic hyperbole. It would be foolish to assert that this work represents the culmination of Beerbohm's career as a visual artist, the end toward which he was tending in the softening of the asperities and the inclination to more realistic portraiture of *Rossetti and His Circle*. It would be foolish because the portfolio is quite anomalous in Max's canon and because he continued to draw true caricatures up to the time of his death a quarter of a century later. Nevertheless, we must observe that *Heroes and Heroines* is the last album of drawings Beerbohm published.

The foregoing experiments, whatever else they may signify, indicate at least that Max was willing to attempt new ventures. And because they involve groups of drawings rather than single ones, they may be symptomatic as well of his desire to break out of the old mold, to strike out in a new direction, albeit not so boldly or dramatically as in *Rossetti and His Circle*. But all this is purely conjectural. What is certain is that none of these experiments was ever repeated or led anywhere beyond itself. In short, they provided him with no new formulas for generating caricatures. The old formulas, however, had never been ends in themselves but rather means of highlighting disparities between profession and performance and between the image of the self projected and that actually received. They were but contrivances enabling Max to convey a highly personal, idiosyncratic response to public celebrities. First his retirement to Italy and then the war itself changed all that, and we have seen with what success personal witness yielded to imaginary witness. But *Ros-*

setti and His Circle was a unique undertaking, long in gestation, not repeatable. What was really called for, if Beerbohm was not to stagnate artistically, was a new set of conventions to convey his altered perspective. The basis of caricature, an awareness of discrepancy, the perception of a gulf between the ideal and the real or between what is anticipated and what is brought to pass, had of course gone unchanged. It was Beerbohm — or rather, his point of view — that had. As a young man, with his notebook jottings of anecdotes and quirks and his sketches drawn on the backs of envelopes, intent on commemorating the instant of time, Max had concentrated on *simultaneous* discrepancy — on the war, for example, in Kipling between a talented fabulist and a worshiper of vulgarity and brute force, or on the intellectual beauty and overwrought intricacy of Henry James's analysis of human behavior. As a middle-aged man, deprived by choice and circumstance of first-hand observation, relying more on the mind's than on the body's eye, Max became more aware of temporal discrepancy, of how things now differed from what they once had been. The most successful of the postwar caricatures are those whose situations accommodate this later principle most skillfully.

A simple formula to deal with contrasts developing over time is to present them in paired drawings — then and now. The first drawing would exemplify things in the good old days; the second, a parallel composition in all respects, would show the change, usually in the form of some degeneracy or corruption of an institution or the loss of elegance or distinction in a person. Hart-Davis lists a number of such paired drawings executed in the early twenties, whose tenor we can extract merely from their titles and descriptions. "Author, Publisher, and Printer," which exists in three states (HD 1993, 1993A, 1994), explores the differing relative conditions of these three collaborators in the production of books "in the dear old recent time" and "at the present time." The author is beggared in both instances, but publisher and printer have traded the roles of patron and client from the first drawing to the second. In "The Average Secretary of State" (HD 1999), the first, in Hart-Davis's words, "is a finished drawing of a slim and elegant aristocrat"; the second "is an outline drawing of a coarse plebeian." If Max required any

The Fading of Memory

visual stimulus to produce these impersonal caricatures, his flying visits to London probably afforded enough. On his return to Rapallo after his exhibition in the spring of 1921, at which he had shown "St. James's Street Yesterday and To-Day" (HD 1997), he wrote to a friend:

> Ah, *Londres!* — *parlons de cet endroit!* — or rather, don't let's! In the year that has elapsed since I saw it, it has sunk much lower. It doesn't look *dingy* any more, certainly. The house-fronts have been freshly painted. But oh the people in the streets! Oh Piccadilly on a May morning! I saw ladies and gentlemen in private houses. But only there. They *never* go out — except perhaps the ladies, unattended, to earn something towards the rent, by night! In the daytime the streets are packed, thanks to the redistribution of what wealth England still has, with perfectly dreadful people — people who were perfectly charming in the old days when one didn't see them, when one had the pleasure of pitying them unseen somewhere in the slums and the sweating-shops, and of feeling how perfectly charming one was not to be forgetting them while one gadded about the brilliant metropolis.[32]

Never utterly devoid of snobbery, some of Max's paired drawings lament the decline of literature as well as the decline of society. In "English Fiction — Ancient and Modern" (HD 2016) what distinguishes the pairs of lovers, apart from their costume, is the loss of sin, which Max conceives as an aesthetic rather than a moral loss. The ancient hero is shown "trying to control a guilty passion (Quite dramatic and interesting, this)," while his modern counterpart is "trying to muster up a guilty passion (Less dramatic, surely, and less interesting)." In "Parerga of Statesmanship" (HD 2024) the doddering old nobleman, when not engaged in the affairs of the nation, devotes himself to "a flat but faithful version of the Georgics, in English hexameters," while his modern counterpart, sweat dripping from his enraged face, dictates, for profit, a serialization of his self-aggrandizing memoirs for an undiscriminating literary public. In all of these instances, however, it is the accompanying text that establishes the contrast; the pictures merely fix them in the mind.

The principal limitation of paired drawings is their obviousness. Little subtlety is possible where the eye moves mechani-

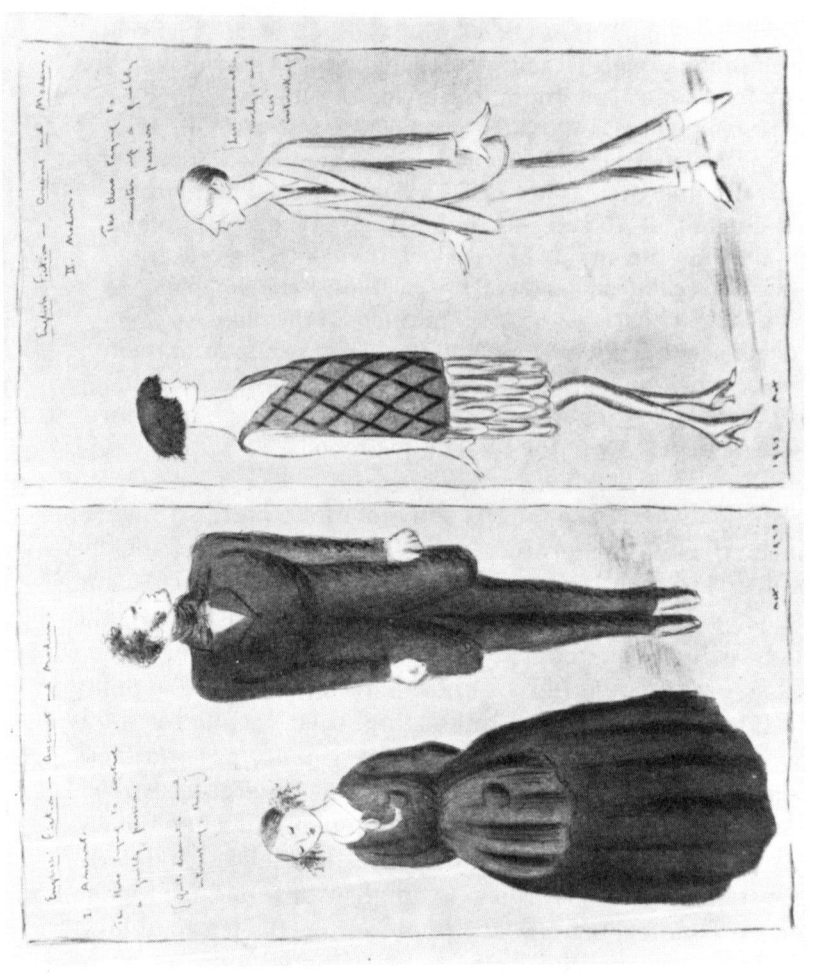

English Fiction — Ancient and New. (1923). Courtesy of Mrs. David Karmel.

cally from left to right and back again, registering correspondences. Moreover, their "point" is invariably the same, that the present constitutes a declension from the past. Without either the richness of particularity or the suddenness of the unexpected, relying heavily on caption to carry the burden of scenic exposition, paired drawings seem longer on instruction than delight. They offer us no occasions to revel in their fancy. A kind of complication is possible by extending the contrasts beyond merely two frames. This possibility admits a more judicious historical perspective, it is true, but does little to reduce the visual tedium induced by knowing exactly what to look for in the drawing and exactly where to find it. In a series of three drawings done in 1920 Beerbohm depicts the future as beheld by the eighteenth, nineteenth, and twentieth centuries (HD 1983–1985). In the first, reflecting a view of the deterioration of civilization, a bewigged and frock-coated worthy scrutinizes a dimmer, less dignified version of himself; in the second, reflecting the liberal idea of material progress, a prosperous bourgeois contemplates an even bigger and more prosperous version of himself; in the third, the gazer into the future wears a black mourning band on his sleeve and betrays not a jot of self-esteem — he beholds nothing other than a question mark. Certainly the three drawings make a more complex statement than a pair might. Yet one feels, particularly in coming upon the question mark, more interest in the abstract idea than in its graphic embodiment. More ambitious and more provocative is the series of nine drawings "Tales of Three Nations" (HD 2007–2015), which was published in the 1923 volume *Things New and Old*. Like the last series, the individual drawings are titled but carry no other explanatory legend. (Paired drawings, on the contrary, are generally accompanied by elaborate captions.) Each drawing contains three figures representing England, France, and Germany at intervals during the nineteenth and early twentieth centuries. Although no labels are attached to any of the figures, the viewer has no difficulty telling them apart; their changing status relative to one another is indicated by positioning, costume, and size. The interpretation of history thus documented seems rather naive and simplistic. Although at least one military figure seems to dominate every picture except the fourth (representing the 1840s), as a soldier England never swaggers and seems to take up arms only in order to finish a fight he has not begun (the second drawing is 1815; the seventh is 1914). At all other times England is represented as a businessman poring over account books. France and Germany alternately puff themselves up in the splendor of uniform. There does not seem much difference between them. Indeed, the most disturbing picture of the series is the last, depicting the status of the three nations in January 1923. In a plumed helmet much the worse for wear, beak-nosed and claw-fingered, a rapacious France swoops down on a hapless Germany, whose open palms indicate that he has no more to give. Both are in tatters, while England sits at his desk behind a spindle piled high with bills. What is remarkable, not about the drawing itself but about its reading of events, is the very harsh judgment implied against France in its policy of exacting reparations and the compassion shown toward Germany in its inability to pay. Moreover, the positions of the three countries in this last drawing — an obsequious Germany on the left, a domineering France in the center, and a preoccupied but not disinterested England observing the scene on the right — recall those of the first one, of the Napoleonic era, suggesting that the whole cycle may be beginning again, the participants older and impoverished but no wiser than a century before.

"Tales of Three Nations" certainly makes a more thoughtful statement than any of its precursors in the representation of temporal change through parallel drawings. Raising the number of "takes" from two or three to nine allows for ampler reflection on the issues under consideration. In the final analysis, however, our judgment of these series drawings rests on our perception of their message rather than on the effectiveness of their execution. We do so because, as in a comic strip, our attention is always directed to the mental space between the drawings rather than to the drawings themselves. The more acute visual impressions of discrepancy are always converted into the duller coin of intellectual abstraction before they become negotiable. This assertion explains why in these drawings Max yielded so readily to allegory — and to that of the least imaginative kind. An arresting scene or an ambiguous one would slow down the mental process of comparison and contrast, dissipating its ef-

The Fading of Memory

fect. The consequence for Beerbohm as a graphic artist, however, was that he was enfeebled in the one capacity in which he really excelled, that of creating memorable ironic fancies.

There is, however, one significant triumph of form among these post-Rossettian caricatures in which Beerbohm overcame the problem of abstraction in dealing with the disparities occasioned by temporal change. Max's solution, moreover, is thoroughly consistent with the artistic premise underlying "The Mirror of the Past," namely, that past and present may be witnessed simultaneously, indeed may be brought into confrontation with each other directly. "The Old and the Young Self" consists of nineteen drawings executed in 1924 and exhibited and published in the following year.[33] As the collective title suggests, their uniform theme is the encounter within a single scene of the mature and immature embodiments of a person across the years. The opportunity here is for more than a contrast between youth and age or energy and weariness, but as much between idealism and pragmatism, struggle and success, and potentiality and achievement. These drawings allow, moreover, the additional possibility of engagement going beyond mere juxtaposition. The mirror between the two figures dissolves as dramatic dialogue ensues. This dissolution is literally the case in the drawing of the painter Walter Sickert (HD 1528), in which the Old Self upbraids the Young Self across an invisible partition that divides the room into squalid and "aesthetic" halves. Although the formula for generating these scenes is nothing more than a specific application of the principle of confrontation, Beerbohm achieves considerable variation by shifting the place and circumstance of the meetings — now placing a memory of the past in the midst of the present, now injecting a vision of the future into the past, mixing private interviews with public occasions — and by isolating qualitatively different kinds of discrepancy.

It is tempting to look for visual sources of inspiration for these drawings of self-encounter, and a likely one leaps to mind in Rossetti's pen and ink and brush composition *How They Met Themselves,* in which a pair of lovers come upon their Doppelgänger in a wood at twilight.[34] Max might have seen it on exhibition at the Tate Gallery in 1923. But literary influences were probably stronger. Certainly the literature of Beerbohm's youth and early manhood provided abundant illustration of supernatural encounters with alter egos and divided selves, and he himself had made a substantial contribution to that literature in *Seven Men*. The confrontation over time, however, was best manifested in Henry James's story "The Jolly Corner" (1908), to which Max had responded so enthusiastically at its first appearance that he wrote James a fan letter and received a gracious acknowledgment in return.[35] He also drew a caricature based on the story (HD 808, pl. 37), which he apparently interpreted as autobiography rather than as fiction, for it is quite obviously James himself, and not the character Spencer Brydon, who meets his other self at the foot of the stairs, a "black stranger" with a pince-nez and two missing fingers, an evil and vulgar presentment of what he might have become had he remained in America. Nine years later Max drew "A Momentary Vision that once befell young Millais" (HD 1039) as one of the eight additional members of the Rossetti series.[36] These two caricatures are the immediate precursors of "The Old and the Young Self" drawings.

Apart from whatever virtues of conception and design these drawings possess, as a series "The Old and the Young Self" enjoys an advantage of intimate familiarity with its subjects that few of Max's other post-Rossettian caricatures can claim. Only four of the "selves" had not been caricatured before on at least ten other occasions. Max had done takeoffs of Shaw in over sixty drawings and sketches of varying degrees of elaborateness and Will Rothenstein in nearly fifty; Balfour, Moore, Kipling, Sickert, and Gosse also rank among the most frequently used of Max's subjects. He had never caricatured Arthur Ponsonby or Stanley Baldwin before, and this omission may partially account for the undistinctiveness of their representations. Indeed, Baldwin may have been included merely to give the series an aura of timeliness, particularly since three former prime ministers are depicted. But for the others, Max had drawn them not only with frequency but over a long period: with the exception of Arnold Bennett, the earliest caricature of whom goes back only to 1911, all of the others had been dismembered and distorted by Max's pen well before he had abandoned England for Italy, many even before the turn of the century. It might almost be argued that Beerbohm had drawn these persons so often that they had virtually ceased to be subjects in their own right but had become models for his vagrant muse to fasten upon. He seems to have entertained such an idea himself, for in 1911 he drew a group portrait of thirty men parading past him in a sinuous queue. The drawing is entitled "One fine morning, or, How they might undo me" (HD 1443) and is described by Hart-Davis as follows: "Max starts back appalled from a procession of his victims, each of whom has adopted a new style of hair or clothing." Max would thus be "undone" if they departed radically from his way of habitually representing them. Significantly, among the group are eight who later appear as old and young selves. But Max was obviously fascinated by more than their physical appearance: he had parodied the styles of Shaw, Bennett, Conrad, Gosse, Kipling, Moore, and Wells in *A Christmas Garland* and had introduced both Balfour and Rothenstein as characters in *Seven Men*. Although the organizing principle of the series precludes our seeing it as reminiscence, certainly the old imaginative engagement with these persons as performers, rather than as mere celebrities, very much pervades the work. That engagement, far more than Beerbohm's accidental discovery of a new mode of generating caricatures of confrontation, contributes to the overall success of "The Old and the Young Self." Because he maintains such sharp impressions of these men as they once were, his hypotheses of what they have become since (or, in some instances, of what they were even earlier) have a forceful credibility. Even this quality, however, is not quite enough to overcome the besetting problem of series drawings, namely, that some specimens may be included, not because of the strength of their execution, but because they round out the set, giving greater luster to more accomplished individual drawings. This problem had arisen with all of Beerbohm's unified groups of caricatures, from the casually assembled literary portraits of *The Poets' Corner* (1904) through the political cartoons of *The Second Childhood of John Bull* (1911) to the near narrative of *Rossetti and His Circle* (1922). A very few drawings of "The Old and the Young Self," Beerbohm's last major experiment in form, would hardly command any attention at all were they not placed near more effective scenes. Their number is not large. What is more remarkable is that the good ones are as good as they are, considering the narrowly circumscribed limits within which they operate.

Variety, as I have suggested, prevents the scenes from falling into repetitiveness. However prepared viewers may be in turning over the leaves of *Observations* to see in each plate a meeting of the young and the old, they can never wholly predict the kind of encounter that will take place. Essentially these encounters are of four types. The simplest of them may be called "the sellout," in which the Old Self is arraigned explicitly or tacitly for having betrayed the idealism of his youth. The prototype for such drawings is Millais's "pre-vision" in *Rossetti and His Circle.* It is not surprising, therefore, that the best manifestation of the type in this series has as its subject another artist, Augustus John, who appears charged with the same offense (HD 828). The Young Self, attired in the miscellaneous bohemian garb of slouch hat, tattered trousers, and knapsack, faces a crowd of prosperous "applicants" to portraiture, who are all costumed according to their rank and station in life and whose geometrical faces with their button eyes betray not the slightest expression. The Old Self, obviously burdened with more than he can manage, implores the Young Self to "take some of them off my hands" but "receives an indignant and a disappointing reply." In the Shaw encounter (HD 1510; BLC 26) the positions of the figures are reversed; it is the Old Self with his back to the viewer who berates his young counterpart with frivolity, irreligion, pertness, and poverty. Somewhat ungenerously Beerbohm implies that worldly success has caused Shaw to repudiate his earlier iconoclasm; yet the playwright's career hardly sustains such a notion. Confrontations of the sellout type tend to be fairly obvious and do not admit a great range of situation. But Beerbohm generally rescues the scene from flatness by the accompanying legend, distributing the best lines of dialogue to the Old Self in his attempted exculpation. In the drawing of the tenth earl of Chesterfield (HD 307), the Young Self casts a sidelong look of disdain at his counterpart for having capitulated to the vulgarity of modern fashion in sporting a billycock rather than a top hat. The Old Self sputters a feeble apology but acknowledges the justice of the rebuke. Here the remorseless intolerance of youth attaches itself not to professional ideals but to sartorial ones. The effect is

The Fading of Memory

ironic, for even though we can hardly take seriously the declination of the dandy, its very depiction in this form causes us to wonder about the appropriateness of youthful self-righteousness in instances of graver apostasy.

The second and largest group consists of drawings emphasizing the magnitude of disparity between the Old and Young Selves. In these drawings, whose prototype is the "Jolly Corner" caricature of Henry James, it is not so much change or development that is noted as the sheer contrast between the two figures sharing a common identity. Who would have dreamt, Max seems to ask, that Arthur Ponsonby, son of General the Right Honourable Sir Henry Ponsonby and great grandson of Earl Grey, who as a lad had served as page to Queen Victoria, would in maturity have evolved into a leading Socialist politician (HD 1181)? A reverse of the sellout, a confrontation of the second type usually depicts the Old Self as rather impatient with the Young Self for his immaturity, and where Beerbohm's sympathies are less than total, this impatience often takes the form of condescension. Thus in the Conrad drawing (HD 362; BLC 87) the shock-haired youth suppliantly questioning the sage about the British Mercantile Marine in a gibberish that purports to be Polish receives a magisterial answer that concludes, "And I've written some books, too . . . but you are hardly old enough to understand them." One is left with the implication that there is something spurious or fraudulent about Conrad because of his failure wholly to embrace his origins. The meeting of the two Kiplings (HD 861; BLC 71) conveys a comparable feeling. The younger, clad in topi and colonial whites with a pencil behind his ear, rushes in from the right, exclaiming, "I *say*! Have you heard the latest about Mrs. Hauksbee?" But there is scarcely a sign of recognition from the elder, who, crowned with laurel and decked in elaborate robes, sits imperially, his left hand resting on a globe as though in benediction, his legs crossed and mounted on a footstool. In the background is a map of the world divided into hemispheres, in front of which on high pedestals are the busts of three authoritarian figures, the central one of which appears to be Moses *cornutus*. The drawing is quite obviously mock-heroic; Kipling's apotheosis is belied by the intrusion of the assiduous, gossipy journalist. Yet the bemedaled

Sir Max Beerbohm

Edmund Gosse, C.B. (he was not knighted until the year after Beerbohm had drawn the caricature), seems not in the least embarrassed by the sudden appearance among his distinguished friends of his infant self as a zealot of the Lord (HD 616; BLC 64). The company looks far more puzzled and disturbed by the ingenuous presence while the Old Self bears an expression neither apologetic nor cordial that seems to acknowledge the Young Self as indeed a part of his past. In a letter to Max, Gosse himself professed delight in the conjuration in terms that the Old Self of the picture might well have used: "The evangelical ardour of the child — most unbecomingly robed in white, and belted in the service of Jesus — is delicious. I thought it one of the very best, where all were good."[37] Few of the confrontations of this type are so good-natured. The elder Sickert is positively abusive to his Young Self, and Lloyd George drops his cigar in wordless disbelief as he beholds the reality of his childhood, a chubby, proper schoolboy, who contrasts violently with the wild, free-spirited youth whose full-length portrait dominates the background (HD 953). The conceit is a fine one, for it needles the former prime minister for overly romanticizing his past. Yet Max nearly destroys the effect by reviving the old wallpaper trick, the motif here being the Welsh national vegetable, the leek. Lloyd George does not dwindle into a mere Taffy, however. But that Max thought it necessary to fortify the caricature in this way may suggest that he felt less sure about the weaknesses and foibles of men he had not really known well.

Not very large numerically, the last two groups contain some of the most engaging drawings of the series, for they seem to baffle the expectations established by the first two groups. We have been led to believe that either the Young Self is censorious of the Old for betrayal of idealism or that the Old Self is intolerant of the Young for callowness and lack of sophistication. We are not quite prepared to see the reversal of roles that we do in the third group, where the elder Asquith, for example, recommends diversion from study to his Young Self at Balliol (HD 51) or (in a total overturning of the Lloyd George confrontation) the younger Stanley Baldwin registers an almost contemptuous incredulity at what the future holds in store for him (HD 55); although the Young and the Old Selves are portrayed in identical poses, legs apart and arms akimbo, that appears to be all they have in common. The Young Self simply cannot conceive of the eventuality that will bring him to Downing Street and can only exclaim, "Prime Minister? *You?* Good Lord!!" The most accomplished drawing of this group is, curiously enough, that of another prime minister, Arthur Balfour (HD 78). As frontispiece to *Observations,* moreover, it is reproduced in color. The Old Self, somewhat plumper than we have been accustomed to seeing him in Max's caricatures, bears his body in the same sinuous posture that Beerbohm had never ceased to observe in him. He appears to have entered the room to engage his Young Self in a tennis match, for he is all in white and carrying a racket. The Young Self, lean and cadaverous, lies recumbent on a lounge, an array of medicaments on a table beside him. We hardly require Max's legend to inform us that young and old have reversed the roles of athlete and invalid. This climax of Beerbohm's thirty years of Balfour-watching virtually illustrates the observations he had made to Reggie Turner four years earlier.

> When he was eighteen years old he believed that he had certainly not more than three more years to live, and made all his arrangements accordingly. . . . And then, many years later, he found himself being somehow a militant Irish Secretary and feeling a little stronger and better, though still far from well and not at all long for this world. And later on he found himself being Prime Minister for ever so long and exasperating and dominating everybody over the Fiscal Question and feeling decidedly better.
>
> And then came the crash when he lost his seat in Manchester and everybody thought his career was ended because the new Parliament, when he did get returned for another borough, wouldn't listen to him. And presently the new Parliament was sitting at his feet. And then, years later, another crash, and Bonar Law took his place. And then, opportunely, the War; England being a maritime power, Balfour must be at the Admiralty; and then, nobody but Balfour could manage Foreign Affairs; and then, Balfour was the only man whom America would welcome. And now he's President or something of the League of Nations, and constantly improving his stroke in tennis, and is plump without being fat, and has a complexion like a blush-rose, and only one ambition is left to him, who started with no ambition at all and yet has achieved so much; only one ambition (barring the

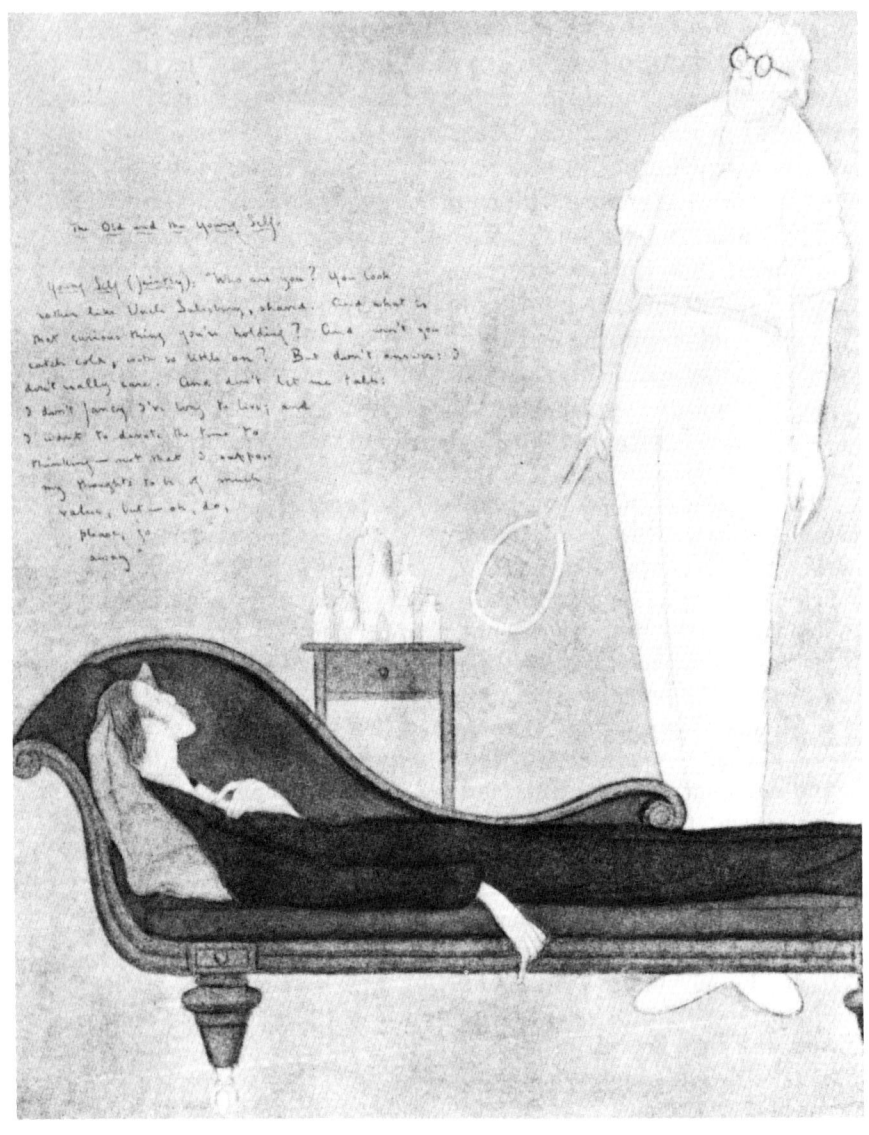

The Old and the Young Self. [Lord Balfour] Observations. (1925).
Courtesy of Lord Cottesloe.

The Fading of Memory

wish to improve still further at tennis), *viz*, to survive *everybody*.[38]

The figure of Balfour as reluctant and unambitious survivor may have had an unusual fascination for Beerbohm. In none of Max's presentments of him does he appear to enjoy public life or the exercise of power, preferring to retreat to retirement. These characteristics alone may have caused Max to feel a particular affinity toward him. At any rate, particularly after the move to Italy, when he began cultivating his mustache, in his self-caricatures Max grew to *resemble* the Balfour he had drawn years earlier.[39]

In confrontations of the Old and the Young Self of the fourth type what are initially perceived as disparities dissolve on reflection into continuities. The simplest way Beerbohm accomplishes this effect is through dialogue. The elder Arnold Bennett, for example, pompously exuding self-satisfaction as his meaty fingers grasp the waistcoat lapels of his dinner clothes, confides patronizingly to his clerkly Young Self: "All gone according to plan, you see" (HD 135; BLC 98). But the young Bennett, unlike the young Conrad or the young Kipling, is not in the least cowed by his elder self's success and retorts, "*My* plan, you know," thereby identifying himself with the energetic and ambitious heroes of his fiction. The effect is somewhat more subtle in the drawing of Will Rothenstein (HD 1321), where the irrepressible and irreverent dandy of the *fin de siècle* has burst into the classroom of the principal of the Royal School of Art, South Kensington, while a group of expressionless students look on. The professor, however, is undaunted and, with a pointing gesture reminiscent of Max's earliest caricatures of him, orders his Young Self to remove his hat and leave the room. Their stations in life are certainly different, but their impetuous behavior has not altered in the least over the years. The finest representative of this group — indeed, what is probably the best of the whole series in conception and execution — is the captionless drawing of R. B. Cunninghame Graham (HD 628; BLC 65). The Young Self, a kilted lad astride a hobbyhorse, salutes the Old Self, who, depicted as a centaur, leaps into the room through an open window in a cloud of dust. The obvious reference is to Graham's

The Old and Young Self. Mr. Cunninghame Graham. 1924. *Observations.* (1925).

horsemanship — as an M.P. "he regularly rode to the House of Commons on his favorite horse"[40] — and the room displays other equine toys to assure us that the connection is not accidental. The drawing is one of the most elaborately detailed of the series, recalling the fine line and delicate shading of *Rossetti and His Circle*. What appear to be religious prints hang on the wall: that on the left suggests the sacrifice of Isaac, and the one on the right, cut off by the border of the larger picture, may be of Isaac blessing Jacob. The care lavished on this composition stimulates us to look beyond the obvious conceit of the boy on a simulacrum of a horse growing into a man turned in to a "real" one. As the meeting takes place in the child's room, it is a fair presumption that the centaur, drawn as a very noble beast and trailing with itself associations ranging from classical mythology to *Gulliver's Travels,* constitutes for the child "some fragment from his dream of human life." If so, few childhood dreams ever came so close to realization. Graham was not merely a horseman, but a writer, politician, and adventurer as well, equally at home riding over the Scottish moors as over the Argentine pampas. Beerbohm's drawing is a genial mockery to which a considerable measure of admiration has been admixed, a tribute from a sedentary recluse to a romantic legend.

Although we have examined "The Old and the Young Self" largely as an experiment in form, Beerbohm's last attempt to achieve in caricature something of the substantiality of *Rossetti and His Circle,* it is quite unlikely that he himself would have seen it in this way. More probably he would have regarded the confrontation across time as a device merely, a concession to the present generation in return for its indulging a middle-aged man in his valediction to his prewar heroes. All pretense of contemporaneity disappeared, however, in Beerbohm's next exhibition of over one hundred drawings in 1928, significantly entitled "Ghosts." Although only five of them had been exhibited before, most of these drawings date from before the war and about a third of them from before the turn of the century. They are all of persons, not an allegory or hypothetical scene among them. Unashamedly retrospective, Max not only assembled his previously recorded impressions, he included among them as well a number of "memories" freshly composed in 1926. Unlike his

Sir Max Beerbohm

earlier shows, however, the 1928 exhibition did not yield a published album; most of the drawings have passed into private hands, therefore, without having been reproduced in any form. Nevertheless, the general character of the 1926 drawings may be extrapolated from those few that have — they seem to hark back to the Spy style of portrait caricature — and even more clearly perhaps by the titles and captions of those that have not. The following is a representative sample:

> A Memory of Mr. Hamilton Aidé, poet, painter, playwright and private gentleman. The Great War, and even more its consequences, would have jarred unspeakably upon him. Always a darling of the Gods, he died before the beginning of it. (HD 4)

> In memory of the famous Wilson Barrett. What would he have made of Tchekov? (HD 100)

> An Oxford memory: 1890: Lord Hugh Cecil and Mr. H. B. Irving walking away from the Union together. (Deeply impressive to a freshman's heart.) (HD 263)

> This would have amused my very dear John Davidson. (HD 409)

> A memory of Henry James and Joseph Conrad conversing at an afternoon party — circa 1904. (HD 814, pl. 38)

> Oxford, 1891. Mr. Walter Pater taking his walk through the meadows. (HD 1146)

Many other of the 1926 drawings might almost serve as illustrations to the "remembering" essays: there are "memories" of Andrew Lang, Sir Henry Irving, Henry James, and one entitled "No 2 The Pines." For after having flirted in the first half of the decade with newer themes, such as international politics and the decay of civilization, in drawings that hovered dangerously near to editorial cartoons, Max retreated in the second half to the more congenial world of personal reminiscence. But the passage of years had blurred both vision and invention. Max was no longer creating; he was trying desperately to embalm rather than to recapture the past. Although in his *Catalogue* Hart-

The Fading of Memory

Davis lists over a hundred items known to be drawn after 1928, most of these are casual sketches. The "Ghosts" exhibition effectively sealed Beerbohm's career as a caricaturist, just as *A Variety of Things,* published as the tenth and last volume of the collected edition in the same year, sealed his career as a writer. Both of these culminations are retrospective; not only do earlier, otherwise fugitive, compositions preponderate in them, but what little new matter there is in them is of an earlier mode in form and content.

Although only in his fifties at the time of his second retirement, Max had clearly abandoned the quest to "do something big." He still undertook commissions from time to time and continued to draw for his own amusement and that of his friends. But the obviously grand work of memory, an autobiography, for which in a sense he had been preparing all his life, was never undertaken, though he appears to have seriously contemplated such a project.[41] The fact of the matter is that for Beerbohm memory had always been prized not for its own sake but as the stuff upon which his visual and verbal imagination could expatiate. Both the stock and the energy appear to have given out at about the same time. But then Max had come to maturity so early, his apprenticeship had been so brief, and his recognition so immediate and sustained that we need not wonder excessively that he spent his last thirty years in relative ease. "He knows the value of what he has done both as a writer and as an artist," Edmund Wilson said of him after a visit to Rapallo in 1954.[42] Not the least of that knowledge lay in knowing where and how far he could go with his "little talents." For Beerbohm's career was unique in that he had practically to invent the forms to contain his idiosyncratic vision. Some of them were quite private — his frescoes and doctored books and photographs. For the public, however, he fashioned those ingenious productions of imaginary reminiscence that will continue to delight long after the more conventional memoirs of greater men have settled into the mold of antiquarian things.

Notes

Notes to the Introduction

1. Edmund Wilson, "An Analysis of Max Beerbohm," *Classics and Commercials,* pp. 431–441, and "A Miscellany of Max Beerbohm," *The Bit Between My Teeth,* pp. 41–58; W. H. Auden, "One of the Family," *Forewords and Afterwords,* pp. 367–383; John Updike, "Rhyming Max," *Assorted Prose,* pp. 256–263. All four of these articles are reprinted in J. G. Riewald, ed., *The Surprise of Excellence.*

2. Bohun Lynch, *Max Beerbohm in Perspective;* David Low, "The Art of Max Beerbohm," *Spectator,* pp. 218–219, and *British Cartoonists, Caricaturists and Comic Artists;* Osbert Lancaster has provided the introduction to Max Beerbohm, *Max's Nineties,* and illustrated a limited edition of Max Beerbohm, *Zuleika Dobson* (Oxford: Shakespeare Head Press, 1975).

3. See Beerbohm's note to the American edition of *A Variety of Things,* pp. viii–x.

4. A. E. Gallatin, *Sir Max Beerbohm: Bibliographical Notes;* A. E. Gallatin and L. M. Oliver, *A Bibliography of the Works of Max Beerbohm.* These two works have been largely superseded by J. G. Riewald, *Sir Max Beerbohm, Man and Writer: A Critical Analysis with a Brief Life and a Bibliography,* and Rupert Hart-Davis, *A Catalogue of the Caricatures of Max Beerbohm.*

5. The indefatigable Sir Rupert Hart-Davis has edited and published two volumes of Beerbohm's drama criticism from the *Saturday Review* to complement *Around Theatres,* the selection that the author made for the collected edition in 1924: *More Theatres, 1898–1903,* and *Last Theatres, 1904–1910;* for the centenary of Beerbohm's birth he edited *A Peep into the Past and Other Prose Pieces by Max Beerbohm.* J. G. Riewald has collected and annotated *Max in Verse,* and most recently he has edited *Beerbohm's Literary Cari-*

catures, from Homer to Huxley, a selection of 104 caricatures from published albums and other sources.
6. Max Beerbohm, *Letters to Reggie Turner* and *Max and Will*.
7. Katherine Lyon Mix, *Max and the Americans*.
8. S. N. Behrman, *Portrait of Max*, published in England as *Conversations with Max*.
9. David Cecil, *Max: A Biography*, p. xiii.
10. *Rossetti and His Circle*, p. vi.
11. Cecil, *Max*, p. 4.

Notes to Chapter I

1. John Felstiner, "Max Beerbohm and the Wings of Henry James," in Riewald, *Surprise of Excellence*, pp. 195–196.
2. Edmund Wilson, "A Miscellany of Max Beerbohm," in Riewald, *Surprise of Excellence*, p. 150.
3. "Whistler's Writing" (1904), *Yet Again*, pp. 109–110.
4. Riewald, *Beerbohm's Literary Caricatures*, p. 16.
5. In addition to citation of the original album in which they were reproduced, each caricature will be further identified by its number in Hart-Davis's compilation, *A Catalogue of the Caricatures of Max Beerbohm* (hereafter HD), and, where appropriate, its plate number in Riewald's edition, *Beerbohm's Literary Caricatures* (hereafter BLC). Thus, the frontispiece to *A Survey* is HD 359; BLC 85.
6. Lynch, *Max Beerbohm*, p. 144; and cited by Riewald, *Beerbohm's Literary Caricatures*, p. 242.
7. Riewald, *Beerbohm's Literary Caricatures*, p. 242.
8. The amusement has the same origin in Beerbohm's two early caricatures of Wordsworth, one in which the poet is seen transcribing a sailor's conversation (HD 1809) and the more famous "Wordsworth in the Lake District, at cross purposes" (HD 1810; BLC 6) from *The Poets' Corner* (1904), where, looking rather like a "dirty old man," he is seen chucking a little girl under the chin.
9. For details see *Letters to Reggie Turner*, pp. 201, 214–215.
10. I did actually find a copy of *Seven Men* classified under biography in the public library of Brattleboro, Vermont, a situation probably not uncommon.
11. G. S. Layard, review in *Bookman* (London), p. 183.
12. *Spectator*, 21 Dec. 1912, p. 1068.
13. *Athenaeum*, 16 Nov. 1912, p. 598.
14. S. W., "The Art of Mr. Beerbohm," *Athenaeum*, p. 1186.
15. Lynch, *Max Beerbohm*, pp. 149–150.

16. Auden, "One of the Family," in Riewald, *Surprise of Excellence*, p. 168.
17. "Music Halls of My Youth," *Mainly on the Air*, p. 46.
18. "Ouida" (1897), *More*, p. 108.
19. From a letter dated 18 May 1920, *Letters to Reggie Turner*, p. 249.
20. The best source of Beerbohm's aversions and prejudices is Behrman, *Portrait of Max*.
21. See *Rossetti and His Circle*, pls. 7 and 14.
22. Behrman, *Portrait of Max*, p. 70.
23. See "Our Lady of 'Pars'" (1896), reprinted in Max Beerbohm, *A Peep into the Past and Other Pieces*, pp. 16–19.
24. Max Beerbohm in an interview with Ada Leverson, *Sketch*, 2 Jan. 1895, p. 439; as cited by Cecil, *Max*, p. 104.
25. See *Max in Verse*.
26. Beerbohm's one-act play, *A Social Success*, was produced in London in 1913 and published in *A Variety of Things* (1928). He had also collaborated on a couple of plays and prepared *The Happy Hypocrite* for the stage (see Cecil, *Max*, p. 188). In addition to *Zuleika Dobson* and *Seven Men*, Beerbohm's fiction must also include his fairy tales.
27. Max Beerbohm, "Punch" (1897), *More*, pp. 23–24.
28. "The Mirror of the Past," MS, p. 59. This manuscript is in the Robert H. Taylor Collection, Princeton University Library.
29. This point is discussed more fully in chapter 5, where Beerbohm's subsequent addition "*and Two Others*" is also considered.
30. F. W. Dupee, "Max Beerbohm and the Rigors of Fantasy," in Riewald, *Surprise of Excellence*, pp. 176–177.
31. *Zuleika Dobson*, chapter 7 of the 1911 London edition, p. 100.
32. Frederic Manning (1882–1935), born in Australia, is now known chiefly for his novel of World War I, an excised version, *Her Privates We*, appearing in 1930 and a large unexpurgated edition, *The Middle Parts of Fortune*, only in 1977. Beerbohm was particularly approving of an earlier book, *Scenes and Portraits* (1909), containing dialogues, among others, between Socrates and Euripides and Pope Leo XIII and Ernest Renan. He recommended the book in a letter to Mabel Beardsley (2 Feb 1914, O'Connell Collection, Princeton University Library) and a year earlier had drawn a caricature of Manning as a ventriloquist with a dummy of a pope on one knee and one of a military officer on the other (HD 1008). This caricature was reproduced in *Things New and Old* (1923).
33. "Madame Tussaud's" (1897), *More*, p. 42.

34. See *Rossetti and His Circle,* pl. 14 (HD 837), discussed in Chapter 6.

35. William Matthews, ed., *British Diaries,* p. 293, s.v. "Soames, Enoch (1862–1897)."

Notes to Chapter II

1. *Letters to Reggie Turner,* p. 102. All further references to this letter are cited in the text.

2. Dated 15 Dec. 1914; this letter accompanies a fourteen-page extract from "No. 2. The Pines," which Beerbohm offered Gosse as a pen portrait of Swinburne. Letter and extract are bound together as Ashley MS 4695 in the British Library.

3. "Actors" (1897), *More,* pp. 33–34.
4. "King George the Fourth," *Works,* pp. 81–82.
5. "Poor Romeo!" (1896), *Works,* pp. 132–133.
6. Behrman, *Portrait of Max,* pp. 135–136.
7. *More,* p. 201.
8. *Works,* p. 37.
9. *More,* p. 130.
10. *More,* p. 157.
11. "Madame Tussaud's" (1897), *More,* p. 44.
12. "Some Words on Royalty" (1898), *More,* pp. 3–13.
13. *More,* pp. 60–61.
14. "Dandies and Dandies" (1896), *Works,* pp. 3–29.
15. "Seeing People Off" (1906), *Yet Again,* pp. 19–26.
16. "Actors" (1897), *More,* pp. 29–35.
17. *Yet Again,* pp. 91–102.
18. "Ouida" (1897), *More,* pp. 107–108.
19. *Yet Again,* p. 298.
20. *Yet Again,* p. 304.

21. This is the central point of Dupee's very perceptive introduction to the novel, "Max Beerbohm and the Rigors of Fantasy," pp. 175–191.

22. In a recently republished essay antedating Beerbohm's first engagement on his novel, we find the following illuminating passage: "Rivers have their uses. They are serviceable for purposes of commerce, scenery, suicide, and the like, but it is a shame that they should pass near a great University" ("The Boat Race" [1897], in Beerbohm, *A Peep into the Past,* p. 23).

23. See particularly Robert Viscusi, "A Dandy's Diary," pp. 234–256.

24. Behrman, *Portrait of Max,* pp. 257–258.

25. John Felstiner, *The Lies of Art,* p. 177. Felstiner's complex and subtle reading of *Zuleika Dobson* (pp. 169–186) emphasizes its parodic and critical aspects.

26. *Zuleika Dobson,* p. 183.

27. George Meredith (d. 1909) is the one anomaly; Beerbohm's parody of him, "Euphemia Clashthought," is an improved version of "The Victory of Aphasia Gibberish," which had originally been published during Meredith's lifetime in 1896.

28. Filson Young, "The Perfect Parodist," *Saturday Review,* p. 578.

29. Felstiner, *Lies of Art,* pp. 142–143.

30. Max Beerbohm, "Perkins and Mankind, by H. G. W*lls," *A Christmas Garland,* p. 34. All further references to this parody are cited in the text.

31. "The Feast, by J*s*ph C*nr*d," *A Christmas Garland,* pp. 125–126.

32. *And Even Now,* pp. 49–50.

33. Behrman, *Portrait of Max,* p. 282.

34. *And Even Now,* p. 52.

35. "A Pathetic Imposture," *Yet Again,* pp. 83–88.

36. Behrman, *Portrait of Max,* pp. 43, 153, 269.

37. Sotheby and Company, *Catalogue of the Library and Literary Manuscripts of the Late Sir Max Beerbohm* (hereafter SC).

38. Walter Pater (1839–1894) and Oscar Wilde (1854–1900) were obviously encountered in the nineteenth century. It is possible that Beerbohm may have begun making entries while still an undergraduate — under "Union of Oxford" he has noted, "Pleasure in election to" — but since there are so few persons of the nineties named (Aubrey Beardsley, for example, is absent, as is Henry Harland, editor of the *Yellow Book*), it is equally likely that those few are retrospective entries.

39. *Mainly on the Air,* pp. 81–98.

40. *And Even Now,* pp. 57–88.

41. *Mainly on the Air,* pp. 131–133.

42. British Library, Ashley MS 4695.

43. *A Variety of Things,* pp. 155–156.

44. "H. B. Irving as a Young Man," *Mainly on the Air,* pp. 117–119.

45. "An Incident," *Mainly on the Air,* pp. 131–133.

46. "Nat Goodwin — and Another," *Mainly on the Air,* p. 68.

Sir Max Beerbohm

47. "George Moore," *Mainly on the Air,* p. 83. All further references to this essay are cited in the text.
48. *And Even Now,* p. 57. All further references to this essay are cited in the text.
49. The fairly recent death of Theodore Watts-Dunton, the solicitor and author who attended both Rossetti and Swinburne in their declines, on 6 June 1914 may have prompted Beerbohm to express more fully than otherwise his "tribute to Watts-Dunton's charm of mind and character, which I think have been a good deal underrated" (penciled note to Edmund Gosse, British Library, Ashley MS 4695).

Notes to Chapter III

1. Hart-Davis, *Catalogue,* pp. 9–10.
2. Bibliographic data on Beerbohm's albums of caricatures are derived from Riewald, *Sir Max Beerbohm,* pp. 255–271.
3. The reprint edition, London and New York: King Penguin Books, 1943.
4. Max Beerbohm, *Observations.* The Haskell House, 1971, reprint unfortunately does not reproduce the colored frontispiece of Balfour.
5. *Caricatures by Max: From the Collection in the Ashmolean Museum* (Oxford: Oxford University Press, 1958).
6. Beerbohm, *Max's Nineties,* dust jacket.
7. Riewald, *Beerbohm's Literary Caricatures.*
8. C. R. Ashbee, *Caricature,* pp. 18–19.
9. "The Spirit of Caricature" (1901), *A Variety of Things,* p. 124. Hereafter cited in the text.
10. Raymond Blathwayt, "The Art of Caricature," *Cassell's Magazine,* pp. 277–278.
11. See particularly Max Beerbohm, *A Book of Caricatures,* pl. 12 (HD 1566).
12. Felstiner, *Lies of Art,* p. 115.
13. Lynch, *Max Beerbohm,* pp. 131–132.
14. "The Spirit of Caricature," *A Variety of Things,* p. 129.
15. Behrman, *Portrait of Max,* p. 170.
16. Felstiner, *Lies of Art,* p. 115.
17. *Max's Nineties,* p. 10; plates 35 through 45 constitute "Mr. Gladstone Goes to Heaven."
18. The series is reproduced for the first time in *Max and Will.*
19. Hart-Davis, following Beerbohm's own enumeration, believes

24. Behrman, *Portrait of Max*, pp. 257–258.

25. John Felstiner, *The Lies of Art*, p. 177. Felstiner's complex and subtle reading of *Zuleika Dobson* (pp. 169–186) emphasizes its parodic and critical aspects.

26. *Zuleika Dobson*, p. 183.

27. George Meredith (d. 1909) is the one anomaly; Beerbohm's parody of him, "Euphemia Clashthought," is an improved version of "The Victory of Aphasia Gibberish," which had originally been published during Meredith's lifetime in 1896.

28. Filson Young, "The Perfect Parodist," *Saturday Review*, p. 578.

29. Felstiner, *Lies of Art*, pp. 142–143.

30. Max Beerbohm, "Perkins and Mankind, by H. G. W*lls," *A Christmas Garland*, p. 34. All further references to this parody are cited in the text.

31. "The Feast, by J*s*ph C*nr*d," *A Christmas Garland*, pp. 125–126.

32. *And Even Now*, pp. 49–50.

33. Behrman, *Portrait of Max*, p. 282.

34. *And Even Now*, p. 52.

35. "A Pathetic Imposture," *Yet Again*, pp. 83–88.

36. Behrman, *Portrait of Max*, pp. 43, 153, 269.

37. Sotheby and Company, *Catalogue of the Library and Literary Manuscripts of the Late Sir Max Beerbohm* (hereafter SC).

38. Walter Pater (1839–1894) and Oscar Wilde (1854–1900) were obviously encountered in the nineteenth century. It is possible that Beerbohm may have begun making entries while still an undergraduate — under "Union of Oxford" he has noted, "Pleasure in election to" — but since there are so few persons of the nineties named (Aubrey Beardsley, for example, is absent, as is Henry Harland, editor of the *Yellow Book*), it is equally likely that those few are retrospective entries.

39. *Mainly on the Air*, pp. 81–98.

40. *And Even Now*, pp. 57–88.

41. *Mainly on the Air*, pp. 131–133.

42. British Library, Ashley MS 4695.

43. *A Variety of Things*, pp. 155–156.

44. "H. B. Irving as a Young Man," *Mainly on the Air*, pp. 117–119.

45. "An Incident," *Mainly on the Air*, pp. 131–133.

46. "Nat Goodwin — and Another," *Mainly on the Air*, p. 68.

47. "George Moore," *Mainly on the Air,* p. 83. All further references to this essay are cited in the text.

48. *And Even Now,* p. 57. All further references to this essay are cited in the text.

49. The fairly recent death of Theodore Watts-Dunton, the solicitor and author who attended both Rossetti and Swinburne in their declines, on 6 June 1914 may have prompted Beerbohm to express more fully than otherwise his "tribute to Watts-Dunton's charm of mind and character, which I think have been a good deal underrated" (penciled note to Edmund Gosse, British Library, Ashley MS 4695).

Notes to Chapter III

1. Hart-Davis, *Catalogue,* pp. 9–10.
2. Bibliographic data on Beerbohm's albums of caricatures are derived from Riewald, *Sir Max Beerbohm,* pp. 255–271.
3. The reprint edition, London and New York: King Penguin Books, 1943.
4. Max Beerbohm, *Observations.* The Haskell House, 1971, reprint unfortunately does not reproduce the colored frontispiece of Balfour.
5. *Caricatures by Max: From the Collection in the Ashmolean Museum* (Oxford: Oxford University Press, 1958).
6. Beerbohm, *Max's Nineties,* dust jacket.
7. Riewald, *Beerbohm's Literary Caricatures.*
8. C. R. Ashbee, *Caricature,* pp. 18–19.
9. "The Spirit of Caricature" (1901), *A Variety of Things,* p. 124. Hereafter cited in the text.
10. Raymond Blathwayt, "The Art of Caricature," *Cassell's Magazine,* pp. 277–278.
11. See particularly Max Beerbohm, *A Book of Caricatures,* pl. 12 (HD 1566).
12. Felstiner, *Lies of Art,* p. 115.
13. Lynch, *Max Beerbohm,* pp. 131–132.
14. "The Spirit of Caricature," *A Variety of Things,* p. 129.
15. Behrman, *Portrait of Max,* p. 170.
16. Felstiner, *Lies of Art,* p. 115.
17. *Max's Nineties,* p. 10; plates 35 through 45 constitute "Mr. Gladstone Goes to Heaven."
18. The series is reproduced for the first time in *Max and Will.*
19. Hart-Davis, following Beerbohm's own enumeration, believes

that one of these drawings (number 3) has disappeared. But the quotation moves without a break from number 2 to number 4, and I am inclined to think that HD 1613 is a "ghost" etherealized by a slip of Beerbohm's pen. This series, indeed a very hasty affair, was in the possession of the late Stephen Greene, who was kind enough to show it to me.

20. Beerbohm thought well enough of this drawing to include it in the 1923 album, *Things New and Old,* where he dated it from 1903. There is a note attached to a reproduction of this drawing in Merton College Library indicating that it had been contributed to the Eights number of the *Oxford Magazine,* 25 May 1905.

21. Beerbohm's own description of Kipling in 1903; Blathwayt, "Art of Caricature," p. 279.

22. Blathwayt, "Art of Caricature," p. 278.

23. Bruce R. McElderry, Jr., "Max Beerbohm," in Riewald, *Surprise of Excellence,* p. 222.

24. For the *Guardian's* objection, see Hart-Davis, *Catalogue,* pp. 39–40, s.v. "Paul Cambon"; the more complicated affair of Beerbohm's proposed illustrations to Sir Sidney Lee's biography of Edward VII is treated by Cecil, *Max,* pp. 398–400.

25. *The Poet's* [sic] *Corner,* the reprint edition (London and New York: King Penguin Books, 1943), p. 16. Perhaps the passionate intercession of John Lane may refer to his extraordinary sensitivity to Watson in the aftermath of the Wilde trial, where Lane summarily dismissed Aubrey Beardsley from the staff of the *Yellow Book* on receiving a cable from Watson. Beerbohm, as usual, seems to have kept out of things, and his relations with Lane after the affair appear to have been no less cordial than before.

26. Letter dated 1 Apr. 1907, *Max and Will,* p. 55.

27. George Moore, *Ave,* pp. 293–294.

28. Hart-Davis, *Catalogue,* p. 57.

Notes to Chapter IV

1. *Around Theatres,* p. 578.

2. Though not to satire. See Beerbohm's "Ballade Tragique à Double Refrain," the offense of which is "said to have delayed Max's knighthood for twenty years," *Max in Verse,* pp. 48–49.

3. Letter dated 15 Apr. 1910, *Letters to Reggie Turner,* p. 183.

4. Letter dated 15 Nov. 1910, *Letters to Reggie Turner,* p. 193.

5. Cited by Hart-Davis, *Catalogue,* p. 126.

6. Letter dated 11 Mar. 1913, *Letters to Reggie Turner,* p. 221.

7. Riewald, *Sir Max Beerbohm.*
8. Behrman, *Portrait of Max,* p. 41.
9. *Mainly on the Air,* pp. 120–130.
10. SC 329; the manuscript is now in the Robert H. Taylor Collection, Princeton University Library.
11. Since this chapter was originally composed, an extensive description and illustration of the manuscript has been published: see Lawrence Danson, "Max Beerbohm and *The Mirror of the Past,*" pp. 77–153.
12. "Quia Imperfectum" (1918), *And Even Now,* p. 197.
13. Behrman, *Portrait of Max,* p. 41.
14. Letter dated 8 Oct. 1913, *Letters to Reggie Turner,* p. 229.
15. Cecil, *Max,* p. 341n.
16. Pencil draft, p. 2. In the manuscript the name is spelled at times with an "i" and at others with a "y." As it is the generally accepted spelling and the one that prevails in the later pages of "The Mirror of the Past," except where the variant occurs in direct quotation, I have chosen to write "Sylvester" throughout.
17. Scenario letter, p. 4.
18. Mix, p. 177.
19. *Herbert Beerbohm Tree: Some Memories of Him and of His Art,* collected by Max Beerbohm.
20. SC 15; now in the Berg Collection of the New York Public Library.
21. *Rossetti and His Circle,* p. vii.
22. Rough notes for the "Mirror of the Past," hereafter cited in the notes and text as "Mirror" with appropriate page numbers. This quotation is "Mirror," p. 56.
23. "Mirror," after p. 33 and verso.
24. Scenario letter, p. 10.
25. Scenario letter, p. 11.
26. "Mirror," Fair copy, p. 1.
27. Pencil draft, p. 4.
28. Scenario letter, pp. 5–6; see also Ira Grushow, "Beerbohm's Lord Runcorn," *N&Q,* pp. 207–208.
29. Cecil, *Max,* p. 324.
30. Pencil draft, p. 6.
31. Scenario letter, pp. 4–5.
32. *Mainly on the Air,* pp. 124–127.
33. *Mainly on the Air,* pp. 122–124.
34. Scenario letter, p. 5.
35. *Mainly on the Air,* p. 130.

36. *And Even Now*, p. 80.
37. Behrman, *Portrait of Max*, p. 41.
38. Cecil, *Max*, p. 340.
39. "Mirror," pp. 34A, 34B, 34C, 34D.
40. Letter to Robert Ross, undated (probably 1916), Margery Ross, ed., *Robert Ross*, p. 259.
41. *Mainly on the Air*, p. 122.
42. Perhaps this is the drawing "on a quasi-Rossettian theme — a thing without merit, but not unfunny" that Beerbohm was referring to in a letter to Robert Ross written "in my present acute stage of Rossettitis" (Ross, *Ross*, pp. 259–260).
43. John Morley, *Recollections*, 1:132.
44. The manuscript, marked "Unpublished — and to remain so," was Beerbohm's contribution to the Red Cross Sale at Christie's in April 1918. Together with a covering letter to E. V. Lucas, it is now in the Robert H. Taylor Collection, Princeton University Library.
45. Cf. *Letters to Reggie Turner*, p. 200.

Notes to Chapter V

1. Even earlier is the date Max attached to the composition of "James Pethel" — 17 Sept. 1912 — though it is by no means to be accepted as authoritative. Pethel, incidentally, professing himself an admirer of Max's work, also urges him to the *chef d'oeuvre*: "He asked what I was writing now, and said that he looked to me to 'do something big, one of these days,' and that he was sure I had it 'in' me. This remark (though of course I pretended to be pleased by it) irritated me very much" (*Seven Men*, pp. 119–120).
2. Letter dated 10 July 1920, *Letters to Reggie Turner*, p. 253.
3. See Chapter 1, note 32 with text.
4. "Diminuendo," *Works*, p. 149.
5. In addition to the last, see "A Cloud of Pinafores" (*More*, p. 173), "The Case of Prometheus" (*More*, p. 197), where Pater's "Apollo in Picardy" (1893) is alluded to, and "Whistler's Writing" and "The Naming of Streets," both in *Yet Again* (pp. 111, 207), where he is discussed as a stylist.
6. "Diminuendo," *Works*, p. 150.
7. *Works*, p. 150.
8. "An Aesthetic Book," review of Arthur Symons's *Plays, Acting and Music*, 19 Sept 1903, *Around Theatres*, pp. 274–275.
9. Harvard University Library, fMS Eng 696.1, p. 1.

10. *Seven Men*, New York, 1920 edition, facing p. 234. On the half-title page of the presentation copy to Bohun Lynch, Max inscribed the "autographs" of all the seven men. Maltby's rather resembles Max's own signature except that there is more backhand to it; Braxton's is heavy and authoritative, done it would almost seem with a worn-out nib; Pethel's is in a nineteenth-century commercial hand; Laider's is shaky, revealing a debilitated physical state; Brown's is deliberate and underlined, as though trying to be assertive; Soames's, though standing first, is, of course, "dim." I am indebted to the late Stephen Greene, who owned it, for showing this curiosity to me. It is now in the Beerbohm Room of the Merton College Library.

11. "Lytton Strachey," *Mainly on the Air*, p. 211.

12. "Enoch Soames," *Seven Men*, p. 39. Hereafter cited in the text.

13. Ira Grushow, "The Chastened Dandy," *Papers on Language and Literature*, pp. 149–164.

14. Cecil, *Max*, p. 341.

15. "Maltby and Braxton," *Seven Men*, p. 57. Hereafter cited in the text.

16. "A Deplorable Affair," 5 Sept. 1908, *Around Theatres*, p. 517.

17. HD 1853 and the sketch reproduced in the World's Classics edition of *Seven Men and Two Others*, London, 1966, p. 45, bear uncanny resemblances to Beerbohm's self-caricatures.

18. The implications of this self-projection are more fully considered in Grushow, "Chastened Dandy," cited earlier.

19. See Chapter 1, note 14 and text.

20. SC 336. This thirty-one-page manuscript is now in the Berg Collection of the New York Public Library.

21. "'Savonarola' Brown," *Seven Men*, p. 183. Hereafter cited in text.

22. "'Herod' as Dramaturgy," *More Theatres*, p. 319.

23. "'Herod,'" p. 316.

24. See William Rothenstein, *Men and Memories, 1872-1900*, p. 283.

25. In addition to a review of *Paolo and Francesca* on 15 Mar. 1902 (*More Theatres*, pp. 445–448), Beerbohm devoted two columns, on 10 and 17 Nov. 1900, to an enthusiastic reception of *Herod* (*More Theatres*, pp. 315–323), and one on 8 Feb. 1902 to a more restrained approval of *Ulysses* (*More Theatres*, pp. 433–436). Phillips's curtain raiser, *Aylmer's Secret*, a modern philosophic fantasy, supposedly written when the author was nineteen, Beerbohm

regarded as an unredeemed failure (15 July 1905, *Last Theatres*, pp. 171–174).

26. "Drama of This Year," *More Theatres*, p. 278.

27. *Kiartan the Icelander* (1902), *Savonarola* (1904), and *Constantine the Great* (1906). Howard's first volume, *Footsteps of Prosperine, and Other Verses and Interludes,* was published in 1897 and his last, *Collected Poems,* in 1913. See Joseph B. Gilder, "A New English Poet," *Bookman*, pp. 30–32. Howard continued to publish occasional poems in magazines during the period 1913–1919. He appears to have been a considerable polymath, for in 1910 he also contributed technical articles on the determination of atomic weights to *Chemical News* and *Nature*.

28. Newman Howard, *Savonarola*, pp. 93, 101.

29. Robert Lynd, "Max Beerbohm, 1922," *Essays on Life and Literature*, ed. Desmond MacCarthy, p. 148.

30. "James Pethel," *Seven Men*, p. 108. Hereafter cited in text.

31. This unromantic and unheroic reading of character is directly opposed to that of Joseph Conrad in "The Shadow-Line," a work nearly contemporary with "James Pethel," in which the cook Ransome drives himself to almost superhuman exertions in time of crisis precisely *because* he has a heart ailment.

32. "A. V. Laider," *Seven Men*, pp. 163–164. Hereafter cited in text.

33. HD 1856, which appears in the first American edition of *Seven Men* (New York, 1920), and another in the World's Classics edition of *Seven Men and Two Others*, p. 123. Hart-Davis lists a third (HD 1857), privately owned, which he has not seen.

34. "Not That I Would Boast," *A Variety of Things*, p. 260; "Felix Argallo and Walter Ledgett," *Seven Men and Two Others* (London, 1966), p. 186. Subsequent references to this story, citing page numbers to *both* editions respectively will be incorporated in the text.

Notes to Chapter VI

1. See Chapter 4. Plate numbers placed first in parenthesis both here and subsequently refer to *Rossetti and His Circle*.

2. Lynch, *Max Beerbohm*, p. 149.

3. Hart-Davis, *Catalogue*, p. 12.

4. See Chapter 4.

5. William Rothenstein, *Men and Memories, 1900–1922*, pp. 312–313; Sir John Rothenstein, *Summer's Lease*, pp. 45–48.

6. See Max's letter of 11 May 1913 gratefully acknowledging this assistance, *Max and Will*, p. 93.

7. Watts-Dunton (as Watts) figures as one of DGR's "guardians" in the most elaborate drawing of the series (pl. 20; HD 1277; BLC 48). Apart from Hall Caine, Sir Edmund Gosse (b. 1849) was the only survivor of those depicted and, though subject to its influence, was strictly speaking far too young to have been admitted to the "circle." His appearance in the company of Swinburne is almost gratuitous (pl. 17; HD 1643; BLC 47), but the drawing is brilliant, and he thanked Max for the kindness "to drag me into the scheme" (Sir Evan Charteris, *The Life and Letters of Sir Edmund Gosse*, p. 415).

8. The phrases are Beerbohm's own, in a letter to Sir Sydney Cockerell, cited by Behrman, *Portrait of Max*, p. 277.

9. "Mirror," p. 37.

10. Lynch, *Max Beerbohm*, p. 146.

11. Felstiner, *Lies of Art*, p. 76.

12. Lynch, *Max Beerbohm*, pp. 149–150.

13. Thomas Craven, "The Drawings of Max Beerbohm," *New Republic*, p. 353.

14. Beerbohm mentions the existence of the Dunn copy in his notes to "The Mirror of the Past" (p. 36), which also contains a sketch of the copy (p. 53A).

15. Oswald Doughty, *A Victorian Romantic*, pp. 34–35.

16. Virginia Surtees, *The Paintings and Drawings of Dante Gabriel Rossetti (1828–1882)*, cat. no. 443, pl. 415.

17. Sylvester Herringham also observes vanity as one of Tennyson's salient characteristics. He tells Max: "I daresay you've often said in an odd hour, 'How many things that mirror must have reflected!' Well, that was said by poor Alfred Tennyson. In '78 he'd come here — it was . . . to consult me about some current scientific theory that he wanted to seem to know all about in a poem he was writing. I came in late. He was looking at himself and he said to excuse himself, 'I was just thinking how many things that old mirror must have reflected.' It was like him to be looking at himself, it was like him to be anxious not to be supposed to be looking at himself, and it was like him to say what he said" ("Mirror," after p. 33).

18. See Chapter 3.

19. Wilson, "Analysis of Max Beerbohm," in Riewald, *Surprise of Excellence*, p. 40.

20. These last details of the drawing bring to mind simultaneously two other of Max's representations of the clash between the aesthet-

ic and the commonplace: the illustration of *the* quatrain of the *Rubaiyat* in *The Poets' Corner* (see Chapter 3) and the description of Swinburne at dinner in "No. 2. The Pines," surely the source of that bottle of ale (see Chapter 2).

21. See Henry Treffry Dunn, *Recollections of Dante Gabriel Rossetti and His Circle*, pp. 24, 43–50.

22. See end of Chapter 4.

23. Surtees, *Paintings and Drawings of DGR*, cat. no. 206, pl. 299.

24. Letter to Max Beerbohm, 14 Nov. 1917, Charteris, *Gosse*, p. 415.

25. Felstiner, *Lies of Art*, p. 75.

26. Dated 16 Sept. 1921, p. 11.

27. "Fenestralia," *Mainly on the Air*, p. 164.

28. Doughty, *Victorian Romantic*, p. 128.

29. Lynch, *Max Beerbohm*, p. 147.

30. Nowhere is this quality better demonstrated graphically than in Beerbohm's drawing for the binding case of *The Poets' Corner* (HD 1420; BLC frontispiece). Ostensibly the bust of an unidentified poet is being illuminated, both above from the sunlight streaming through the Gothic window and below from the lesser light beaming from Max's electric torch. The face of the statue, however, is expressionless — lofty and impenetrable. Beerbohm's glance, on the other hand, is sensitive and searching.

31. Harry Quilter, "The Art of Rossetti," *Contemporary Review*, pp. 200–201.

32. Ross, *Ross*, p. 259.

Notes to Chapter VII

1. "Lytton Strachey," *Mainly on the Air*, p. 198.

2. This is the title of one of Beerbohm's radio broadcasts, delivered on 26 July 1936, *Mainly on the Air*, pp. 24–35.

3. Max described the genesis of the edition in the following words: "One day in the autumn of 1919 I laughed quite spontaneously when dear William Heinemann of a sudden suggested to me that an uniform edition of me would not be amiss. He told me that the idea was not his own — had been conceived by Mr Macrae, of the firm of Dutton & Co., New York. He said that the proposal was that Messrs Dutton should publish one such edition of me over there, and he another such edition over here. Also, I remember, he showed me a letter in which Mr Macrae spoke of me as 'that splen-

did old lion, Max Beerbohm.' That I was old I knew. That I was splendid and leonine was a revelation; dazzled by the light of which I made a feebler resistance than I should otherwise have made to the whole scheme. No matter. I should anyway have yielded in the end." ("Uniform Editions," *A Peep into the Past*, p. 44.)

4. Riewald, *Sir Max Beerbohm*, p. 214.

5. "My Ambitions" (1940), *A Peep into the Past*, p. 89.

6. June 1928, pp. 1–11; reprinted in *A Peep into the Past*, pp. 68–76.

7. SC 332. *Unberufen*, the German equivalent to "Touch wood!" is an expression Max frequently used in letters (and presumably in conversation) before the war. Cf. *Letters to Reggie Turner*, p. 134, n. 5.

8. *A Peep into the Past*, p. 69.

9. Dated 6 Jan. 1925; reprinted in *A Peep into the Past*, pp. 52–53.

10. Max's introduction is reprinted as "William Rothenstein" in *A Peep into the Past*, pp. 54–61.

11. The posthumous edition of *Mainly on the Air* (New York, 1958) gathers up both broadcasts and essays of this period. Their titles well convey the shift of purpose in invoking memory: "Old Carthusian Memories" (1920), "London Revisited" (1935), "A Small Boy Seeing Giants" (1936), "Speed" (1936), "The Top Hat" (1940), "Music Halls of My Youth" (1942), and "Playgoing" (1945).

12. "T. Fenning Dodworth," *A Variety of Things*, p. 135. Hereafter cited in text as "Dodworth."

13. Behrman, *Portrait of Max*, p. 129.

14. *A Peep into the Past*, pp. 105–108. Hereafter cited in the text as "Dustworth."

15. "Then and Now," *A Peep into the Past*, p. 96. Hereafter cited by this title in text.

16. Tischbein's artistic infatuation with Lady Hamilton as a subject for historical paintings was real enough. See his autobiography, *Aus meinem Leben*, pp. 292 ff.

17. "Quia Imperfectum," *And Even Now*, p. 199. Hereafter cited by this title in text.

18. Riewald, *Sir Max Beerbohm*, p. 297.

19. Wolfgang von Oettingen, *Goethe und Tischbein*, p. 35. See also the pamphlet published for a special exhibition of the painting, *Goethe gemalt von Tischbein — ein Porträt und seine Geschichte* (Frankfurt: Städelsches Kunstinstitut, 1974).

20. "'A Clergyman,'" *And Even Now*, p. 233.

Notes for Pages 211-253

21. James Boswell, *Life of Johnson*, 3:518.
22. Riewald, *Sir Max Beerbohm*, p. 79.
23. Cecil, *Max*, p. 382.
24. "A Relic," *And Even Now*, p. 7.
25. This number includes the drawings of *A Survey*, which, it will be remembered, was published in 1921, actually a year before the publication of *Rossetti and His Circle* but four years after the first exhibition of fifteen of the series and three months after the exhibition of the full set of twenty-three.
26. Michael Holroyd, *Lytton Strachey*, 2:393.
27. See Chapter 4, note 44 and text. The drawing itself is reproduced in H. C. Marillier, *"Christie's," 1766 to 1925*.
28. Reproduced in Charteris, *Gosse*.
29. See HD 324 in *A Survey*, where the shade of Lord Randolph Churchill muses over his hapless son, who stands sheepishly in the foreground.
30. In at least one instance Max indulges in self-parody. His 1923 caricature of Strachey, called "Echo" (HD 1603; BLC 76), consciously recreates the postures and dialogue of his drawing of Matthew Arnold in *The Poets' Corner* (HD 37; BLC 61).
31. Desmond MacCarthy, "Max," *New Statesman*, p. 236.
32. Dated 20 June 1921, *Letters to Reggie Turner*, p. 256.
33. A twentieth drawing, that of Lord Curzon (HD 391), in both content and manner appears to belong to the series yet was neither publicly shown nor reproduced in *Observations*. It is not a particularly forceful caricature compared to some of the others and may not have been included for artistic reasons. It seems more likely that it was omitted because of the death of the former viceroy in 1925; with the sole exception of Joseph Conrad (d. 1924), all the personages caricatured were alive at the time of the April 1925 show.
34. Surtees, *Paintings and Drawings of DGR*, cat. no. 118, pl. 182.
35. See *Letters to Reggie Turner*, p. 178.
36. See Chapter 6.
37. Charteris, *Gosse*, pp. 478–479.
38. Dated 18 May 1920, *Letters to Reggie Turner*, pp. 246–247.
39. The likeness is even more pronounced in the work of the political cartoonist F. Carruthers Gould, in whose album *Political Caricatures, 1905*, Balfour's face might well be mistaken for that of Beerbohm in 1911.
40. Riewald, *Beerbohm's Literary Caricatures*, p. 188.
41. Letter dated 7 Sept. 1935, *Letters to Reggie Turner*, p. 276.
42. Behrman, *Portrait of Max*, p. 262.

Bibliography

The following bibliography makes no pretense to completeness, confining itself essentially to a compilation of editions cited and other printed sources consulted more than casually in the preparation of this study. Among the omissions are short unsigned notices in newspapers, literary journals, and exhibition catalogues, for which notices the reader is referred to the bibliographic works listed below. Nor are there here itemized the unpublished letters, manuscripts, and drawings that have been consulted in the following collections: the British Library; the Houghton Library, Harvard University; the Berg Collection, New York Public Library; the Ashmolean Museum and the Merton College Library, Oxford University; the O'Connell and Taylor collections, Princeton University Library; and the Tate Gallery.

I. Bibliographic Works

Gallatin, A. E. *Sir Max Beerbohm: Bibliographical Notes.* Cambridge, Mass.: Harvard University Press, 1944.
——— and L. M. Oliver. *A Bibliography of the Works of Max Beerbohm.* London: Rupert Hart-Davis; Cambridge, Mass.: Harvard University Press, 1952.
Hart-Davis, Rupert. *A Catalogue of the Caricatures of Max Beerbohm.* London: Macmillan & Co.; Cambridge, Mass.: Harvard University Press, 1972.
Riewald, J. G. *Sir Max Beerbohm, Man and Writer: A Critical Analysis with a Brief Life and a Bibliography.* The Hague: Martinus Nijhoff, 1953. Rpt. Brattleboro, Vt.: Stephen Greene Press, 1961.
Sotheby and Company. *Catalogue of the Library and Literary Manuscripts of the Late Sir Max Beerbohm.* London: Sotheby & Company, 1960.

II. Works by Beerbohm

And Even Now. London: William Heinemann, 1920.
Around Theatres. London: Rupert Hart-Davis, 1953.
A Book of Caricatures. London: Methuen & Co., 1907.
Caricatures by Max: From the Collection in the Ashmolean Museum. Oxford: Oxford University Press, 1958.
Caricatures of Twenty-Five Gentlemen. Introd. L. Raven-Hill. London: Leonard Smithers, 1896.
Cartoons "The Second Childhood of John Bull." London: Stephen Swift & Co., 1911.
A Christmas Garland. London: William Heinemann, 1912.
Fifty Caricatures. London: William Heinemann, 1913.
Herbert Beerbohm Tree: Some Memories of Him and of His Art. Comp. Max Beerbohm. London: Hutchinson & Co., 1920.
Heroes and Heroines of Bitter Sweet. London: Messrs. Leadlay, 1931.
Last Theatres, 1904–1910. London: Rupert Hart-Davis, 1970.
Letters to Reggie Turner. Ed. Rupert Hart-Davis. London: Rupert Hart-Davis, 1964.
Mainly on the Air. London: William Heinemann, 1946. Enl. ed. New York: Alfred A. Knopf, 1958.
Max in Verse: Rhymes and Parodies. Ed. J. G. Riewald. Brattleboro, Vt.: Stephen Greene Press, 1963; London: William Heinemann, 1964.
Max's Nineties: Drawings 1892–1899. London: Rupert Hart-Davis; Philadelphia and New York: J. B. Lippincott Company, 1958.
More. London and New York: John Lane, 1899.
More Theatres, 1898–1903. London: Rupert Hart-Davis, 1969.
Observations. London: William Heinemann, 1925. Rpt. New York: Haskell House Publishers, 1971.
A Peep into the Past and Other Prose Pieces. Ed. Rupert Hart-Davis. London: William Heinemann; Brattleboro, Vt.: Stephen Greene Press, 1972.
The Poets' Corner. London: William Heinemann, 1904. Rpt. London and New York: King Penguin Books, 1943.
Rossetti and His Circle. London: William Heinemann, 1922.
Seven Men. London: William Heinemann, 1919; New York: Alfred A. Knopf, 1920. Enl. ed. rpt. as *Seven Men and Two Others.* London: Oxford University Press, 1966.
A Survey. London: William Heinemann, 1921.
Things New and Old. London: William Heinemann, 1923.

A Variety of Things. New York: Alfred A. Knopf, 1928.
Works. London: John Lane; New York: Charles Scribners' Sons, 1896.
The Works of Max Beerbohm. 10 vols. London: William Heinemann, 1922–1928.
Yet Again. London: Chapman and Hall, 1909.
Zuleika Dobson. London: William Heinemann, 1911. Oxford: Shakespeare Head Press, 1975.
Beerbohm, Max, and Will Rothenstein. *Max and Will: Max Beerbohm and William Rothenstein, Their Friendship and Letters, 1893–1945.* Ed. Mary M. Lago and Karl Beckson. London: John Murray, 1975.

III. Other Works

Ashbee, C. R. *Caricature.* London: Chapman and Hall, 1928.
Auden, W. H. "One of the Family." *Forewords and Afterwords.* New York: Random House, 1973, pp. 367–383. Rpt. in Riewald, *The Surprise of Excellence,* pp. 159–174.
Behrman, S. N. *Portrait of Max: An Intimate Memoir.* New York: Random House, 1960. Publ. in England as *Conversations with Max.* London: Hamish Hamilton, 1960.
Benson, Arthur Christopher. *From a College Window.* New York and London: G. P. Putnam's Sons, 1906.
Blathwayt, Raymond. "The Art of Caricature: A Talk with Mr. Max Beerbohm." *Cassell's Magazine,* February 1903, pp. 275–279.
Boswell, James. *Life of Johnson.* Ed. George Birkbeck Hill. Rev. L. F. Powell. 6 vols. Oxford: Clarendon Press, 1934–1950.
Burdett, Osbert. *The Beardsley Period.* London: John Lane, 1925.
Caine, Hall. *Recollections of Dante Gabriel Rossetti.* London: Elliott Stock, 1882.
Cecil, David. *Max: A Biography.* London: Constable, 1964; Boston: Houghton Mifflin, 1965.
Charteris, Evan. *The Life and Letters of Sir Edmund Gosse.* London: William Heinemann, 1931.
Craven, Thomas. "The Drawings of Max Beerbohm." *New Republic,* 21 February 1923, pp. 353–354.
Danson, Lawrence. "Max Beerbohm and *The Mirror of the Past.*" *Princeton University Library Chronicle* 43 (Winter 1982): 77–153.
Delaware Art Museum. *Occasional Paper Number One.* (A discussion of Rossetti's *Found.*) Wilmington: Delaware Art Museum, 1976.

Doughty, Oswald. *A Victorian Romantic: Dante Gabriel Rossetti*. 2d ed. London: Oxford University Press, 1960.

Dunn, Henry Treffry. *Recollections of Dante Gabriel Rossetti and His Circle*. London: Elkin Mathews, 1904.

Dupee, F. W. "Beerbohm: The Rigors of Fantasy." *New York Review of Books*, 9 June 1966, pp. 12–17. Rpt. as "Max Beerbohm and the Rigors of Fantasy" in Riewald, *The Surprise of Excellence*, pp. 175–191.

Felstiner, John. "Changing Faces in Max Beerbohm's Caricature." *Princeton University Library Chronicle* 33 (Winter 1972): 73–88.

———. *The Lies of Art: Max Beerbohm's Parody and Caricature*. New York: Alfred A. Knopf, 1972.

———. "Max Beerbohm and the Wings of Henry James." *Kenyon Review* 29 (1967): 449–471. Rpt. in Riewald, *The Surprise of Excellence*, pp. 192–213.

Gaunt, William. *The Aesthetic Adventure*. London: Jonathan Cape, 1945.

Gilder, Joseph B. "A New English Poet." *Bookman* (London), September 1902, pp. 30–32.

Goethe, Johann Wolfgang von. *Travels in Italy*. Trans. from the German. London: George Bell & Sons, 1883.

Gould, F. Carruthers. *Political Caricatures, 1905*. London: Edward Arnold, 1905.

Grushow, Ira. "Beerbohm's Lord Runcorn." *Notes and Queries*, n.s. 22, no. 5 (May 1975): 207–208.

———. "The Chastened Dandy: Beerbohm's 'Hilary Maltby and Stephen Braxton.'" *Papers on Language and Literature* 8, supp. (Fall 1972): 149–164.

Henderson, Marina. *Dante Gabriel Rossetti*. London: Academy Editions, 1973.

Hilton, Timothy. *The Pre-Raphaelites*. London: Thames and Hudson, 1970.

Holroyd, Michael. *Lytton Strachey: A Critical Biography*. 2 vols. New York: Holt, Rinehart, and Winston, 1968.

Howard, Newman. *Savonarola: A City's Tragedy*. London: J. M. Dent & Co., 1904.

Hunt, W. Holman. *Pre-Raphaelitism and the Pre-Raphaelite Brotherhood*. 2 vols. New York: Macmillan Co., 1905.

Jackson, Holbrook. *The Eighteen Nineties: A Review of Art and Ideas at the Close of the Nineteenth Century*. London: Grant Richards, 1913.

Layard, George Somes. "Max Beerbohm; or Art and Semolina."

Bibliography

Bookman (London), August 1911, pp. 201–208.

――――. Review of *A Christmans Garland*. *Bookman* (London), December 1912, pp. 182–183.

Low, David. "The Art of Max Beerbohm." *Spectator*, 14 February 1931, pp. 218–219.

――――. *British Cartoonists, Caricaturists and Comic Artists*. London: William Collins, 1942.

Lynch, Bohun. *Max Beerbohm in Perspective*. London: William Heinemann, 1921; New York: Alfred A. Knopf, 1922.

Lynd, Robert. "Max Beerbohm, 1922." In *Essays on Life and Literature*, ed. Desmond MacCarthy. London: J. M. Dent & Sons, 1951, pp. 147–155.

MacCarthy, Desmond. "Max." *New Statesman*, 2 June 1923, p. 236.

McElderry, Bruce R., Jr. "Max Beerbohm: Essayist, Caricaturist, Novelist." In *On Stage and Off: Eight Essays in English Literature Presented to Dr. Emmett L. Avery*, ed. John W. Ehrstine, John R. Elwood, and Robert C. McLean. Pullman: Washington State University Press, 1968, pp. 76–86. Rpt. in Riewald, *The Surprise of Excellence*, pp. 215–227.

――――. *Max Beerbohm*. New York: Twayne Publishers, 1972.

Manning, Frederic. *Scenes and Portraits*. Rev. ed. London: Peter Davies, 1930.

Marillier, H. C. *"Christie's," 1766 to 1925*. London: Constable & Company, 1926.

――――. *Dante Gabriel Rossetti: An Illustrated Memorial of his Art and Life*. 3d ed., rev. London: George Bell & Sons, 1904.

Matthews, William, ed. *British Diaries: An Annotated Bibliography of British Diaries Written between 1442 and 1942*. Berkeley and Los Angeles: University of California Press; London: Cambridge University Press, 1950.

Mix, Katherine Lyon. *Max and the Americans*. Brattleboro, Vt.: Stephen Greene Press, 1974.

――――. "Max on Shaw." *Shaw Review* 6 (September 1963): 100–104. Rpt. in Riewald, *The Surprise of Excellence*, pp. 131–137.

Moers, Ellen. *The Dandy: Brummell to Beerbohm*. New York: Viking Press, 1960.

Moore, George. *Ave*. London: William Heinemann, 1911.

Morley, John. *Recollections*. 2 vols. New York: Macmillan Co., 1917.

Nicoll, John. *Dante Gabriel Rossetti*. London: Studio Vista, 1975.

Oettingen, Wolfgang von. *Goethe und Tischbein*. Schriften der

Goethe-Gesellschaft, vol. 25. Weimar: Verlag der Goethe-Gesellschaft, 1910.

Panter-Downes, Mollie. *At the Pines: Swinburne and Watts-Dunton in Putney.* Boston: Gambit Incorporated, 1971.

Pater, Walter. *The Works of Walter Pater.* 10 vols. London: Macmillan & Co., 1910.

Pocock, Tom. *Chelsea Reach: The Brutal Friendship of Whistler and Walter Greaves.* London: Hodder and Stoughton, 1970.

Pritchett, V. S. "Max Beerbohm: A Dandy," in *The Tale Bearers.* New York: Random House, 1980.

Quilter, Harry. "The Art of Rossetti." *Contemporary Review* 43 (February 1883): 190–203.

Riewald, J. G., ed. *Beerbohm's Literary Caricatures, from Homer to Huxley.* Hamden, Conn.: Archon Books, 1977.

———, ed. *The Surprise of Excellence: Modern Essays on Max Beerbohm.* Hamden, Conn.: Archon Books, 1974.

Ross, Margery, ed. *Robert Ross: Friend of Friends. Letters to Robert Ross, Art Critic and Writer, together with Extracts from his Published Articles.* London: Jonathan Cape, 1952.

Rossetti, Dante Gabriel. *Works.* Ed. William M. Rossetti. London: Ellis, 1911.

Rossetti, William Michael. *The P.R.B. Journal: William Michael Rossetti's Diary of the Pre-Raphaelite Brotherhood, 1849–1853.* Ed. William E. Fredeman. Oxford: Clarendon Press, 1975.

———, ed. *Praeraphaelite Diaries and Letters.* London: Hurst and Blackett, 1900.

———, ed. *Ruskin: Rossetti: Praeraphaelitism: Papers, 1854 to 1862.* New York: Dodd, Mead and Company; London: George Allen, 1899.

Rothenstein, John. *Summer's Lease: Autobiography, 1901–1938.* London: Hamish Hamilton, 1965.

Rothenstein, William. *Men and Memories, 1872–1900.* London: Faber & Faber; New York: Coward-McCann, 1931.

———. *Men and Memories, 1900–1922.* London: Faber & Faber; New York: Coward-McCann, 1932.

———. *Since Fifty; Men and Memories, 1922–1938.* London: Faber & Faber, 1939; New York: Macmillan Co., 1940.

S. W. "The Art of Mr. Beerbohm." *Athenaeum,* 19 November 1919, p. 1186.

Städelsches Kunstinstitut. *Goethe gemalt von Tischbein— ein Porträt und seine Geschichte.* Frankfurt: Städelsches Kunstinstitut, 1974.

Bibliography

Surtees, Virginia. *The Paintings and Drawings of Dante Gabriel Rossetti (1828–1882): A Catalogue Raisonné.* 2 vols. Oxford: Clarendon Press, 1971.

Tischbein, Wilhelm. *Aus meinem Leben.* Ed. Kuno Mittelstadt. Berlin: Henschelverlag, 1956.

Updike, John. "Rhyming Max." In *Assorted Prose.* New York: Alfred A. Knopf, 1965, pp. 256–263. Rpt. in Riewald, *The Surprise of Excellence,* pp. 152–157.

Viscusi, Robert. "A Dandy's Diary: The Manuscripts of Max Beerbohm's *Zuleika Dobson.*" *Princeton University Library Chronicle* 40 (Spring 1979): 234–256.

Watts-Dunton, Theodore. *Aylwin.* London: Oxford University Press, 1929.

Wilson, Edmund. "An Analysis of Max Beerbohm." In *Classics and Commercials: A Literary Chronicle of the Forties.* New York: Farrar, Straus, 1950, pp. 431–441. Rpt. in Riewald, *The Surprise of Excellence,* pp. 38–46.

———. "A Miscellany of Max Beerbohm." In *The Bit Between My Teeth: A Literary Chronicle of 1950–1965.* New York: Farrar, Straus & Giroux, 1965, pp. 41–58. Rpt. in Riewald, *The Surprise of Excellence,* pp. 138–151.

Young, Filson. "The Perfect Parodist." *Saturday Review,* 9 November 1912, p. 578.

Index

Note: References to illustrations are followed by an asterisk (*).

Abdul Hamid II, 82
acting, 34
Aidé, Hamilton, 252
Alexander, George, 94
Alexandra, Queen, 66
Alfonso XIII, 228
And Even Now, 17, 208, 209, 211, 212, 220, 223, 226-27
"Ape." *See* Pellegrini, Carlo
Archer, William, 48, 75, 76*, 88, 214
"Argallo and Ledgett," 129, 136, 158-63, 161*, 209, 215, 222
"Arise, Sir —!" 36
Around Theatres, 208
art in writing, 35-36
Ashmolean Museum, 59, 60
Asquith, Herbert, 246
"At Covent Garden," 35
Auden, W. H., xi, 9
"A. V. Laider," 33, 134, 136, 154-58

Baldwin, Stanley, 12, 231, 242, 246-47
Balfour, Arthur, 8, 67-68, 69*, 128, 242-43, 247-49, 248*

Barnato, Barney, 49
Barrett, Wilson, 252
BBC broadcasts, 10, 14, 28, 48, 50, 95, 221
Beardsley, Aubrey, 50-51, 230
Beerbohm, Florence Kahn, 93-94, 99, 105, 167, 218
Beerbohm, Max: as caricaturist, 5-6, 15-16, 227; composing in two media, xiv, 1-3; as critic of performances, 12-13, 24, 25, 26-27, 140, 207, 243; as dramatist, 14; as essayist, 5-6, 14, 212; and Dr. Johnson, 11, 14; literary preferences of, 10, 15, 47; his marriages, 93-94, 170; as a modernist, 18-19, 22, 164; as novelist, 14-15, 125-27; reputation of, xi-xii, xiv; and Rossetti, 169-70; technique of caricature, 61, 91, 175, 199-200; theory of caricature, 62; works, availability of, 59-61
Behrman, S. N., xii, 31, 95, 96, 112, 215

279

Bellini, Giovanni, 37
Belloc, Hilaire, 48, 73*, 232
Benedict XV (pope), 232
Bennett, Arnold, 7, 46, 242, 243, 249
Benson, A. C., 5, 41
Berg Collection, New York Public Library, 48
Betjeman, John, 14
biography and fiction, 25, 111, 134, 220
"Blight on the Music Halls, The," 36
Boer War, 6, 84
Book of Caricatures, A, 6, 59, 74, 87, 91
Borges, Jorge Luis, 164
Boswell, James, 220, 222-23, 224
Brandes, Georg, 77
British Museum, 22, 105, 138
Brown, Ford Madox, 114, 168, 184, 185*, 197
Browning, Oscar, 71
Browning, Robert, 42, 74-75, 184, 198, 204
Burdett, Osbert, 230
Burne-Jones, Edward, 70, 108, 184, 185*, 187*, 188, 198, 201, 205
Burns, Robert, 88
Byron, George Gordon, 72, 89

Caine, Hall, 12, 114, 162, 198, 223; caricatures of, 65, 66, 70, 71, 162, 202; imaginary reminiscence of, 109; recollections of, 49-50, 51-52, 212
caricature and parody, 5, 41-42
caricatures: allegorical, 80-81, 231-32, 233, 240-41; allusion in, 81-87; of confrontation, 6, 74-78, 186, 231-33, 251; discrepancy the basis of, 236; group, 68-74, 229-30; of introduction, 78-79, 186, 192-93, 233-34; literary, 88, 170-73; paired drawings, 236-39; portrait, 6, 228-29; series, 65-66, 90-91, 234-35
Caricatures of Twenty-Five Gentlemen, 5, 17, 59, 63, 64, 207
Carlos I (king of Portugal), 66
Carlyle, Thomas, 107, 188-89, 198
Carson, Edward, 231
"Case of Prometheus, The," 31-32
Cecil, David, xii-xiii, 93, 105, 113, 128, 141, 224-25
Cecil, Hugh, 252
Century (magazine), 98
Century Company, 134
Chamberlain, Joseph, 64, 66
characters: "found," 127, 144; generated by parody, 127; "invented," 127-28; and persons, 20
Chelsea, 105, 122, 169
Chesterfield, Tenth Earl of, 244-45
Chesterton, G. K., 42, 68, 71, 73*, 77
Christmas Garland, A, 5, 6, 7-8, 17, 41-46, 95, 243
Churchill, Randolph, 231
Churchill, Winston, 11, 48, 115, 231
"Clergyman, A," 222-23, 224
collected edition, 210-11, 212
Conrad, Joseph, 3-5, 45, 136, 243, 245, 252

Index

convention in art, 21
Corder, Rosa, 179
Corelli, Marie, 12, 223
Cornforth, Fanny, 114, 176, 192-93, 197, 205
Corot, Jean Baptiste, 37
Coward, Noel, 235
Craven, Thomas, 175-76
"Crime, The," 212

D'Annunzio, Gabriele, 232
Dante Alighieri, 170
Daumier, Honoré, 80
Davidson, John, 252
"Decline of the Graces, The," 35
Desborough, Lady, 48
Disraeli, Benjamiin, 2, 66, 170-73, 172*, 198, 219
Don Quixote, 199
Dostoevsky, Fyodor, 47
"Doubles" (drawings), 234
Douglas, Lord Alfred, 24
Du Maurier, George, 232
"Dulcedo Judiciorum," 35
Dunn, Henry Treffry, 168, 179

Eden, William, 48
Edward VII, 11, 66, 86, 94; as Prince of Wales, 116-17, 118*, 232
Edward VIII, as Prince of Wales, 32, 227, 232-33
"Edwardyssey, The" (drawings), 66, 90, 117
"1880," 31, 101
Einstein, Albert, 226
"Encaenia of 1908, The" (drawing), 71, 162
"English Fiction—Ancient and Modern" (drawing), 237, 238*

"Enoch Soames," 7, 128, 136, 137-41, 217, 224; authenticity of, 22, 105; and Yeats, 28, 230

Far Oakridge, 167
Faraday, Michael, 106
Faust legend, 138, 140
Feiffer, Jules, 179
Felstiner, John, xv, 1-2, 63, 174, 195
"Fenestralia," 226
fiction and reality, 22
Fielding, Henry, 39
Fifty Caricatures, 6, 7, 81, 87, 91
FitzGerald, Edward, 87

Galsworthy, John, 48, 73*, 223
"General Elections," 35
genres, fusion of, 6-7, 8
George V, 94, 233-34; as Duke of York, 64-65
"Ghosts" (exhibition), 251-53
Gladstone, William E., 65-66, 90
Goethe, Johann von, 220-22, 224
"Going Back to School," 33
"Going Out for a Walk," 212
"Golden Drugget, The," 212
"Good Prince, A," 32
Goodwin, Nat, 49-50, 51
Gordon, General Charles, 66
Gorki, Maxim, 47
Gosse, Edmund, 14, 28, 48, 50, 195, 198; caricatures of, 72, 73*, 88, 168, 189, 230, 242, 246; friendship with Beerbohm, 9, 105, 167; *Life of Swinburne*, 55, 212; parody of, 42, 243

281

Graham, R. B. Cunninghame, 65, 73*, 229, 249-51, 250*
Gray, Thomas, 33
Greaves, Walter, 124
Grosvenor Gallery, 166
Guedalla, Philip, 233

Hamilton, Lady, 220
Happy Hypocrite, The, 31
Harcourt, William, 64
Hardy, Thomas, 7
Harris, Frank, 9, 42, 65
Hart-Davis, Rupert, 59, 68, 72, 86, 122, 234, 236, 243
Haydon, B. R., 113
Heroes and Heroines of Bitter Sweet (drawings), 235
"Hethway Speaking," 95, 106, 107, 111, 114, 117, 124
Hewlett, Maurice, 41, 73*
history and fiction, 19, 27, 38-40
Hogarth, William, 68, 200, 203
holograph notebook, 48-50, 212
Homer, 66, 81-82
Horace, 66
"Hosts and Guests," 212
"How Shall I Word It?" 46
Howard, Newman, 149-50
Howell, Charles Augustus, 108, 117, 179, 188, 198
Hunt, Holman, 70, 114, 168, 171, 172*, 197
Huxley, Aldous, 228

Ibsen, Henrik, 42, 75, 76*, 77, 88, 183
imaginary reminiscence: as caricature, 89-91; defined, 16, 220; as satiric fiction, 17
"Incident, An," 50

"Infamous Brigade, An," 35
Irving, H. B., 49-50, 51, 252
Irving, Sir Henry, 159, 252

Jackson, Holbrook, 128, 129, 138, 139, 224, 230
James, Henry, 2; Beerbohm's admiration of, 15, 236, 242; caricatures of, 71, 79, 86, 115, 233, 242, 252; "The Jolly Corner," 242, 245; parodies of, 7, 41, 42-43; recollection of, 50, 51
"James Pethel," 136, 151-54
Jerome, Jerome K., 142
John, Augustus, 244
Johnson, Samuel, 11, 14, 223
Jowett, Benjamin, 22, 168, 177*, 179, 182, 197, 198, 201, 204
Joyce, James, 15, 164

Kahn, Florence. *See* Beerbohm, Florence Kahn
"King George the Fourth," 13, 29-30
Kipling, Rudyard, 236; Beerbohm's aversion to, 11, 12, 63; caricatures of, 63, 66-67, 73*, 88, 245; parody of, 7, 41, 43, 243
Kitchener, Earl, 65
Knewstub, Walter J., 168
"Kolniyatsch," 46-67, 217

Lancaster, Osbert, xi, 66
Landor, Walter Savage, 130
Lane, John, 82, 211
Lang, Andrew, 49, 213, 220, 252
Lee, Sidney, 117, 227
Leech, John, 104

LeGallienne, Richard, 131
Leicester Galleries, 6, 94, 122, 166, 227
Leighton, Frederic, 175, 176, 179, 198
Leo XIII (pope), 66
Leverson, Ada, 24
Leverson, Ernest, 24
Lewis, George, 64
Liberty, Arthur Lasenby, 166
Life and Letters (journal), 213
Lloyd George, David, 228, 246
Low, David, xi
Lucian, 130
Lynch, Bohun, xi, 166, 173, 175

MacCarthy, Desmond, 213, 235
MacColl, D. S., 70, 82, 83*, 105
Machiavelli, Niccolo, 150
Mainly on the Air, 17, 28, 50, 213
"Maltby and Braxton," 7, 8, 20, 136, 141-45
Manning, Frederic, 21, 130-31
Martyn, Edward, 68, 84
Maupassant, Guy de, 225
"Memory of a Midnight Express, A," 33
Meredith, George, 10; caricatures of, 70, 88, 91, 114, 165, 198; imaginary reminiscences of, 100, 107, 114, 116, 117, 127, 199; parodies of, 7, 107, 159; recollections of, 48
Merton College, Oxford, 122
Mill, John Stuart, 120, 166, 193, 194*, 198, 204
Millais, John Everett, 88, 171, 172*, 189-92, 190*, 197, 242, 244
"Mirror of the Past, The," 5, 48, 95-116, 117, 126-27, 208; abandonment of, 112-13; cited, 16; composition of, 97-99, 103; description of, 95, 104, 110*, 124; narrative devices of, 97, 99-100, 111, 217; origins of, 31, 97; premise of, 241; research for, 105, 114; and *Rossetti and His Circle*, 99, 108, 116, 124, 129, 165, 192
mirrors, fascination with, 96-97, 99, 111, 170
"Miss Dustworth and Miss Libman," 217-18, 219
Moore, George: caricatures of, 7, 71, 78-79, 84-86, 85*, 88, 242; parody of, 243; recollections of, 11, 48-50, 52-54, 212; sketch of, 115
More, 5, 6, 17, 35
Morland, George, 37
Morley, John, 120-22, 121*, 166, 167, 193, 194*, 204, 229
Morris, Jane, 117, 193, 197, 205
Morris, William, 105, 198, 205; caricatures of, 70, 184, 185*, 187*, 188, 201; imaginary reminiscences of, 107, 108, 127
Mussolini, Benito, 233-34

Nabokov, Vladimir, 164
narrator as character, xiii, 136, 218, 220
New English Art Club, 70-71, 84, 94

New Yorker, xii
Nietzsche, Friedrich, 77
"Not That I Would Boast," See "Argallo and Ledgett"
"Note on the Einstein Theory, A," 226
"No. 2. The Pines," 7, 49, 50, 55-58, 95, 112, 206, 212

Observations (drawings), 91, 140, 167, 208, 228, 231, 244
"Old and the Young Self, The" (drawings), 91, 231, 241-51
"On Speaking French," 212
"One Fine Morning" (drawing), 243
Orpen, William, 71
Oxford, 38, 132, 168, 209
Oxford Union, 108, 114, 179, 182, 197, 201
Paderewski, Ignace, 232
"Parallel, A," 35
Parnell, Charles Stewart, 66
Pater, Walter, 26, 131-33, 184, 185*, 198, 252
Patmore, Coventry, 159, 166, 183, 188, 198, 204
Pellegrini, Carlo, 5, 15, 91
Pennell, Joseph, 86-87
Phillips, Stephen, 148-49
Pinero, Arthur Wing, 64, 71, 115
Poe, Edgar Allen, 125
Poets' Corner, The (drawings): innovation in, 6, 16, 63, 74, 81; as miscellany, 17, 184, 243; popularity of, 59-60, 78, 87; restraint in, 65
"Point to be Remembered by Very Eminent Men, A," 226
Ponsonby, Arthur, 242, 245
"Poor Romeo!" 30-31

"Prangley Valley," 32
Pre-Raphaelite Brotherhood, 168-69, 173, 192, 197, 205
"Pretending," 34
"Princeps Triplumiferus" (drawing), 116-17, 118*
Punch, 16

Queensberry, Marquis of, 23
"Quia Imperfectum" 220-22, 224

Rapallo, 9, 94, 96, 98, 103, 210, 212, 227, 237
"Red Cross Sale at Christie's, The" (drawing), 229-30
"Relic, A," 225
"remembering" essays, 27-28, 49-58, 95, 97, 126, 209, 212, 214, 219
Reynolds, Joshua, 233
Riewald, J. G., 3, 4, 60, 95
Rosebery, Earl of, 12, 66, 115, 231
Ross, Robert, 9, 205
Rossetti, Christina, 166
Rossetti, Dante Gabriel: beauty, his conception of, 20; Beerbohm's notes on, 105, 114, 115; compared to Beerbohm, 169-70; compared to Disraeli, 170-73; as hero, 11; imaginary reminiscences of, 112, 120, 124; in "The Mirror of the Past," 101, 102, 104, 108-9, 127, 162, 170; myth of, 167, 173, 198, 203-6; painting in oils of, 122, 123*; in *Rossetti and His Circle,* 166, 168, 172*, 177*, 179, 180*, 183-84,

Index

185*, 192, 193-95, 194*, 196-97; sketch of, 122; as a source for Beerbohm's drawings, 241; his style imitated, 114, 116-17
Rossetti, Gabriele, 180*, 181*, 182
Rossetti, William Michael, 114, 168, 182, 195
Rossetti and His Circle (drawings): composition of, 167-68, 208; decoration in, 201-3; exhibitions of, 166, 209; fenestration in 200-201; as imaginary reminiscence, xv, 67, 179, 197, 209; introduction scenes in, 78, 192; irony in, 132, 182-83, 186, 188, 203; and "The Mirror of the Past," 99, 116, 124, 165; narrative in, 18, 176, 196, 203, 205; preface to, 99, 167; research for, 168; stimuli to drawings, 166-67; technique of, 61, 173-75, 228, 229, 235; theme of, 173, 186; uniqueness of, 8, 179, 251; unity of, 165-66, 167, 196, 210, 243; verisimilitude of, 182, 223
Rostand, Edmond, 56
Rothenstein, Alice, 167-68
Rothenstein, John, 167, 214
Rothenstein, William, 15, 82, 214; caricatures of, 70, 230, 242, 249; as character in Beerbohm's fiction, 20, 22, 128, 138, 243; hosted Beerbohms during W. W. I, 129, 167-68
Rothschild, Alfred de, 83*, 84
Ruskin, John, 11, 70, 114, 192-93, 198
Russell, Bertrand, 233
Rutherston, Albert, 71, 82

Sala, George Augustus, 165, 175, 198, 204
Sandys, Frederick, 103
Sarasate, Pablo de, 115
Sargent, John, 71, 74
satire, 17
Saturday Review, 6, 17, 41, 93-94, 150, 207
"'Savonarola' Brown," 21, 127, 128, 136, 145-51, 219
Schopenhauer, Arthur, 77
Scott, William Bell, 11, 114, 168, 184, 185*
Second Childhood of John Bull, The (drawings), 6, 65, 94, 243
"Servants," 212
Seven Men, 7, 98, 128-37, 208, 214, 219, 242; analogues to, 130-33; augmented edition, 129, 158, 209; Beerbohm's presence in, xiii, 18, 136, 158, 216; as burlesque, 133; characters in, 8, 11, 12, 127-28, 161*, 226, 243; as imaginary reminiscences, xv, 163-64, 207; as stories, 134; unity of, 141, 210; verisimilitude of, 134, 135*, 140
Shakespeare, William, 21, 37, 42, 88, 128, 142, 147, 148, 192
Shaw, George Bernard, 13, 42, 48, 71, 73*, 75-78, 229, 242, 243, 244
Shelley, Percy, 4
Shields, Frederick, 198, 202

285

Sickert, Walter, 20, 53, 85*, 241, 242, 246
Siddal, Elizabeth, 101, 114, 176, 183, 193, 196-97, 201, 205
Social Success, A, 94, 95
"Some Persons of 'the Nineties'" (drawing), 22, 140, 230
"Something Defeasible," 212
Soveral, Luis de, 20, 49, 62, 71
Spectator, 228
Spencer, Earl, 68
"Spy." *See* Ward, Leslie
Städelsches Kunstinstitut, 221
Steer, Wilson, 53, 70, 85*
Stevenson, Robert Louis, 72, 73*, 97, 159
Strachey, Lytton, 11, 21, 137, 210, 228
Street, G. S., 41, 66
"Studies in the Eighteen-Seventies" (drawings), 234-35
Survey, A (drawings), 59, 167, 208, 209. 228, 229, 231
Swift, Jonathan, 39, 44
Swinburne, Algernon Charles: Beerbohm's notes on, 48, 49; caricatures of, 63, 68, 70, 88; imaginary reminiscences of, 102; *Life of* (Gosse), 55, 212; parody of, 57; *Poems and Ballads*, 195; recollections of, 7, 10, 50, 55-58, 162, 193, 206; in *Rossetti and His Circle*, 102, 184, 185*, 189, 195, 198-99, 202; sketch of, 114

"Tales of Three Nations" (drawings), 91, 239-40
Tate Gallery, 59, 174, 241

Tenniel, John, 16
Tennyson, Alfred, 75, 179, 183, 198, 204
"T. Fenning Dodworth," 215-17, 219
Thackeray, William Makepeace, 13, 14
"Then and Now," 218-19
Things New and Old (drawings) 91, 208, 228, 239
Tischbein, Wilhelm, 220-22, 224
Tonks, Henry, 53, 70, 85*
Tree, Herbert Beerbohm, 23, 48, 98
Trollope, Anthony, 14
Turner, Reginald, 23, 24, 247
Twain, Mark, 48

Updike, John, xi

Vanity Fair, 5, 15, 91, 234
Variety of Things, A, 17, 208, 211, 253
Verlaine, Paul, 89
Victor Emmanuel III, 233-34
Victoria, Queen, 66, 75, 232

Ward, Leslie, 5, 15, 175, 252
Watson, William, 82
Watts-Dunton, Theodore, 20, 50, 55-57, 68-70, 88, 168, 173, 193, 198, 202, 206
Webb, Sidney, 229
Wells, H. G., 41, 43-45, 62, 73*, 113, 223, 229
Whistler, James, 11, 87, 105, 124, 219; caricatures of, 68, 70, 88, 188-89, 198; imaginary reminiscences of, 101, 107, 115, 117, 127; as writer, 36
Whitman, Walt, 72, 89

Index

Wilde, Oscar, 18, 53, 131, 206, 219; caricatures of, 63, 88, 174, 196, 198, 202-3; imaginary reminiscence of, 199; influence on Beerbohm, 31, 97; recollections of, 48; trial of, 23-25, 26
Wilding, Alexa, 114
Wilhelm II, 228
"William and Mary," 224-25
Wilson, Edmund, xi, 2, 186, 253
Windsor, Duke of. *See* Edward VIII
Woolf, Virginia, 15, 164
Woolner, Thomas, 166, 183, 197
"Words for Pictures," 36
Wordsworth, William, 4-5, 33, 88

Works, 5, 17, 36, 103, 131, 211

Yeats, William Butler, 8-9, 84, 212; caricatures of, 22, 68, 78-79, 88, 230; recollections of, 28, 48, 49-50, 54, 212, 224
Yet Again, 6, 17, 35, 36

Zangwill, Israel, 73*
Zuleika Dobson, 6, 8, 11, 37-40, 94, 132; characters of, 128; as criticism of novelistic conventions, 40-41; fame of, 19, 37; peripheral to imaginary reminiscence, 208-9; self-conscious narration in, xiii, 14, 20-21